Practical Beginning Theory
A Fundamentals Worktext

Sixth Edition

Practical Beginning Theory
A Fundamentals Worktext

Bruce Benward
University of Wisconsin, Madison, Wisconsin

Barbara Garvey Jackson
University of Arkansas, Fayetteville, Arkansas

wcb
Wm. C. Brown Publishers
Dubuque, Iowa

Book Team
Editor, Karen Speerstra
Assistant Editor, Carol Mills
Editorial Assistant, Sharon R. Nesteby
Permissions Editor, Carla D. Arnold
Product Manager, Marcia Stout

wcb group
Wm. C. Brown, Chairman of the Board
Mark C. Falb, President and Chief Executive Officer

wcb
Wm. C. Brown Publishers, College Division

G. Franklin Lewis, Executive Vice-President, General Manager
George Wm. Bergquist, Editor in Chief
Edward G. Jaffe, Executive Editor
Beverly Kolz, Director of Production
Bob McLaughlin, National Sales Manager
Marilyn A. Phelps, Manager of Design
Colleen A. Yonda, Production Editorial Manager
Faye M. Schilling, Photo Research Manager

Consulting Editor
Frederick W. Westphal
California State University, Sacramento

Acknowledgments

We wish to thank the following professors who assisted us in the revision of *Practical Beginning Theory,* sixth edition:

Janis B. Kindred
Stetson University, Florida

Paul Nahay
Stanford University, California

Michael Hamman
University of Maryland, College Park

Dan Beaty
Stephen F. Austin State University, Texas

Susan Cohn Lackman
Rollins College, Florida

Anthony Tommasini
Emerson College, Massachusetts

Contents

Preface

To the Instructor

While the revision process allows authors an excellent opportunity to update and improve their texts, it is essential that the authors maintain the characteristics that were most useful in the previous editions. For that reason, instructors and students will continue to find this text straightforward and thorough. It is demanding—yet rewarding. Further, the significant background material, always a feature of past editions, has not been compromised, nor has the authors' strict attention to detail.

This sixth edition of *Practical Beginning Theory* is an appropriate text for use in music fundamentals courses at the junior college and college level. It is also well-suited to the students who are preparing for entrance to college or professional school as music majors.

The text assumes no prior musical training, poses no threat to beginning students, and sets a flexible pace suitable to the average student as well as to the gifted. A major improvement is the reorganization of the format to make it shorter and more efficient. Headings have been accentuated; key terms have been boldfaced and can be found quickly in the new Glossary; and the Chronology at the back of the book aids in developing a time perspective for music in the course.

The music included in the listening list from which many text examples are drawn can also be used as an excellent resource for students who wish to begin or enhance their own collections. Thus, the listening experience not only involves listening for academic achievement but for pleasure as well.

The harmony section has been completely rewritten, with an emphasis on practicality, utility, and above all, clarity.

Considerable prominence is given to the integration of music theory with keyboard instruments (piano, organ, synthesizers, and so on) guitar, and autoharp. Such coordination between theory and actual practice has been expanded throughout the entire text.

Practical Beginning Theory is designed to be flexible, supporting whatever musical preference you as the course instructor may cherish—classical music, piece of the European tradition, folk literature, popular music, and sacred compositions.

Because of the variety and diverse types of assignments, this text can be used even when outside-of-class learning facilities are minimal. A valuable learning environment may be sustained even where there is no access to a keyboard laboratory, listening room for ear training, computer lab, or adequate music library. While these learning opportunities are valuable, the textbook contains other options (such as written assignments and sight singing material) that help offset the absence of desirable equipment.

Included throughout the text are perforated pages that are especially helpful in tearing out assignments for grading.

And finally, seven appendixes offer supplemental material in such areas as popular music, chord symbols, musical forms, and nonharmonic tones.

Instructor's Manual

The *Instructor's Manual* serves two purposes: it is a repository of music for the ear training segment of the course, and it offers a number of suggested strategies and applications for instructors who may find them valuable.

This instructor's manual, through the ear training assignments, provides tactics to help students develop a step-by-step rationale that narrows the gap between musical theories and their applications. Experienced instructors may already employ many of the strategies described here or have found others equally effective, while those who may be teaching the course for the first time will find the strategies a stimulating aid in incubating ideas of their own.

Audiocassettes

Most of the ear training exercises are available on audiocassette recordings (as well as the set of microcomputer disks described next). Both the audiocassettes and computer disks are keyed to individual assignments throughout this *text*. All ancillary material is available from the publisher.

Microcomputer Software

In schools where computer labs are available, the publisher offers a set of nine floppy disks entitled *Music Fundamentals,* which run on the Apple II, IIe, or II+ (with 48K and an Applesoft Language card). A music board with speakers or headphones is required. Clear on-screen instructions and simple operations offer students multiple opportunities to learn harmony, intervals, melodic concepts, meter, rhythm, scales, and drills.

Practical Beginning Theory
A Fundamentals Worktext

Introduction

What Is Music?

Music is the art of sound moving through time to form a structure that evokes a response from the feelings and senses of the hearer. The sound elements selected to create this structure vary in different cultures and historical periods. Within any given culture there is a common practice that determines which combinations of sounds will be accepted by the listener as logical, and a body of principles codifying their use.

How Is It Used?

The uses of music are many. Ancient cultures considered music to have healing powers, and the Greeks and others believed that it had an effect on the development of good or bad qualities of character, and so thought its regulated use important for education. Music has been used as part of worship in every culture, it has urged troops on to battle and heroism (drums and bugles even provided means of sending messages in the field in the days before telephone and radio communication), it has provided for entertainment of all social classes, and it even has an important symbolic role in governments (national feelings aroused by national songs) and revolutions (the "Marseillaise" in the French Revolution). Though the practice of going to a special hall open to the public (a concert hall) to hear music is relatively modern, public concerts and recitals have made music of all kinds available to a very wide public. The development of recordings in the twentieth century has also made it possible for a listener practically anywhere in the world to hear almost any kind of music simply by playing a record!

What Is Music Theory?

Whatever the purpose for which the music was originally produced, musicians use certain common principles to manipulate the sound material. It is the use of these materials that is generally included in the study of **music theory.** Although theory includes some study of the physical laws of sound, full investigation of the physical laws is reserved for the study of physics or **acoustics** (the science of sound).

In this course you will learn about the sound materials used in the Western World in modern times. Be aware, however, that the music of ancient times and the music of other cultures of the modern world, such as the various Oriental and African civilizations, is often organized along quite different lines, and that, from these different principles, coherent and intelligible art-forms result.

Traditionally the study of music theory is divided into three parts: *rhythm, melody,* and *harmony.* The study of **rhythm** covers the time relationships between beats, patterns of note values, meter, and so on. **Melody,** since it is the movement from one pitch to another in a time relationship, involves both rhythm and pitch. Melodic patterns often use broken chords or imply harmonic relationships, so the study of melody also involves harmony. **Harmony** is the study of arrangements of pitches that sound together (*chords*) and the movement from one chord to another. Since movement is involved, rhythmic relationships also enter into the study of harmony; as one chord moves to another, the separate members of the chord create melodic patterns as they move to the following notes, so melody also enters the division of harmony.

Where Did the Examples in the Text Come from?

Awareness of style differences and of the purposes for which different kinds of music have been written also helps to make music speak more intensely to you. We have provided some guides for helping you see the examples in the book in a historical setting. You will find more extensive treatment of this aspect of music in the courses in *music appreciation, music literature,* or *music history* that are offered in your school. We have given you a listening list of complete works that can be heard as a supplement to the examples drawn from them in the text, and we have also added a chronology of musical people and events correlated with other historical and cultural movements, events, and people. Listen to the complete works in your listening list as much as you can, for the examples are not merely exercises but small excerpts from whole works of art which can be the source of much pleasure and artistic impact for you when heard complete.

As you begin this course in the handling of the musician's materials, try to think of as many situations as possible in the lives of the class members in which music is necessary or desirable. You might find it interesting to think of this question again at the end of the course and see if you have discovered any new ways you use music or have noticed it being used around you.

The Musician's Raw Materials   Part I

All music must manipulate certain basic elements—the pitch, duration, intensity, and timbre of each tone, and the rhythmic relationships that result from combining tones in succession. In this first part of your study you will study the properties of sound, and the notation of individual sounds that show their relation to each other in pitch and rhythm.

Chapter 1   The Properties of Individual Sounds

Pitch, Duration, Intensity, Timbre

Every isolated musical sound has four properties that give it its particular character: *pitch, duration, intensity,* and *timbre.*

Pitch is the property that the ear perceives as the *high* or *low* character of the sound. The sensation of *highness* or *lowness* is the ear's response to the frequency of the vibrations of the sounding body; the more rapidly the object vibrates, the higher the sound will be heard to be. Pitch is perceived only when the sounding body vibrates with a regular number of vibrations per second. If the vibrations are irregular, the sound is without pitch and is called *noise.*

Duration is simply the length of time the tone sounds.

Intensity is what the ear perceives as the *loudness* or *softness* of the sounds.

Timbre is the property which distinguishes the sound of a violin from that of the human voice, or that of the oboe from the clarinet. It is often referred to as *tone color* or *tone quality.* It is caused by the complex components of each sound called *overtones.* Overtones are a series of higher pitches which are mixed in the sound of every musical tone and which maintain invariable pitch relations to the *fundamental tone.* The tones of different instruments contain these overtones in varying degrees of intensity. The ear does not usually perceive them as separate pitches but as a total sound property called *timbre.* The notes that make up the first part of the overtone series for the note A follow. The series goes on to infinity, theoretically, although the extreme upper limits of the series would then be beyond the range of human hearing.

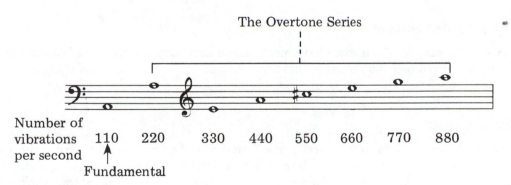

The Overtone Series

| Number of vibrations per second | 110 | 220 | 330 | 440 | 550 | 660 | 770 | 880 |

↑ Fundamental

The most important aspect of these properties to the musician is the aural effect perceived. In the exercises that follow, you will be asked to hear changes in the various properties of sound from one tone to another.

The Instruments That Produce the Different Timbres

Musical instruments are classified into families on the basis of the methods by which the sound is produced. *String instruments* are those that sound when a bow is drawn across the string causing the string to vibrate. Instruments of this family can also be sounded by plucking their strings. *Wind instruments* sound by means of a vibrating column of air in a tube or pipe. There are two groups of wind instruments: the *brass* family in whose instruments lengths of tubing produce the notes of the overtone series, and the *woodwind* family in which fingerholes are used in a pipe to produce different pitches by changing the length of the column of air. Instruments in which the sound is produced by striking the sounding body are called *percussion* instruments.

Members of the *string* family played with a bow include the violin, the viola, the cello, the string bass, and earlier instruments from the Renaissance and Baroque eras, such as the viola da gamba. All these instruments are sometimes played by plucking the strings. Some string instruments are always played by plucking the strings. Members of the *plucked string* family also have *frets,* that is, division points on the fingerboard behind which the finger is placed to produce the desired pitch. Members of this family (also often called the family of *fretted* instruments) include the guitar, lute, banjo, ukelele, and balalaika. The harp is another type of instrument with strings whose sound is produced by plucking.

Members of the *brass* family include the bugle (which has only one possible length of tubing, and can thus only play the notes of *one* overtone series), the trumpet (which like most instruments of this family can change the length of the tubing by means of valves, and which thus, unlike the bugle, has a complete scale), the cornet, the tuba, the trombone (which changes the length of its tubing by means of a slide), French horn, and euphonium.

Members of the *woodwind* family include the flute, clarinet, oboe, bassoon, English horn, and the various saxophones. All these instruments except the flute use a reed.

Members of the *percussion* family include tympani, snare drums, castanets, chimes, cymbals, triangle, and a variety of other drums and special instruments. One large and important category of percussion instruments include those with bars arranged like keyboards and struck with mallets; these include the xylophone, marimba, and vibraphone.

A very important group of instruments uses a *keyboard* to activate the sound producing agent. Among the *keyboard instruments,* the piano produces its sound by means of hammers striking the strings, the organ uses air columns in pipes to produce its sound, and the harpsichord sound results from *plectra* that pluck the strings.

In the twentieth century some instruments have been adapted or invented to use electric means of producing or enhancing the sounds they make. *Electronic sounds* may be amplifications of natural sounds, they may be electrically produced sounds similar to the sounds of natural instruments, or they may be completely new qualities of sound. Many popular music groups of the present day use electronic means of producing sounds. There are various electronic plucked and keyboard instruments. An instrument which can use electronic techniques to put together synthetic sounds of various sorts is the Moog synthesizer which has been useful to both serious composers and composers in the popular music field.

Music made up entirely or in part by electronic sound may be preserved on tape. Some music is composed especially for tape, using sounds and adaptations of sounds that are only possible by this means. The effects and combinations of sound of such *electronic music* cannot be represented adequately by standard musical notation.

Class Demonstration Assignment

Members of the class who play various musical instruments should demonstrate their instruments to the class, showing how the sound is produced and how the various pitches are obtained.

Sight Singing Assignment

You must be able to use your own voice to express yourself musically. An important first step is the ability to match pitches, whatever the timbre producing the pitch to be matched. A series of tones will be played by different instruments. Each tone will be played twice. After the second sound is played, sing it back, using the neutral syllable "la." The pitch will then be sounded again to give you a chance to check yourself. There will be ten different pitches in all, as in the following example. The examples are all recorded on the cassettes that are available for use with this text. They may also be played by your teacher.

You hear:

You sing:

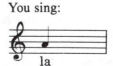

You hear again:

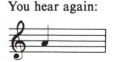

Ear Training Assignment

A. In each of the following exercises you hear two tones, one followed closely by the other. In each exercise *one* of the four properties of musical sound has been altered. The four properties of musical sound are:

   1. Pitch   2. Duration   3. Intensity   4. Timbre

Three of the properties will remain the same in each exercise; only *one* property will be changed. Place a line under the one that has been altered. The example is worked correctly for you.

EXAMPLE: (Two different timbres)

Answer: † 1. Pitch   Duration   Intensity   <u>Timbre</u>

           † 2. Pitch   Duration   Intensity   Timbre

           † 3. Pitch   Duration   Intensity   Timbre

           † 4. Pitch   Duration   Intensity   Timbre

           † 5. Pitch   Duration   Intensity   Timbre

           † 6. Pitch   Duration   Intensity   Timbre

           † 7. Pitch   Duration   Intensity   Timbre

           † 8. Pitch   Duration   Intensity   Timbre

           † 9. Pitch   Duration   Intensity   Timbre

          †10. Pitch   Duration   Intensity   Timbre

B. In each of these exercises you will hear two tones, one followed closely by the other. *Two* of the four properties of musical sound have been altered. Remember that *two* of the properties will remain the same in each exercise; *two* will change. Underline the two that have been altered:

           † 1. Pitch   Duration   Intensity   Timbre

           † 2. Pitch   Duration   Intensity   Timbre

           † 3. Pitch   Duration   Intensity   Timbre

           † 4. Pitch   Duration   Intensity   Timbre

           † 5. Pitch   Duration   Intensity   Timbre

           † 6. Pitch   Duration   Intensity   Timbre

           † 7. Pitch   Duration   Intensity   Timbre

           † 8. Pitch   Duration   Intensity   Timbre

           † 9. Pitch   Duration   Intensity   Timbre

          †10. Pitch   Duration   Intensity   Timbre

†Indicates examples recorded on the cassettes available for use with this text.

Chapter 2   The Notation of Musical Sounds: Pitch

Notes on the Staff

The most common type of musical notation shows pitch by placing symbols called **notes** on a graph of *five lines and four spaces* known as the **staff.** The location of the note on the staff represents the highness or lowness of the pitch. The principle of the staff was adopted in Europe in the eleventh century. Although the shape of the notes was different then, the graph principle has remained the same.

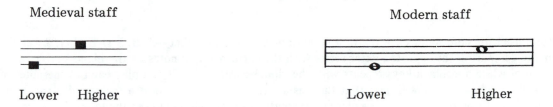

Medieval staff	Modern staff
Lower Higher	Lower Higher

Clefs

The actual pitch of the note has always been determined by referring to a sign placed at the left end of the staff called the **clef.** It designates the exact pitch of the line on which it stands, and all the other lines and spaces are related to that line. Since the range of notes on any one staff is limited, various clefs are used to notate music at different pitch levels. The clef commonly used for pitches in the range of women's voices and the upper half of the piano keyboard is called the **treble clef.** It is placed on the second line of the staff, making that line represent G just above the middle of the piano keyboard. The form of the modern sign is derived from an ancient ornate letter G, with the lower circular portion enclosing the second line of the staff—the note G.

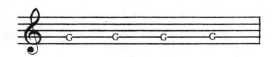

The clef used for notes in the male voice range and the lower half of the piano keyboard is called the **bass clef.** It marks the position of the F below the middle of the piano keyboard and takes its shape from an old form of the letter F.

Other clefs in common use are the **C clefs** which mark the position of middle C. The most common positions for the C clef are:

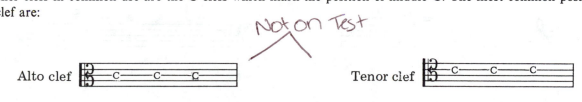

Alto clef	Tenor clef

Today C clefs are most often used for instrumental music. The viola reads alto clef and the cello, bassoon, and trombone use tenor clef for their upper ranges. In this book the exercises will all be in treble or bass clef.

The Names of the Notes

When the clef sign is in place, every other line and space acquires an exact pitch in relation to it. Each pitch is given a letter name, going up in alphabetical order.

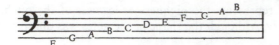   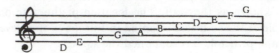

The letters used for note names are the first seven letters of the alphabet—A B C D E F G. After G, the series begins again. By comparing the repeated letter series with the corresponding notes on the piano keyboard, you will see that the pattern of white and black keys repeats with the alphabetical series. If you play each of the notes of the same letter name on the keyboard, you will hear that there is a strong similarity, almost a feeling of identity, between the notes. The similarity of sound is evidence of a close mathematical relationship between the tones, for as you go from left to right on the keyboard (that is, *up* in relation to the pitches) each repeated letter has exactly twice as many vibrations as the one preceding it.

Each line and space corresponds to a white key of the piano keyboard, as shown on the following diagram. Play each note on the piano, using the diagram as a guide.

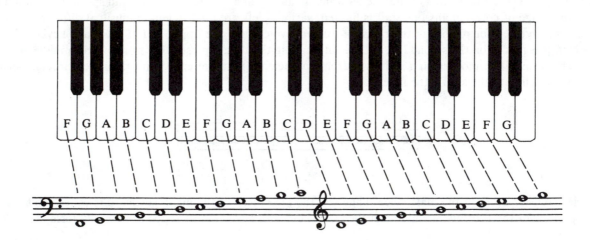

For notes beyond the range of the five line staff, small line segments called **leger lines** are used above or below the staff so that higher or lower notes may be written.

   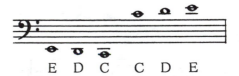

The Interval of the Octave

The distance between any two musical tones is called an **interval.** If two notes of an interval are sounded together, the interval is a **harmonic interval.** When they are sounded successively, the interval is a **melodic interval.** The interval from a tone to the next note with the same letter name is called an **octave.**

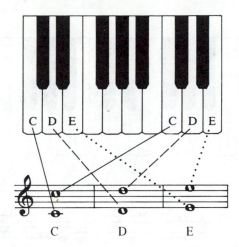

In music for the piano and other keyboard instruments, two staves are used, forming the **grand staff.** The lower staff is usually notated in bass clef, and the upper is written in treble clef. The note which is on the first leger line below the treble clef is known as **middle C.** That same pitch is the first leger line above the bass clef.

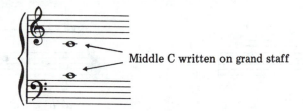

Middle C written on grand staff

The System for Naming Specific Pitches

There is a convenient system for referring to specific notes in their proper octave without using staff notation. The octave beginning with *middle C* (one-line octave) uses the symbols *c'*, *d'*, *e'*, etc.; the next octave uses *c''*, *d''*, *e''* and so on; the octave above that is *c'''*, *d'''*, *e'''*, and so on. The octave below *c'* is notated *c, d, e,* and so on; the next octave down is *C, D, E,* and so on; and the octave below that would be *C'.* The whole system is shown in the following. (The system using c^1, c^2, c^3, c^4 is also used by many writers.)

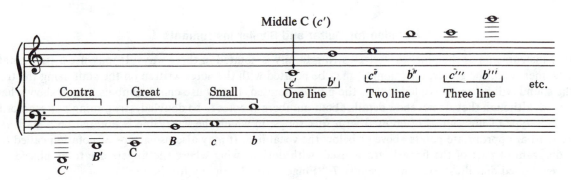

This system will be used (in *italic print*) when referring to a specific pitch throughout the text. If a general pitch name (not referring to a specific note in a particular octave) is used, a capital Roman letter will be used, as in the sentence "A piece in the key of C major usually ends on a C." This system is the one now preferred for writing about music.

Label the following example with the correct letter symbols for each note in its proper octave. Underline letters that would be printed as italics. Play each note in the proper octave on the keyboard. As you can see, the example does not cover the whole keyboard.

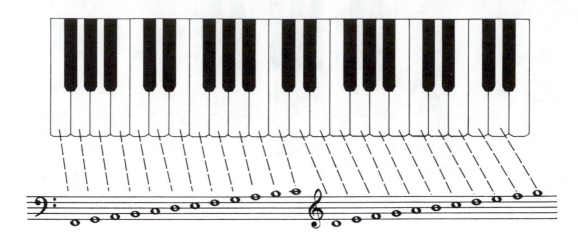

Octave is sometimes abbreviated 8ᵛᵃ. The range of the staff can be extended by using an *octave sign* (8ᵛᵃ‒‒‒‒‒ ⌐) to show that notes included in the bracket are played an octave higher when the sign is above the notes and an octave lower when it is below them.

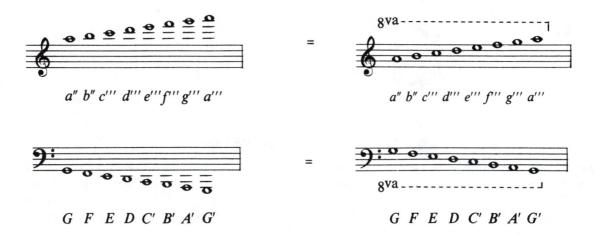

Notation for Guitar and Similar Instruments

Music for the instruments of the plucked, fretted string family is notated in three ways. It may use a staff notation just as other instruments do; the guitar, for example, may be notated with the notes written on the staff using the treble clef, although the sound will be an octave lower than the pitches notated. It may use chord symbols, which show what chords are to be played, although they do not show details about numbers of notes to be doubled, strumming patterns, or rhythms to be used. This type of notation is often used with folk songs, in which the vocal line is notated on a staff and chord symbols are used at appropriate points above or below the vocal line. It may also use a type of notation called **tablature,** in which a diagram of part of the fingerboard is used, with dots showing where the fingers are to be placed. All these systems are explained and illustrated in Appendix 7, "Fingerboard Harmony for Guitar."

Sight Singing Assignment

A pitch will be given you on the piano. Sing that pitch, then sing the note an octave higher, and then sing the first pitch again. These exercises may be worked out in two different ways.

1. *For the classroom:* The instructor plays the whole notes, and the student immediately sings the black notes.
2. *For individual drill:* The student plays the whole notes on an instrument (outside class) and immediately sings the black notes. It is advisable also for the student to play the black notes on a pitchpipe, on the piano, or on another instrument *after* singing them. This acts as a final check on the accuracy of singing.

To be sung by students with treble voices:

To be sung by students with lower voices:

Written Assignment

A clear and legible musical handwriting is essential to the musician. The purpose of these exercises is not simply to acquaint you with the shape of the notes, with which you may already be familiar, but to give you practice in perfecting the legible musical manuscript, which is so important in communicating musical ideas to the performer who reads your manuscript. You should continue to practice and perfect a clear and legible manuscript in all subsequent written drills, even when it is not specifically mentioned in the instructions.

A. 1. The steps in writing a treble clef are:

Step 1   Step 2   Step 3   Step 4   Step 5   Step 6

Following this method, write ten treble clefs on the following staff. Be sure that the relation of the parts of the clef to the staff lines is kept exact in all the clefs you write.

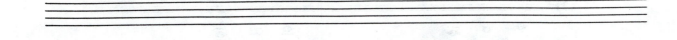

2. The steps in writing a bass clef are:

Step 1   Step 2   Step 3   Step 4   Step 5

Following this method, write ten bass clefs on the following staff. Be careful to see that the two dots to the right of the clef sign are on either side of the fourth line of the staff.

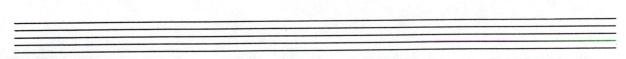

B. Whole notes are written as:

Stroke 1 + Stroke 2 = Whole note   Stroke 1 + Stroke 2 = Whole note

Using this method, write one whole note on each line and each space of the staff provided. Then write the proper letter symbol for each note in its proper octave.

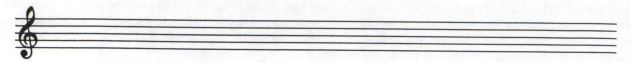

C. Leger lines are spaced with the same distance between them as that between the lines of the staff. They are just long enough to extend slightly beyond the note on each side.

Place the note on the last leger line or in the space beyond the last leger line. *Never* use a leger line beyond the note.

Correct   Incorrect

Write the notes called for in the following exercises. Be sure to use the correct notation for notes with leger lines. Then write the proper letter symbol for each note in its proper octave.

EXAMPLE:

1. Write the note an octave above the note given. Use a treble clef.

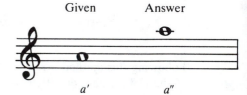

2. Write the note an octave below the note given. Use a bass clef.

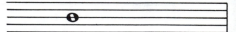

3. Write the note an octave above the note given. Use a bass clef.

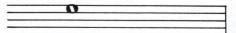

4. Write the note an octave above the note given. Use a treble clef.

Written Assignment (cont.)

5. Write the note an octave below the note given. Use a bass clef.

6. Write the note an octave below the note given. Use a treble clef.

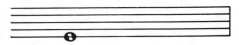

D. Here you see a series of notes. Label each with its letter name showing the correct octave. The first example is worked correctly for you.

1 _e'_ 2 _____ 3 _____ 4 _____ 5 _____ 6 _____ 7 _____ 8 _____

1 _____ 2 _____ 3 _____ 4 _____ 5 _____ 6 _____ 7 _____ 8 _____

Under the staff is a series of note names. Write each note in its proper place on the staff.

EXAMPLE:

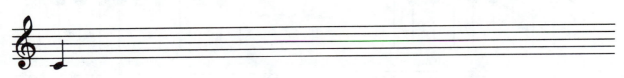

1 _c'_   2 _f'_   3 _g"_   4 _d'_   5 _a"_   6 _e'_   7 _b'_

1 _b_   2 _f_   3 _E_   4 _C_   5 _d_   6 _g_   7 _a_

E. A diagram of a keyboard accompanies each of the following groups of notes. Draw a line from each note to the appropriate key on the diagram. After finding each group of notes on the diagram, play them on the piano. The example is worked correctly for you.

EXAMPLE:

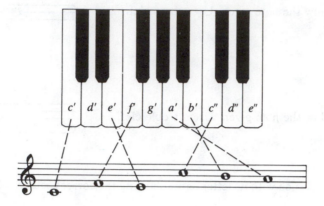

2.

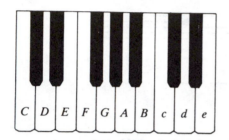

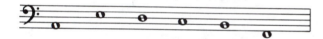

3.

4.

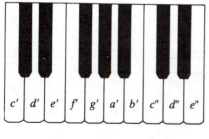

5.

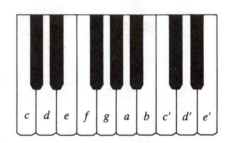

6.

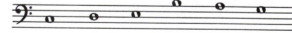

Ear Training Assignment

A. Generally speaking, tones sounding *higher than middle c′* are written in the *treble clef*. In each exercise you will hear middle C (the C in the middle of the piano keyboard) *first*, followed by a group of three other tones. Indicate which of the three tones should be written in the treble clef and which should be written in the bass clef by circling the proper clef in each instance. The example is illustrated and worked correctly for you.

EXAMPLE: The instructor plays this:

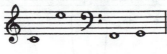

a.   b.   c.   d.

Answer:

1. a. Middle C
   b.
   c.
   d.

2. a. Middle C
   b.
   c.
   d.

3. a. Middle C
   b.
   c.
   d.

4. a. Middle C
   b.
   c.
   d.

5. a. Middle C
   b.
   c.
   d.

† 6. a. Middle C
   b.
   c.
   d.

† 7. a. Middle C
   b.
   c.
   d.

† 8. a. Middle C
   b.
   c.
   d.

† 9. a. Middle C
   b.
   c.
   d.

†10. a. Middle C
   b.
   c.
   d.

Computer Program Disk: Intervals 1, Lesson B

B. In each of the following exercises you will hear four harmonic intervals. *Three* will be octaves, and *one* will be some other interval. Circle the letters here that represent the octaves. Each exercise will be played twice. The example is illustrated and is worked correctly.

EXAMPLE: 1. (a.)   (b.)   c.   (d.)   † 6. a.   b.   c.   d.

2. a.   b.   c.   d.   † 7. a.   b.   c.   d.

3. a.   b.   c.   d.   † 8. a.   b.   c.   d.

4. a.   b.   c.   d.   † 9. a.   b.   c.   d.

5. a.   b.   c.   d.   †10. a.   b.   c.   d

Computer Program Disk: Intervals 1, Lesson B

†Indicates examples recorded on the cassettes available for use with this text.

C. In each of the following exercises you will hear a group of three melodic intervals. *Two* will be octaves, and one will be some other interval. Circle the following letters that represent the interval of an octave. The example is illustrated and is worked correctly. Each exercise will be played twice.

EXAMPLE: You will hear:

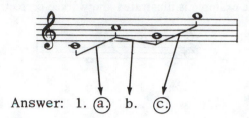

Answer: 1. (a.) b. (c.)

2. a. Between the 1st and 2nd note
   b. Between the 2nd and 3rd note
   c. Between the 3rd and 4th note

3. a. Between the 1st and 2nd note
   b. Between the 2nd and 3rd note
   c. Between the 3rd and 4th note

4. a. Between the 1st and 2nd note
   b. Between the 2nd and 3rd note
   c. Between the 3rd and 4th note

5. a. Between the 1st and 2nd note
   b. Between the 2nd and 3rd note
   c. Between the 3rd and 4th note

† 6. a. Between the 1st and 2nd note
   b. Between the 2nd and 3rd note
   c. Between the 3rd and 4th note

† 7. a. Between the 1st and 2nd note
   b. Between the 2nd and 3rd note
   c. Between the 3rd and 4th note

† 8. a. Between the 1st and 2nd note
   b. Between the 2nd and 3rd note
   c. Between the 3rd and 4th note

† 9. a. Between the 1st and 2nd note
   b. Between the 2nd and 3rd note
   c. Between the 3rd and 4th note

†10. a. Between the 1st and 2nd note
   b. Between the 2nd and 3rd note
   c. Between the 3rd and 4th note

Computer Program Disk: Intervals 1, Lesson C

Chapter 3 Pitch and the Keyboard

The Octave, the Half Step, and the Whole Step

Within each octave of the piano keyboard there is a fixed relationship between the black and white keys. The octave whose lowest note is *middle C* (the note on the first leger line below the treble clef staff) is the middle octave of the keyboard (c'–c'').

The interval between notes of the same letter name is the *octave*. This relationship gives order to the larger divisions of the pitch range. The *smallest* division in use in most of the music of Western civilization is the distance between *two adjacent keys on the piano*. This distance is called a **half step** or a *semitone*.

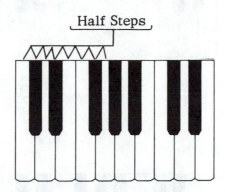

Intervals smaller than the half step and slides or **glissandi** through a continuous pitch stream are used in music in other parts of the world and in some twentieth century European and American music.

There are two places within any octave from C to C in which the adjacent keys on the piano are both white keys; E and F, and B and C. These are the only white keys with *only one half step* between them. All other white keys are separated by a black key, so the distance between them is *two* half steps or a **whole step** (also called a *whole tone*).

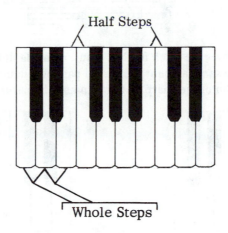

Sharps, Flats, and Naturals

To notate all the possible pitches on the keyboard, additional signs are needed to raise or lower the pitch of the seven letter names (A B C D E F G).

The pitch is raised a half step when a **sharp** (♯) is placed in front of the note and lowered a half step when a **flat** (♭) is placed before the note.

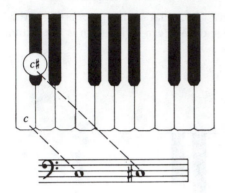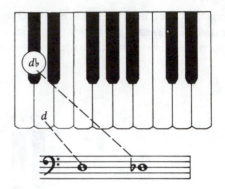

A **natural** (♮) cancels the preceding sharp or flat.

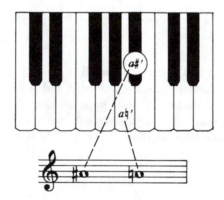

A double sign is used to raise or lower the pitch further. Thus, a **double flat** (♭♭) lowers the note by two half steps, and a **double sharp** (𝗫) raises it by the same amount. To cancel part of a double flat or double sharp, so that one half step of alteration remains, a combination of the sharp or flat sign and the natural sign is used.

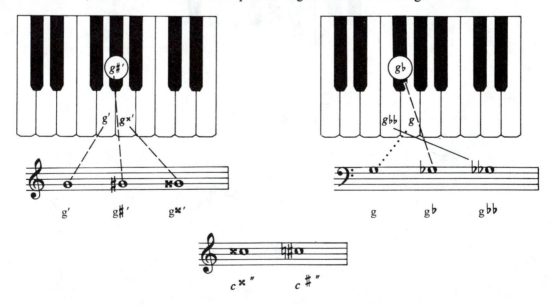

Enharmonic Spellings

As you see, the same key of the keyboard may be given different names, depending on the way it is notated. Notes that sound alike but are notated differently are said to be **enharmonic.**

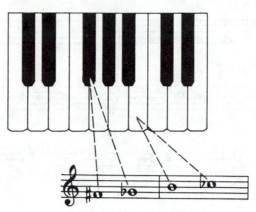

Enharmonic spellings

The Scale

A **scale** is an orderly sequence of the notes within an octave. It summarizes the notes available for use in a particular context. You will learn many specific patterns later.

The Chromatic Scale

When all twelve different notes within the octave are arranged in order, the result is a **chromatic scale.** Sharps are used to notate the ascending scale; flats, the descending scale.

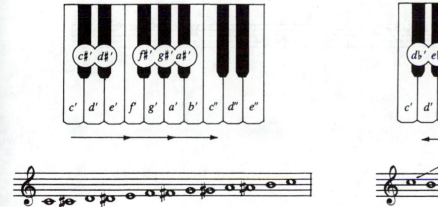
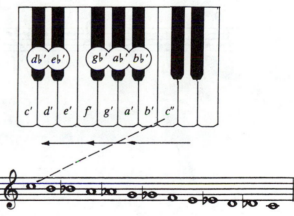

When you write a chromatic scale, be sure that the white-key half step pairs (E–F and B–C) are notated as natural notes.

Wrong

Right

Sight Singing Assignment

A. A pitch will be given to you from the piano or pitchpipe. Sing that pitch, then sing the half step up or down from that pitch as shown by the notation, then sing the first pitch again.

B. The next exercise is for singing half steps and whole steps. When you hear the note played, sing that pitch; then sing the *half step above* it, return to the first pitch, sing the *whole step above* it, and return to the starting pitch. For exercises 7 through 12 practice the same pattern *descending* from the given note.

Written Assignment

Developing a good musical handwriting helps everything you need to do in preparing a musical score.

A.   1.   Sharps are notated as follows:

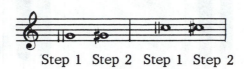

Step 1   Step 2   Step 1   Step 2

Be sure that the sharp is to the *left* of the note, and that the lines enclose the line or space on which the note is placed. Using the above method, write a sharp in front of each of the following notes.

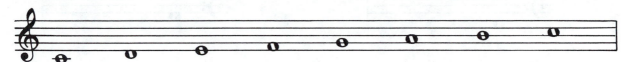

2.   Flats are notated as follows:

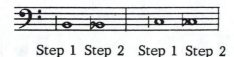

Step 1   Step 2   Step 1   Step 2

Be sure that the flat is to the *left* of the note and that the line or space on which the note stands is enclosed by the curved section of the sign. Using the above method, write a flat in front of each of the following notes.

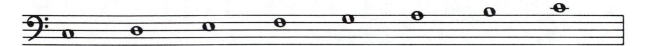

3.   Naturals are notated as follows:

Step 1   Step 2   Step 1   Step 2

The square section of the sign should enclose the line or space on which the note stands. Using the preceding method, write a natural in front of the following notes.

A. After each of the following notes, write the sharped note a half step above the given note. Locate each note of the pair on the keyboard diagram.

1.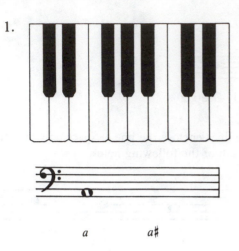

        a   *a♯*

2.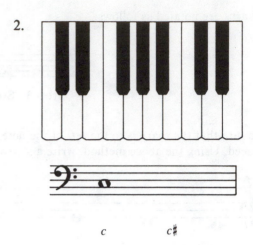

        c   *c♯*

B. After each of the following notes, write the flatted note a half step below the given note. Locate each note of the pair on the keyboard diagram.

1.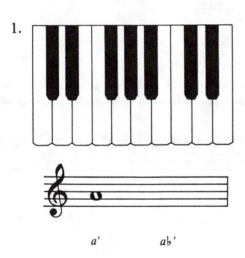

        a'   *a♭'*

2.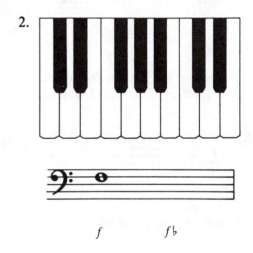

        f   *f♭*

C. Write a chromatic scale, using the correct spelling in sharps for the ascending scale and flats for the descending scale on each of the given tones. After writing the examples, play each scale on the piano.

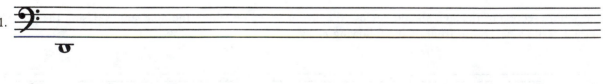

1.

2.

Written Assignment (cont.)

D. Following are several pairs of notes. Some are enharmonic spellings of the same sound and others are not. Locate the correct enharmonic pairs and circle them. Change the second note of the other pairs to make them enharmonic also. Locate the key on the keyboard diagram that would be used to play both notes of all the enharmonic pairs of notes.

1.
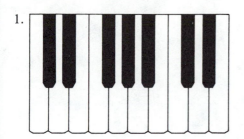

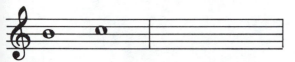

4.

2.
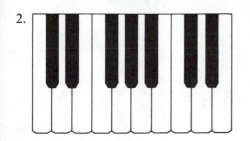

5.

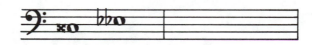

3.

Ear Training Assignment

A. You will hear three isolated melodic intervals. In each exercise *one* of these will be a half step, while the other two intervals will be larger than a half step. Circle the letter designating the half step.

EXAMPLE:

You will hear:

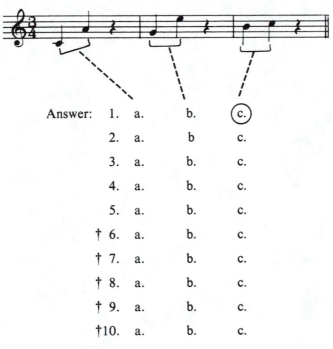

Answer:	1.	a.	b.	(c.)
	2.	a.	b	c.
	3.	a.	b.	c.
	4.	a.	b.	c.
	5.	a.	b.	c.
	† 6.	a.	b.	c.
	† 7.	a.	b.	c.
	† 8.	a.	b.	c.
	† 9.	a.	b.	c.
	†10.	a.	b.	c.

Computer Program Disk: Intervals 1, Lesson D

B. You will hear three isolated melodic intervals. Two will be whole steps, and one will be a half step. Circle the letter designating the half step.

1.	a.	b.	c.
2.	a.	b.	c.
3.	a.	b.	c.
4.	a.	b.	c.
5.	a.	b.	c.
† 6.	a.	b.	c.
† 7.	a.	b.	c.
† 8.	a.	b.	c.
† 9.	a.	b.	c.
†10.	a.	b.	c.

Computer Program Disk: Intervals 1, Lesson E

Chapter 4   The Notation of Musical Sounds: Rhythm

What is Rhythm?

Music is the art of sound organized in time. **Rhythm** is the force that generates, controls, and organizes movement and time relationships. Rhythmic organization is not limited to music; we perceive it as a life-giving force in our own bodies in the regularity of our heartbeat, breathing, walking, sleeping, and waking. We feel day and night, the turn of the seasons, even birth and death, to be rhythmic organizations of experience. The arts of poetry, drama, and dance also depend for their effect on the organization of materials in time. The drive for rhythmic organization is so strong that the concept is even extended to arts such as painting and sculpture where the relation of the parts to each other and to the whole object is seen as a kind of "movement."

The Beat

Rhythm in music involves all time relationships. It includes the progression from one large division of a musical form to another to the underlying pulse, which, like the heartbeat, is present continuously in most music. The study of rhythm begins with the underlying pulse or **beat.**

The *beat* is a regularly recurring pulse which measures the duration of musical events. It also has the property of forming groups with an **accent** or stress for the principal beat of the group. The stressed beat is called **1,** and the remaining beats in the group are counted from the accented beat.

1 2 **1** 2 **1** 2 **1** 2 or **1** 2 3 **1** 2 3 **1** 2 3 **1** 2 3

This grouping of beats can be felt even in a series of pulses of absolutely equal intensity. It probably results from an inner human need to organize experience into patterns. It is this urge to organize that causes optical illusions. If you look at a series of equidistant dots, you may see them group themselves in twos or threes at will.

. . . .

If some of the dots are slightly darkened or *accented* one grouping will be seen.

· . **·** . **·** . **·** . **·** . **·** . **·**

Grouping I

By changing the accent, another grouping appears.

· . . **·** . . **·** . . **·** . .

Grouping II

In musical notation, these groups would be expressed as in the examples below. The > (*accent mark*) shows the stressed notes.

Grouping I (**duple meter**)

Grouping II (**triple meter**)

It is important to remember that these natural stresses are generally very subtle. It would be unmusical to over-emphasize them in playing!

Meter

The simplest groups of beats contain two or three beats. Larger groups are the result of combining the smaller groups. When groups of beats with regularly recurring accents occur in music, we call it **meter.** If the groups fall in groups of *two* pulses, the meter is *duple;* when in groups of three, the meter is **triple.** Each group of beats with a regularly recurring accent is called a **measure** or **bar.** In music notation, the end of each measure is indicated by a vertical line drawn through the staff and known as the **bar line** (see the previous examples).

Not all music is **metric.** Some of the old music of the Catholic Church (Gregorian chant) is not measured in this way, and electronic music and some other twentieth century music uses **nonmetric** means of organizing musical time. In the ear training exercises you will hear some examples.

Notes and Their Values

In modern musical notation, the relative duration of each individual note is shown by its shape and coloring.

Breve	𝆸	double whole note
Whole note	o	
Half note	𝅗𝅥	= 1/2 of o
Quarter note	♩	= 1/4 of o or 1/2 of 𝅗𝅥
Eighth note	♪	= 1/8 of o or 1/2 of ♩
Sixteenth note	𝅘𝅥𝅯	= 1/16 of o or 1/2 of ♪
Thirty-second note	𝅘𝅥𝅰	= 1/32 of o or 1/2 of 𝅘𝅥𝅯
Sixty-fourth note	𝅘𝅥𝅱	= 1/64 of o or 1/2 of 𝅘𝅥𝅰

There are three parts which can be assembled to write a note. These are: **note head o** or **●**, the **stem** |, and the **flag** ❬ .

❬ flag

| stem

● note head

The note heads of whole and half notes are not filled in, but all note values smaller than the half note have black note heads. All notes except the whole note have a stem. Flags are added to the eighth notes and all smaller note values. Each flag added to the stem decreases the value by one-half.

eighth note   sixteenth note   thirty-second note

Adding Length to a Note with a Dot or a Tie

In the preceding chapter all the note values were related to each other in a *one to two relationship:* that is, each note value was equal to two of the next smaller value unit. A new symbol is necessary to express a value equal to *three* of the next unit. This symbol is the **dot** added to the right of the note head to increase the value of the note by one-half.

When a note is placed on a space, the dot is written on the space. For clarity, if the note is on a line, the dot is placed on the space above.

A **tie,** a curved line connecting the note heads of two notes of the same pitch, is used to indicate that the note values are to be added together. By means of the tie, a note of any duration can be written.

Tie

3 Beats   1 1/2 Beats   3 1/2 Beats

The Rest

Silence is also a means of musical expression. The **rest** shows the duration of the silence. The values of rests correspond exactly to the notes with the same name.

whole rest   = o   whole note

half rest   = ♩   half note

quarter rest	𝄽		=	♩	quarter note
eighth rest	𝄾		=	♪	eighth note
sixteenth rest	𝄿		=	𝅘𝅥𝅯	sixteenth note
thirty-second rest	𝅀		=	𝅘𝅥𝅰	thirty-second note

Dotted rests have the same value as dotted notes.

$$𝄾\cdot \quad = \quad 𝄾 \;\; + \;\; 𝄿 \quad = \quad ♪\cdot$$

Rests are never tied, since a succession of rests produces an uninterrupted silence without an additional sign.

Beat Units and the Time Signature

Any note value may serve as the *unit* that receives the beat, and all other values are related to it in accordance with the preceding table of values. The most common **beat units** are the quarter note and the eighth note. The beat unit is always shown at the beginning of the piece by the lower one of two numbers found at the right of the clef sign. The top figure shows the number of beats in each measure.

Johann Sebastian Bach (1685–1750),
Minuet, Orchestra Suite No. 1 in C Major (about 1720)

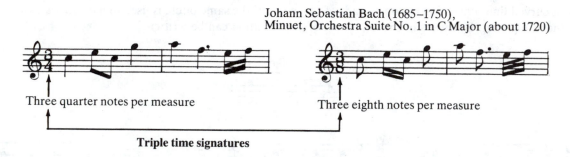

Three quarter notes per measure   Three eighth notes per measure

Triple time signatures

The basic plan of the note unit and the number of beats in each measure is called the *meter*. The pair of numbers which shows the meter is the **time signature.** The numbers of the time signature are always written so that the middle line of the staff comes between them. The time signature is placed at the beginning of a piece of music, just to the right of the clef sign. Unlike the clef sign, *it is not repeated on any of the following lines unless there is a change in the meter.*

Franz Schubert (1797–1828), "Heiden-Röslein," ("Hedge-Rose") (1815)

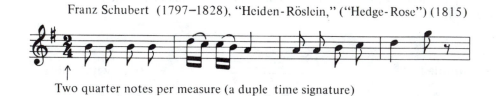

Two quarter notes per measure (a duple time signature)

*The examples are labeled with the composer's name, the dates of birth and death, the part of the work from which the excerpt is drawn, the title of the complete work, and, where possible, the date or approximate date of composition. In this case, Bach's "Suite" (a **suite** is a piece made up of several **movements**) consists of several dances; this example is from the **minuet.** See Appendix 3 for more information on the form names used in this text.

Simple Meter

When the regular division of the unit is into two subdivisions, as in all the preceding examples, the meter is called **simple meter.**

Clara Schumann (1819–1896), Allegretto,
Trio in G Minor, Op. 17 (1847)

Simple duple meter

The abbreviation *op.* stands for **opus,** an Italian word meaning *work*. It is often found after the title of a composition to refer to a musical work or group of works that were published together, and it indicates the order of publication—that is, this is the *seventeenth* work published by this composer. If another number is found after the opus number, it will indicate the number of the piece within a group of works published together.

The Up-beat

If beats or parts of beats occur before the first bar line, it is called an **up-beat, anacrusis,** or **pick-up.** The preceding example has an eighth note anacrusis.

Compound Meter

In certain meters, however, the beat unit has *three* subdivisions. The beat unit in this kind of meter is always a dotted note, and the lower number of the time signature refers to the *subdivision unit* rather than to the *beat unit*. This type of meter is called **compound meter.**

Six eighth notes per measure as shown by the time signature.

Two beat units of one dotted quarter note each.

In all compound meters, the upper number of the time signature is a number divisible by three, that is, 6, 9, or 12. The number of beat units in compound meter is the upper number divided by *three*.

Joseph Haydn (1732–1809), "With Verdure Clad,"
The Creation (1796–8)

With ver-dure clad the fields ap-pear, De-light-ful to the ra-vish'd sense.

Compound duple meter

Richard Wagner (1813–1883), "The Ride of the Valkyries,"
Die Walküre (1852–6)

Compound triple meter

Triplets

To divide a note that normally has two subdivisions into three parts, three notes are written as a group with the numeral 3 above them. The same principle is used for more unusual groups such as five or seven subdivisions. The group of three, which is by far the most common, is called a **triplet.**

Triplets

Eduard Lalo (1823–1892), Allegro non troppo, *Symphonie Espagnole*, Op. 21 (1875)

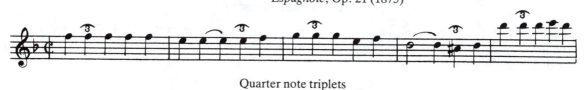

Quarter note triplets

Johannes Brahms (1833–1897), Third Movement, *Sonata in E Minor for Cello and Piano*, Op. 38 (1862–65)

Eighth note triplets

Grouping Notes with Beams

When several notes with flags are grouped together, they may be connected by a heavy line called a **beam** in place of the individual flags. If the notes have more than one flag, they are replaced by an equal number of beams. In instrumental music, beams are used to show the grouping of notes in relation to the beat, as in the following example. In vocal music, the choice of beams or flags depends on the syllable division.

The beam can be used with notes of different values, so long as they all have values smaller than a quarter note.

The grouping of notes within the meter is shown by beams.

More about Meter

As you remember, rhythmic pulses tend to be grouped in twos or threes. Meters are classified by the number of beats per measure. The most common meters are **duple** (two beats per measure), **triple** (three beats per measure), and **quadruple** (four beats per measure, a multiple of duple meter). Such unusual meters as quintuple or septuple meter (with five or seven beats in a measure) are actually combinations of groups of two and three beats within one measure. These meters are called **mixed meters** or **asymmetric meters.**

Piotr Ilyitch Tschaikovsky (1840–1893), Second Movement,
Symphony No. 6 in B Minor (Pathétique), (1893)

Quintuple meter

Some folk music and some twentieth century music use meters that change frequently (**changing meter**), which can have fascinating results.

Béla Bartók (1881–1945), Intermezzo Interotto (Interrupted
Intermezzo), *Concerto for Orchestra* (1944)

Violin

Tempo

The pace at which the beat moves may be fast or slow. The speed or **tempo** of the beat is usually indicated by Italian words. For example, **andante** means a slow, walking tempo; **moderato** means a moderate speed; **allegro** means rapidly, and so on. Some French and German composers use terms in their native languages rather than Italian. In the twentieth century, a few English-speaking composers use English tempo markings. The Italian words, however, are in such universal use that they can be understood easily by all composers and performers throughout the world, no matter what language they speak.

Tempo may be indicated precisely by referring to the **metronome**, a machine invented in 1816 by Beethoven's friend, Maelzel. It can be adjusted to beat any desired number of regular pulses per minute.

If the notation "M.M. ♩ = 60" appears at the beginning of a composition, the tempo of the music is sixty quarter note beats per minute. The initials stand for Maelzel's Metronome. Metronome markings are not always given by the composer and are not found in any music before Beethoven, since he was the first composer to use the machine. Any marking of this kind you see in earlier music has been added by a more recent editor and was not originally provided by the composer.

Sight Singing Assignment

A. The following exercises are for rhythm. Sing or say the regular meter beat indicated, and at the same time clap the note values as shown. These exercises may also be practiced by tapping the rhythm with one hand while beating time with the other hand or with your foot.

B. Sustain the following notes for the durations called for by the notation. Tap the beat as you sing. Sing the syllable *la* or *ta* for the pitch indicated. Sing exercises on a single pitch. They may also be practiced by tapping the rhythm with one hand while beating time with your other hand or with your foot.

Written Assignment

A. There are two methods of notating quarter notes in music manuscript.

Method 1: For use with ordinary pen or pencil and for rapid writing in dictation or written assignments.

In this method the notes are constructed of straight line segments ("stick method"). Use the following procedure:

Step 1   Step 2   Step 1   Step 2   Step 1   Step 2   Step 1   Step 2

Notes on or below the center line have the stem going up on the right.

Notes on or above the center line have the stem going down on the left.

Use the staff provided to make a quarter note on each line and space. Middle C (*c′*) is written as an example.

Method 2: For use with a special music manuscript or drawing pen. With a manuscript pen it is possible to make oval filled-in note heads with two strokes of the pen, using the same method used for writing whole notes or half notes, but turning the pen so that the ink covers the whole note head. Oval note heads may also be written with a pencil by drawing an empty note head and coloring in the space with a pencil.

Use the staff provided to make quarter notes with oval note heads on each line and space. Middle C (*c′*) is written as an example.

B. Eighth notes are formed by adding a flag to a quarter note as in the following examples:

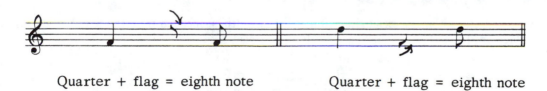

Quarter + flag = eighth note   Quarter + flag = eighth note

The flag is placed on the right side of the stem, no matter which way the stem is pointed.

Use the staff provided to write an eighth note on each line and space. *c′* is given as an example.

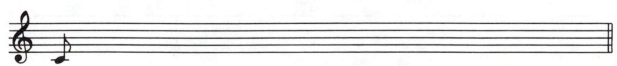

C. Smaller note values add flags or beams as necessary. Make each of the eighth notes on the staff provided into a sixteenth note. The examples are worked correctly for you.

EXAMPLES:

Flag added   Beam added

Write a single sixteenth note on each line and each space of the staff below. *c'* is given as an example.

Using the following note heads, make eighth note groups with a beam connecting each group of four notes. The example is worked correctly for you. The direction of stems is shown by the first note of each group.

Example   Solution

Using the following note heads, make sixteenth note groups with a beam connecting each group of four notes. The example is worked correctly for you. The direction of stems is shown by the first note of each group.

Example   Solution

D. The *whole rest* is written as a heavy rectangle, half a space in width, suspended from the fourth line of the staff. It is in the same place on the staff for all clefs, as are all other rests.

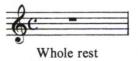

Whole rest

Write a whole rest in each measure on the staff provided.

Written Assignment (cont.)

The *half rest* is written as a heavy rectangle, half a space in width, resting above the middle line of the staff.

Half rest

Write two half rests in each measure on the staff provided.

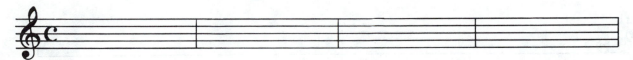

The *quarter rest* is written in music manuscript as shown here. In printed music, it has a somewhat different form, as shown.

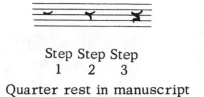

Step Step Step
  1   2   3

Quarter rest in manuscript

Quarter rest, printed form

Write four quarter rests, using the manuscript method just illustrated, in each measure of the staff provided.

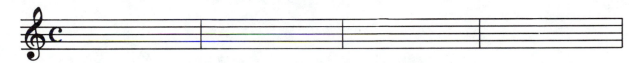

The method for writing an *eighth rest* is shown here.

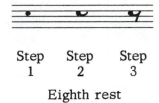

Step   Step   Step
 1   2   3

Eighth rest

Write four eighth rests in each measure provided.

To make smaller note values, extend the long line farther down and add additional flags below the top one.

Sixteenth rest Thirty-second rest

Write four sixteenth rests in each measure provided.

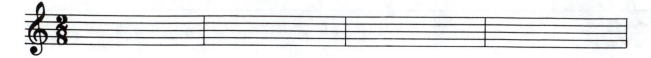

Ear Training Assignment

A. You will hear ten short melodies. Each melody is either in $\frac{2}{4}$ time or $\frac{3}{4}$ time (duple meter or triple meter).

In each exercise, indicate the meter by circling the correct time signature. Each exercise should be played twice.

† 1.	$\frac{2}{4}$	$\frac{3}{4}$		† 6.	$\frac{2}{4}$	$\frac{3}{4}$
† 2.	$\frac{2}{4}$	$\frac{3}{4}$		† 7.	$\frac{2}{4}$	$\frac{3}{4}$
† 3.	$\frac{2}{4}$	$\frac{3}{4}$		† 8.	$\frac{2}{4}$	$\frac{3}{4}$
† 4.	$\frac{2}{4}$	$\frac{3}{4}$		† 9.	$\frac{2}{4}$	$\frac{3}{4}$
† 5.	$\frac{2}{4}$	$\frac{3}{4}$		†10.	$\frac{2}{4}$	$\frac{3}{4}$

Computer Program Disk: Rhythm, Lesson B

B. *Recognition of Tempi.* In each of the following exercises you will hear a short excerpt of music in one of the tempi described in the text. Underline the correct tempo. The tempo markings used are:

Adagio = Very slow

Andante = Slow (walking tempo)

Moderato = Moderate

Allegro = Fast

Presto = Very fast

1. a. Andante	b. Moderato	c. Presto
2. a. Andante	b. Allegro	c. Presto
3. a. Andante	b. Allegro	c. Presto
† 4. a. Adagio	b. Andante	c. Presto
† 5. a. Adagio	b. Moderato	c. Allegro
† 6. a. Adagio	b. Moderato	c. Presto

Computer Program Disk: Rhythm, Lesson A

C. *Recognition of Meter.* In each exercise you will hear a short excerpt of music in one of the meters described in the text. Underline the correct meter.

1. a. duple	b. triple	c. quintuple
2. a. compound duple	b. compound triple	c. neither
† 3. a. duple	b. triple	c. changing meter
† 4. a. triple	b. quintuple	c. duple
† 5. a. triple	b. quadruple	c. neither

Computer Program Disk: Rhythm, Lesson B

Chapter 5   Other Notational Signs

Dynamic Signs

The level of intensity of the sound, changes in level, and variations in the amount of sound are expressed by **dynamic signs.** Those in most common use are given in the following list. Italian is the conventional language for describing the dynamics of a composition.

SYMBOL	TERM	EFFECT
p	**piano**	soft
pp	**pianissimo**	very soft
f	**forte**	loud
ff	**fortissimo**	very loud
mp	**mezzo piano**	moderately soft
mf	**mezzo forte**	moderately loud
▭ or cresc.	**crescendo**	gradually get louder
▭ or decresc. or dim	**decrescendo** or **diminuendo**	gradually get softer
fp	**forte piano**	loud, then suddenly soft
sf or *sfz*	**sforzando**	a sudden strong accent on the note marked
<	**accent**	a strong stress on the note marked

The Double Bar

The **double bar** is used to mark the end of important sections or the end of a piece. It consists of a pair of bar lines placed close together.

Fryderyk Chopin (1810–1849), *Prelude No. 7* (for piano), Op. 28 (1839)

When it is used for the end of a piece, the second line is heavier than the first, as shown here; when it appears at the end of the section within the piece, the two lines are the same.

Repeat Signs

If a section is to be repeated, two dots are placed in front of a double bar, and a double bar with two dots facing the opposite direction is placed at the beginning of the section being repeated. This is called a **repeat sign.**

Clara Schumann (1819–1896), Scherzo, *Trio in G Minor,*
Op. 17 (1847)

Lengthening a Note with a Fermata

There are also signs which show changes of rhythm or tempo. If a single note or rest is to be held longer than its notated value a sign called a **fermata** is placed over it. The length of the note with a fermata depends on the context in the composition.

Joseph Haydn (1732–1809), "Rolling in Foaming Billows,"
The Creation (1796–8)

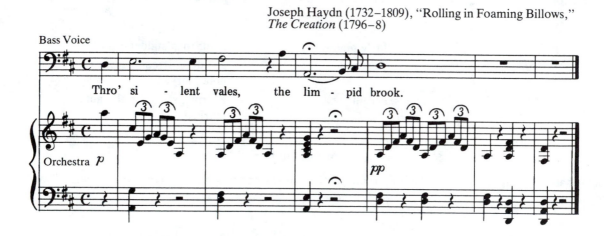

Gradual Change of Tempo

If the tempo is to be increased gradually, the score is marked **accelerando** (*accel.*); if decreased, **ritardando** or *ritenuto* (*rit.*).

Staccato and Legato

Some signs indicate the style of performance—for example, whether notes are to be played smoothly (**legato**) or in a detached manner (**staccato**). A curved line called a **slur** shows legato groups of notes. Dots or wedges placed above or below the note heads indicate staccato notes.

Ludwig van Beethoven (1770–1827), Fourth Movement,
Symphony No. 5 in C Minor, Op. 67 (1807–8)

Embellishment Signs

The Beethoven example you just saw also uses small **embellishments** called **grace notes,** which in 19th and 20th century music are shown in small type with a slash through the stem. They are played *quickly before the beat* and are used to give a spicy accent to the note they decorate.

Many other embellishment signs—*trills, turns,* and so forth—are used in music. Bring examples to class from music you are learning!

Written Assignment

Many terms and signs not discussed in this chapter are probably used in music you are playing or singing. Bring to class ten or twelve signs or terms you have found which are not given here. Look them up in a music dictionary if you do not know what they mean, and see how many different terms and signs the class can find and define.* Compile the definitions that the class finds.

*Become familiar with a good music dictionary, such as Willi Apel, *Harvard Dictionary of Music* or Don Randel, *The New Harvard Dictionary of Music.*

Ear Training Assignment

Recognition of Performance Techniques. Each of the following exercises consists of a short phrase of music. Each composition will be performed in *one* of the two following manners:

1. *Staccato*—shortening the duration of the note, producing a detached, separated effect with a short silence between notes.

2. *Legato*—no interruption of sound between notes. One note is followed immediately by the next with no silence between. One note blends into the next.

In each exercise underline the answer which best describes the manner of performance.

1. Staccato	Legato	† 3. Staccato	Legato
2. Staccato	Legato	† 4. Staccato	Legato

†Indicates examples recorded on the cassettes available for use with this text.

Combinations of Materials to Create Tonality, Scales, Key Signatures, Intervals, and Triads

Part II

The second part of the text treats the way the basic materials you learned in Part I can be combined to create the feeling of a **tonal center** (**tonality**), organized in *scales,* with **key signatures** that show immediately what tonal materials can be expected in a piece of music, and placed together simultaneously to produce intervals (two pitches sounded together) or **chords** (more than two pitches at once). The most important of all chords are those three-note chords whose members are three notes apart (the **triad**). Most of the music with which you are familiar is harmonized with triads, and part of what creates the feeling that one particular note, the **tonic,** is the center or resting place of a tonality is the way in which those chords are arranged in relation to each other.

When you have learned these basic combinations you can see how the broad categories of *rhythm, melody,* and *harmony* function, using the raw materials you learned in Part I of the text and the combinations you are about to explore in Part II.

Chapter 6   Introduction to the Tonal Center

What Is Tonality?

Just as time relations in music are given shape by the beat and meter, pitch relations are given a sense of direction by a tonal center to which the composition returns at the end to give a feeling of completion. The tonic, or note that serves as a tonal center, exercises a strong pull on the other tones used with it, so that moving away from the tonic produces a somewhat restless feeling, while arrival at the tonal center gives a sense of relaxation and stability. The organization of music around a tonal center is called tonality.

To illustrate the strong pull of the tonal center, sing the whole tune for "My Country 'Tis of Thee". . . and stop on the next to the last note. You will feel that the impetus to move on and resolve the tension by singing the last note is extremely strong.

The notes which are used with any given tone to create the feeling that it is the tonal center must be chosen with care. When these tones are arranged in alphabetical order within the octave of the tonal center, the result is a *scale.* The tonal center, or *tonic,* is always the first and last note of the scale in the well-known modern scales.

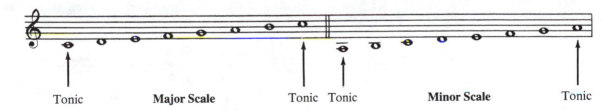

Tonic   **Major Scale**   Tonic   Tonic   **Minor Scale**   Tonic

Two different scales using the white keys

Much music uses other scale systems than the two illustrated. Following are two melodies using other scales. Play them over on the piano or another instrument and note how the tonal atmosphere differs as the scale on which the melody is based is changed.

Modest Moussorgsky (1839–1881), Promenade Theme
from *Pictures at an Exhibition* (1874)

Pentatonic (five-note) scale   Melody based on pentatonic scale shown.

Gregorian chant, some folk music, and some popular music use scales called *modes*. Here is one of these scales and a piece of music which is in that mode.

Gregorian Chant "Dies Irae" ("Day of Wrath") from the *Requiem* (13th Century)

Dorian mode

Note that the example does not have a time signature. Here is how that same melody looks in Medieval notation. The notes are the same pitches, but the shapes of the notes do not show rhythm nor is there any time signature as in more recent music.

Di - es ir - ae, di - es il - la, Sol - vet sae - clum in fa - vil - la.

Can Tonality Be Avoided?

Some music of the twentieth century avoids creating the feeling of a tonal center by using all the twelve chromatic tones in a prearranged order that does not lay particular emphasis on any one pitch in the composition as a whole. This method of composing is based on a **twelve tone row** rather than on a scale. Following is a melody based on a twelve tone row with numbers showing the pitch order used in this piece.

Arnold Schoenberg (1874–1951), First Movement, *String Quartet No. 4*,
(no key) (1933)

1   2   3   4 5   6   7   8 9   10   11   12

Music that avoids the feeling of a tonal center by this means or by any other means is said to be **atonal**, that is, without a tonal center. Much electronic music does not use a tonal center.

Ear Training Assignment

In each of the following exercises you will hear a short melody. Some of these melodies will end on the tonal center and some will end elsewhere. *All will begin on the tonal center.* Underline the proper answer in each exercise. For example, you will hear:

EXAMPLE:

Answer: 1. <u>Ends on the tonic.</u>   Ends elsewhere.

         2. Ends on the tonic.   Ends elsewhere.

         3. Ends on the tonic.   Ends elsewhere.

         4. Ends on the tonic.   Ends elsewhere.

         5. Ends on the tonic.   Ends elsewhere.

         6. Ends on the tonic.   Ends elsewhere.

         7. Ends on the tonic.   Ends elsewhere.

  † 8. Ends on the tonic.   Ends elsewhere.

  † 9. Ends on the tonic.   Ends elsewhere.

  †10. Ends on the tonic.   Ends elsewhere.

†Indicates examples recorded on the cassettes available for use with this text.

Chapter 7   The Major Scale: Major and Minor Seconds

The Major Scale

The composers of the past 300 years have used two arrangements of tones around a tonal center (scales) in preference to any others. These two are the **major scale** and the **minor scale.** Each scale has its own pattern of whole and half steps. Composers of the present day also use many other scale patterns in addition to the major and minor scales.

Scales are described by the arrangement of whole and half steps between the scale tones. A typical major scale is produced by playing all the white keys from C to the next C on the piano. Half steps occur between the third and fourth notes (E and F), and between the seventh and eighth notes (B and C) of the scale. Remember that the tonal center (C) is also called the *tonic.*

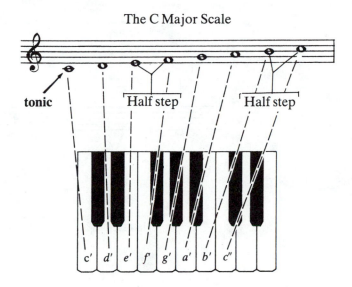

The C Major Scale

Every note of the C major scale is used in this melody in the key of C major. Notice that it begins and ends on the tonic.

Philipp Nicolai (1556–1608), "Wachet auf!" ("Sleepers Awake!"), 1599
(a hymn tune used by Johann Sebastian Bach and many other composers)

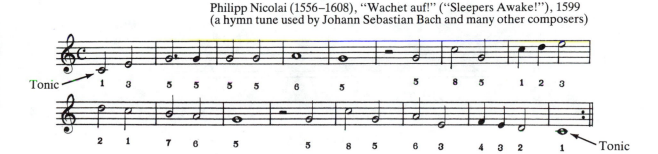

The major scale may have any note as its tonic, so long as sharps or flats are used to make the scale have *half steps between the third and fourth and the seventh and eighth degrees,* and *whole steps between all the other scale degrees.*

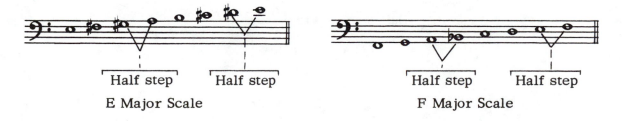

E Major Scale   F Major Scale

Each **scale degree** (note of the scale) is named by number, counting up from the tonic.

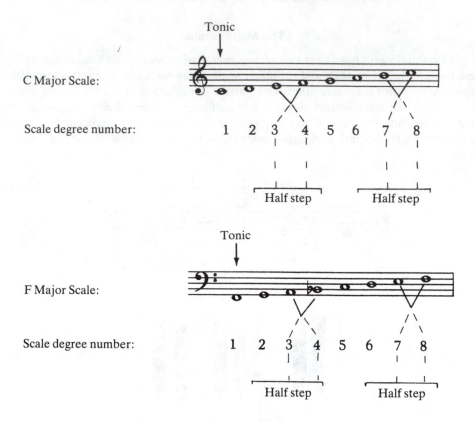

Scale names always include the letter name of the tonic note and the term describing their structure (whether major, minor, or some other mode or pattern). Thus, it is *wrong* to speak simply of the "C scale"; one *must* distinguish between the "C major scale" and "C minor scale." Both parts of the name *must* be used, since other scales could be written with the same beginning note (tonic).

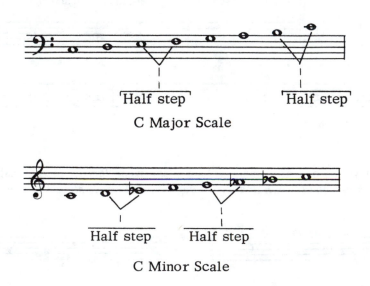

In writing major and minor scales, be careful to keep the letter names of the notes in *alphabetical order,* even though other ways of spelling some sounds might seem more practical at the moment.

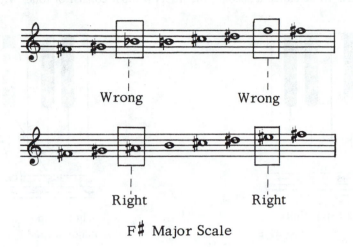

F♯ Major Scale

Major and Minor Seconds

As mentioned earlier, the difference in pitch between two notes is an *interval.* The distance from one letter name to the next letter name is called a **second.** If this distance is a half step, the interval is a *minor* (small) *second;* if it is a whole step, it is a *major* (large) *second.*

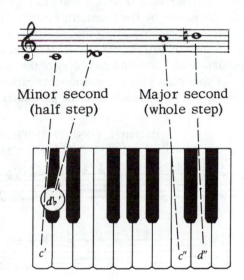

Minor second (half step)   Major second (whole step)

Major second is abbreviated *M2;* minor second, *m2.* In the major scale, major and minor seconds are found in the following order.

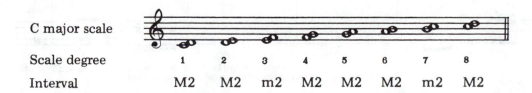

	1	2	3	4	5	6	7	8
C major scale								
Scale degree	1	2	3	4	5	6	7	8
Interval	M2	M2	m2	M2	M2	M2	m2	M2

Half step is a more general term than *minor second;* the distance between any two adjacent keys on the keyboard is a half step, while minor seconds are half steps in which each note has a different letter name. The same is true for whole steps and major seconds. To be called a second, the interval must consist of tones with adjacent letter names.

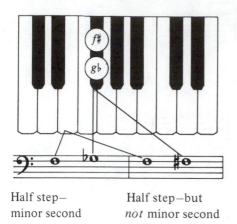

Half step—
minor second

Half step—but
not minor second

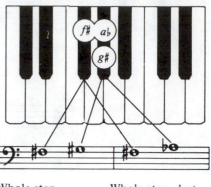

Whole step—
major second

Whole step—but
not major second

Thus, the rule that in major and minor scales the letter names must be in alphabetical order may also be worded to read: *in major and minor scales the adjacent intervals must all be seconds.*

Melodic and Harmonic Intervals

The seconds in scales and melodies are *melodic intervals*. Intervals sounded together are *harmonic intervals*. There is a wonderful movement in the *Concerto for Orchestra* by the twentieth century Hungarian composer Béla Bartók that presents several melodies, using pairs of like instruments playing the melodies set in parallel lines, with a different harmonic interval between the lines for each new pair of instruments. As we study each interval we shall see how that interval sounds in this piece in the passage in which it is used. Listen to a recording of the whole movement to see how the examples fit into the larger whole. If two members of your class play the instruments called for in the example, play the example in class and see how the interval between the two lines sounds with the particular instruments Bartók has chosen.

Béla Bartók, (1881–1945) "Giuoco delle Coppie" ("Game of Pairs"), *Concerto for Orchestra* (1944), Trumpets in C

Are all the seconds that are used as harmonic intervals in this example the same size? What size are they?

Sight Singing Assignment

Note: For those students and teachers who prefer to sight sing with a syllable system, two systems in common use are given here for reference. The syllables themselves originated in the Middle Ages as an aid to learning relationships between notes and learning the large repertory of Church chant easily and quickly. They were originally the first syllables of the words beginning each line of a well-known hymn of the period that happened to begin each line with a different note of the scale.

System I (movable do):
In this syllable system, each syllable belongs to a note of the scale, with the tonic note (1) as *do* in major and *la* in minor:

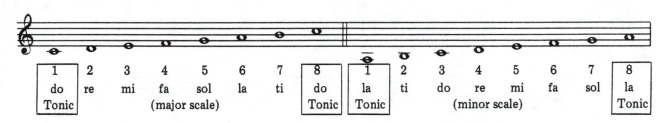

In all keys these syllables may be substituted for the corresponding numbers to sing any of the exercises given, so long as *tonic* is *do* in major and *tonic* is *la* in minor.

System II (fixed do):
In this system, the syllables are used for fixed pitches. Thus C is always *do*, D is always *re,* and so on. The complete system also has syllables for chromatic notes:

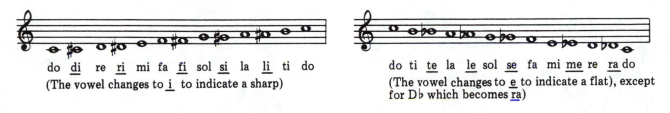

do di re ri mi fa fi sol si la li ti do
(The vowel changes to <u>i</u> to indicate a sharp)

do ti <u>te</u> la <u>le</u> sol <u>se</u> fa mi <u>me</u> re <u>ra</u> do
(The vowel changes to <u>e</u> to indicate a flat), except for D♭ which becomes <u>ra</u>)

Syllables are not given elsewhere in the text to leave the instructor free to choose whichever system is preferred.

A. Sing the following short melodies using the scale numbers as provided under the notes. You may sing syllables by one of the systems just described instead.

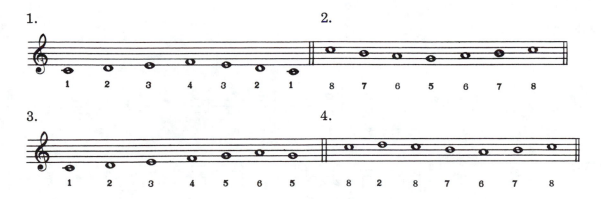

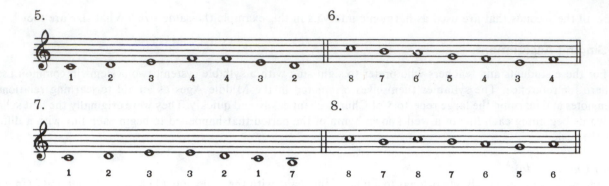

5. 1 2 3 4 4 3 2

6. 8 7 6 5 4 3 4

7. 1 2 3 3 2 1 7

8. 8 7 8 7 6 5 6

B. Sing the following short melodies providing the correct scale numbers (or syllables) as you sing.

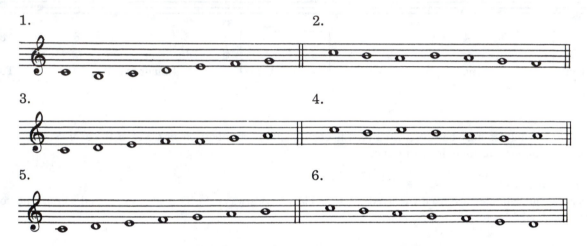

1.

2.

3.

4.

5.

6.

C. In this set of exercises only the numbers of the scale steps are indicated. The number 1 refers to the tonic (first note) of a major scale and so on. Choose any beginning pitch you wish and sing these just as you sang the exercises in the two previous sets of sight singing assignments.

1. 1 2 3 2 3 4 5

2. 8 7 6 5 4 5 6

3. 1 2 2 3 4 5 6

4. 8 7 7 6 5 6 7

5. 1 2 3 4 5 6 7

D. Sing the following melodies.

1.

1 2 3 4 5 5 5 6 6 5 4 3 2 1

2.

1 1 1 2 1 7 6 6 7 1 2 2 2 3 2 1 1 7 7 1

3.

4.

Arr. from Gregorian Chant by Lowell Mason (1792–1872),
hymn tune, "Hamburg"[+]

5.

Johann Crüger (1598–1662), "Nun danket alle Gott"
("Now Thank We All Our God")

6.

Lowell Mason, Hymn tune, "Bealoth," *Mason's Sacred Harp* (1943)[+]

7.

Traditional French Christmas carol, "Picardy"

8.

Martin Luther (1483–1546), "Gloria," *German Mass* (1524)

9.

Glo - ry to God in the high - est, and on earth peace to men in whom

He is well pleas - ed

This melody is without a time signature—that is, it is non-metric.

Gregorian Chant (Medieval)

10.

Glo - ri - a in ex - cel - sis De - o

Glory to God in the Highest

+Denotes American composer.

11.

Glo - ri - a in ex - cel - sis De - o

Notice that three of these melodies are nonmetric and have no bar lines. Sing the even quarter notes smoothly and without accent. The words are given for these three examples. The Latin words in the Gregorian chant examples mean the same as the first phrase of Luther's melody.

Written Assignment

A. *Identifying Major and Minor Seconds.* Following is a series of major and minor seconds. Identify each interval using the abbreviation *M2* for major second and *m2* for minor second. The example is worked correctly for you.

EXAMPLE:

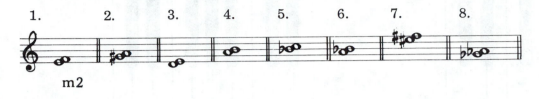

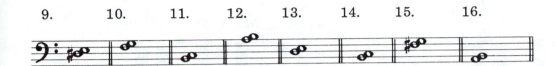

B. *Writing Major and Minor Seconds.* Following is a series of single notes. Write a major second and a minor second above each note in the spaces provided. The example is worked correctly for you.

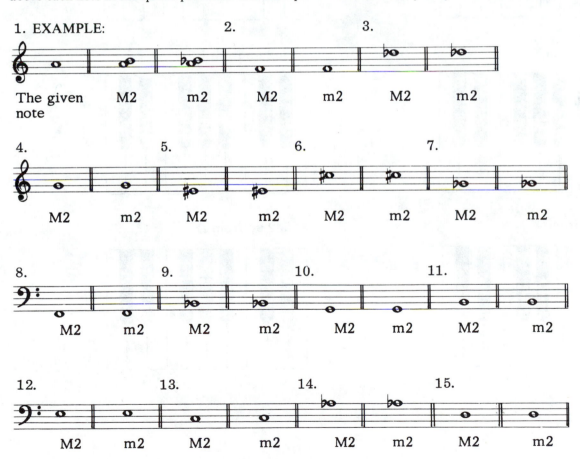

C. *Placing Major and Minor Seconds on the Keyboard.* Using the letter names write the intervals requested on the keyboard diagrams. The example has been worked correctly for you. Play all the examples as melodic intervals on the piano in several octaves.

1. EXAMPLE: m2 up from G♯

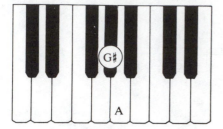

5. M2 up from G

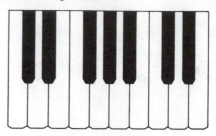

2. M2 up from C

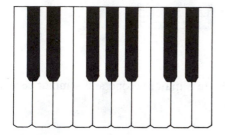

6. m2 up from C♯

3. m2 up from E

7. m2 up from F♯

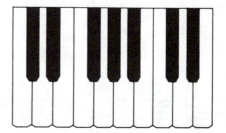

4. M2 up from A

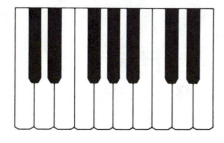

8. M2 up from D♭

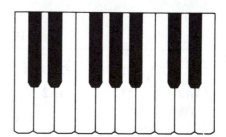

Written Assignment (cont.)

Special Instructions for Finding Whole Steps and Half Steps on Guitar

D. On fretted instruments like the guitar all **frets** are a half step apart.

The guitar is tuned as follows:

When guitar music is written on a staff, it is notated an octave higher and is read in treble clef.

When guitar music is notated to show fingering and finger patterns instead of pitches, the notation is called *tablature*. Each vertical line corresponds to a string with the lowest string at the left. Each horizontal line represents a fret, with the top line representing the end of the string.

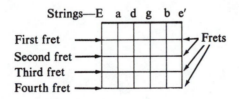

The first fret is a half step above each open string. Write the names of each note on the first fret: ____ ____

____ ____ ____ ____ .

The second fret is a whole step above each open string. Write the names of each note on the second fret:

____ ____ ____ ____ ____ ____ .

The third fret is a half step above the second fret. Write the names of each note on the third fret: ____ ____

____ ____ ____ .

The fourth fret is a whole step above the second fret. Write the names of each note on the fourth fret: ____

____ ____ ____ ____ ____ .

Ear Training Assignment

A. In each of the following exercises you will hear four scales played. Only one of these scales is a *major* scale. Place a circle around the letter that indicates the *major* scale. For example, you will hear:

Answer: 1. (a.)   b.   c.   d.

          2. a.   b.   c.   d.

          3. a.   b.   c.   d.

          4. a.   b.   c.   d.

          5. a.   b.   c.   d.

          6. a.   b.   c.   d.

          7. a.   b.   c.   d.

      † 8. a.   b.   c.   d.

      † 9. a.   b.   c.   d.

      †10. a.   b.   c.   d.

Computer Program Disk: Scales and Keys, Lesson G

B. In each of the following exercises you will hear a short melody played in three different ways. Only one will use the notes of the *major* scale. The other two versions will use notes of other scales. Circle the letter that indicates the version that uses the *major* scale.

    1. a.   b.   c.

    2. a.   b.   c.

    3. a.   b.   c.

  † 4. a.   b.   c.

  † 5. a.   b.   c.

  † 6. a.   b.   c.

Computer Program Disk: Scales and Keys, Lesson H

C. In each of the following exercises you will hear three intervals.

One interval will be a *major second.* (M2)

One interval will be a *minor second.* (m2)

One interval will be an interval larger than a second. (X)

Fill in the blank with the correct symbol for each second you hear.

           1. a. _____ b. _____ c. _____

           2. a. _____ b. _____ c. _____

           3. a. _____ b. _____ c. _____

           4. a. _____ b. _____ c. _____

           5. a. _____ b. _____ c. _____

† 6. a. _____ b. _____ c. _____

† 7. a. _____ b. _____ c. _____

† 8. a. _____ b. _____ c. _____

† 9. a. _____ b. _____ c. _____

†10. a. _____ b. _____ c. _____

Computer Program Disk: Intervals 1, Lesson F

D. In each of the following exercises you will hear a series of four notes. The intervals created between these notes will always be either a *major second* (M2) or a *minor second* (m2).

Two of the intervals will be *major seconds*.
One of the intervals will be a *minor second*.

As you listen, mark the correct intervals in the spaces provided.

1. 1. _____ 2. _____ 3. _____ 4.

2. 1. _____ 2. _____ 3. _____ 4.

3. 1. _____ 2. _____ 3. _____ 4.

† 4. 1. _____ 2. _____ 3. _____ 4.

† 5. 1. _____ 2. _____ 3. _____ 4.

† 6. 1. _____ 2. _____ 3. _____ 4.

Computer Program Disk: Intervals 1, Lesson G

E. In each of the following exercises you will hear a melody of seven notes. You are to:

1. Mark a "+" between the numbers indicating the notes which form either a *major* or a *minor second* (M2 or m2).

2. Do not mark between the notes that form other intervals.

EXAMPLE:

Answer:

1. 1. + 2. + 3. + 4. + 5. ___ 6. ___ 7.

2. 1. ___ 2. ___ 3. ___ 4. ___ 5. ___ 6. ___ 7.

† 3. 1. ___ 2. ___ 3. ___ 4. ___ 5. ___ 6. ___ 7.

† 4. 1. ___ 2. ___ 3. ___ 4. ___ 5. ___ 6. ___ 7.

† 5. 1. ___ 2. ___ 3. ___ 4. ___ 5. ___ 6. ___ 7.

† 6. 1. ___ 2. ___ 3. ___ 4. ___ 5. ___ 6. ___ 7.

Computer Program Disk: Intervals 1, Lesson G

†Indicates examples recorded on the cassettes available for use with this text.

Chapter 8 Intervals: Unison, Octave, and Major and Minor Thirds

Interval Names

Interval names consist of two parts: a general name, such as **second** or **third** and a qualifying term such as *major, minor* or *perfect,* which shows the exact size and **quality** of sound of the interval. The general name is found by counting the number of scale degrees on the staff between the two tones, starting from the bottom note and counting the top note also. A summary of all the intervals is given in a chart on page 135. Each interval will be studied separately first in order for you to have a good opportunity to learn how each interval looks and sounds, and how to sing it before moving on to the next interval.

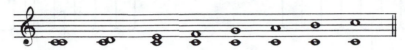

unison second third fourth fifth sixth seventh octave
(prime)

Perfect Intervals: The Unison

The smallest interval is that formed by repeating a tone or by sounding the tone in two voices at the same time. This is called the **unison,** and it contains *no* half steps.

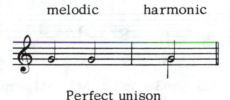

melodic   harmonic

Perfect unison

Perfect Intervals: The Octave

The interval formed by two notes with the same letter name, eight scale degrees apart, is the octave. It contains twelve half steps. These intervals have such a close relationship between the two component tones that neither can be raised or lowered without producing a completely new quality of sound. Intervals that have only one normal size are perfect intervals. Perfect unison is abbreviated P 1; perfect octave, P 8.

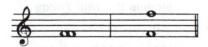

Perfect unison Perfect octave
P 1   P 8

Major and Minor Thirds

Thirds are intervals including three degrees of the scale. If the bottom note of a third is on a line, the top note will be on the next line; if the lower note is in a space, the upper will be in the next space.

Thirds are normally found in two sizes: the major third which has four half steps (two whole steps) and the minor third with three half steps (one and a half whole steps). The symbol for a major third is M3; for a minor third, m3.

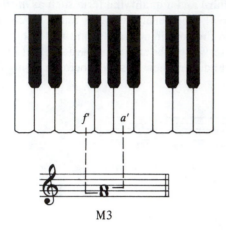

M3

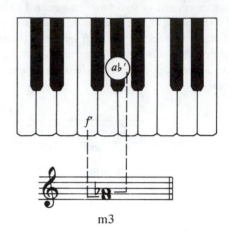

m3

Major and minor thirds are both found in the major scale. If a third is built on each scale degree, using only the notes of the scale, major and minor thirds appear in the following order:

C major scale								
Scale degree	1	2	3	4	5	6	7	8
Interval	M3	m3	m3	M3	M3	m3	m3	M3

Dissonance and Consonance

In playing all the intervals as harmonic intervals, you will notice a striking difference in the amount of tension in the sound. Intervals like seconds, which have a harsh, restless quality, are called **dissonances.** Smooth-sounding intervals such as thirds and octaves are called **consonances.** The smoothest and most closely related intervals, such as the octave and the unison, are called **perfect consonances.**

Melodies Set with Thirds

Here are two melodies set with a parallel line of thirds. The first uses only the thirds within the G major scale, so it contains both major and minor thirds. It is written for two oboes; if you have two oboe players in your class, play the example.

Antonin Dvořák (1841–1904), Fourth Movement, Symphony No. 9 in E Minor, (*From the New World*) (1893), Oboes I and II

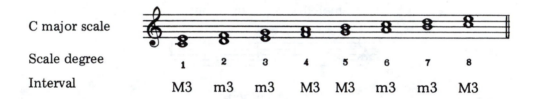

The Czech composer Dvořák wrote his *New World Symphony* in 1893 while he was living in New York. Nearly fifty years later, Béla Bartók was living in New York as a refugee from the Nazis during World War II. There he wrote the *Concerto for Orchestra*. By then the musical language had changed, and although both Dvořák's *Symphony* and Bartók's *Concerto* use folk-like melodies and rhythms, they sound very different. In the passage below, also for two oboes, Bartók writes two lines a third apart; but instead of keeping both lines within the same scale and thus having both major and minor thirds, he uses only one size of third. Have the oboe players in your class play this passage and compare the sound of this passage with the previous example. Compare both with the passage in seconds at the end of the previous chapter. Try to fix the very different sounds of these intervals in your memory.

Béla Bartók (1881–1945), "Giuoco delle Coppie," ("Game of Pairs"), *Concerto for Orchestra* (1944), Oboes I and II

What size *are* the thirds in this passage?

Sight Singing Assignment

A. Sing the following short melodies using the scale numbers as provided under the notes. If you prefer you may use syllables (see page 57). Always be aware of the interval you are singing (M2, m2, M3, m3, and so on).

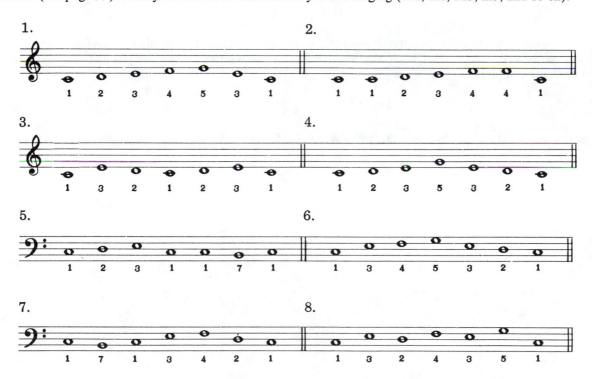

Following is a very useful exercise that can be sung in any major scale. It is shown here in C major.

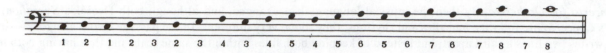

B. Sing the following short melodies providing the correct scale numbers as you sing.

1.

2.

3.

4.

5.

6.

7.

8.

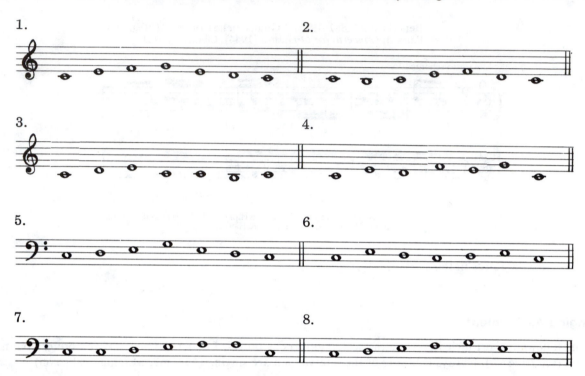

C. In this set of exercises only the numbers of the scale steps are indicated. The number "1" refers to the tonic (first note) of a major scale, and so on. Choose any beginning pitch you wish and sing these just as you sang the exercises in two previous sets of sight singing assignments.

1.	1	2	3	4	5	4	2	3	1
2.	1	3	2	3	4	5	3	2	1
3.	1	2	4	3	5	5	4	2	1
4.	1	3	5	5	2	4	3	2	1
5.	1	3	1	3	5	4	2	3	1

D. Sing the following melodies.

1.

1 2 3 4 5 4 3 4 3 2 1

2.

1 3 3 3 2 1 7 2 7 1

3.

1 3 4 5 5 5 6 4 3 2 1

4.

1 3 2 1 3 5 4 2 3 1 2 7 1

5.

1 3 2 1 7 2 5 1 5 3 1 2 7 1

6.

1 7 6 5 3 5 6 7 1 2 7 1

7.   New Orleans Black Funeral Spiritual, "When the Saints Go Marching In" +

8.   English Folk Song, "Greensleeves"

9.

10.

American Shaker Hymn, "Simple Gifts" (1848)+

Aaron Copland used this old hymn tune in his ballet *Appalachian Spring,* a work on the suggested listening list at the end of this book. You might like to hear how it sounds in that version!

Arnold de Lantins (flourished around 1430), "Puisque je voy" ("Since I Saw Her")

11.

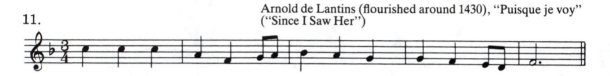

The next group of melodies are all different versions of the same succession of pitches, but very different rhythms are used. All the melodies are from a **mass** by Palestrina, an Italian composer of the Renaissance (16th century). See how well you can read the different rhythms in which the same melodic pattern is set.

Giovanni Pierluigi da Palestrina (1525–1594), Mass on the Gregorian chant "Aeterna Christi Munera" (1590)

12.

13.

14.

15.

16.

Written Assignment

A. *Identifying Major and Minor Thirds.* Following is a series of major and minor thirds. Identify each interval using the abbreviation M3 for major third and m3 for minor third. The example is worked correctly for you.

EXAMPLE:

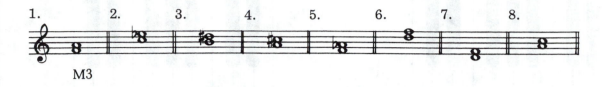

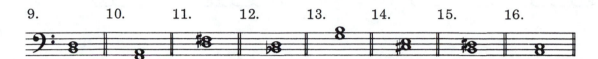

B. *Writing Major and Minor Thirds.* Following is a series of single notes. Write a major third and a minor third above each note in the spaces provided. The example is worked correctly for you.

EXAMPLE:

C. *Placing Major and Minor Thirds on the Keyboard.* Using the letter names, write the intervals requested on the following keyboard diagrams. The example is worked correctly for you. Play all the examples on a piano. Play them both as melodic intervals and as harmonic intervals. Listen carefully.

1. EXAMPLE: m3 up from E

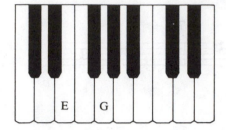

2. M3 up from A

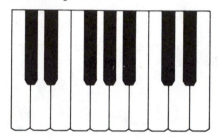

3. m3 up from G♯

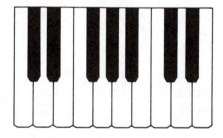

4. M3 up from F

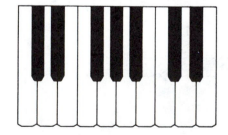

5. m3 up from C♯

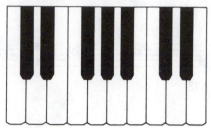

6. m3 up from F

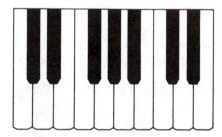

7. M3 up from C

8. M3 up from G♭

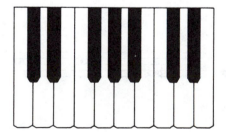

Written Assignment (cont.)

D. Use the guitar tablature to locate major and minor thirds on the fingerboard. The third fret is a minor third above the open strings. Write the names of the notes a minor third above each open string ____ ____ ____ ____ ____ ____ .

The fourth fret is a major third above the open strings. Write the names of the notes a major third above each open string. ____ ____ ____ ____ ____ ____ . Play the intervals you have found.

Which strings of the guitar form the interval of a *third?* _____

Is it a major or a minor third? _____

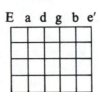

E   a   d   g   b   e′

Ear Training Assignment

A. In each of the following exercises the teacher will play an interval. This interval will be either a major or a minor third. Underline the name of the interval you hear played. See the example.

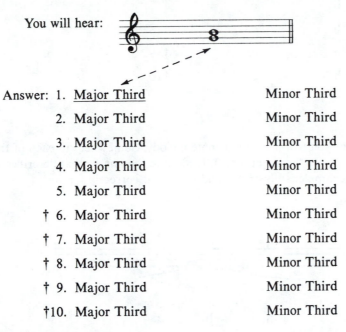

You will hear:

Answer: 1. <u>Major Third</u>   Minor Third

2. Major Third   Minor Third

3. Major Third   Minor Third

4. Major Third   Minor Third

5. Major Third   Minor Third

† 6. Major Third   Minor Third

† 7. Major Third   Minor Third

† 8. Major Third   Minor Third

† 9. Major Third   Minor Third

†10. Major Third   Minor Third

Computer Program Disk: Intervals 1, Lesson H

B. In each of the following exercises the teacher will play three intervals. One of these three will be a major third. Circle the letter that shows which is the major third.

1. a.   b.   c.

2. a.   b.   c.

3. a.   b.   c.

4. a.   b.   c.

5. a.   b.   c.

† 6. a.   b.   c.

† 7. a.   b.   c.

† 8. a.   b.   c.

† 9. a.   b.   c.

†10. a.   b.   c.

Computer Program Disk: Intervals 1, Lesson I; also Intervals 2, Lesson A

C. In each of the following exercises the teacher will play three intervals. One of these three will be a minor third. Circle the letter that shows which one is the minor third.

1. a.	b.	c.	† 6. a.	b.	c.
2. a.	b.	c.	† 7. a.	b.	c.
3. a.	b.	c.	† 8. a.	b.	c.
4. a.	b.	c.	† 9. a.	b.	c.
5. a.	b.	c.	†10. a.	b.	c.

Computer Program Disk: Intervals 1, Lesson I

D. In each of the following exercises you will hear a four note melody. Somewhere in each of these melodies you will hear the leap of a major third (between adjacent tones). Underline the phrase that describes where the major third is located in each exercise. The example is illustrated and is worked correctly for you.

EXAMPLE:

You will hear:

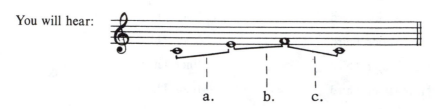

a.   b.   c.

Answer: 1. a. <u>Between 1st and 2nd note</u>
           b. Between 2nd and 3rd note
           c. Between 3rd and 4th note

2. a. Between 1st and 2nd note
    b. Between 2nd and 3rd note
    c. Between 3rd and 4th note

3. a. Between 1st and 2nd note
    b. Between 2nd and 3rd note
    c. Between 3rd and 4th note

4. a. Between 1st and 2nd note
    b. Between 2nd and 3rd note
    c. Between 3rd and 4th note

5. a. Between 1st and 2nd note
    b. Between 2nd and 3rd note
    c. Between 3rd and 4th note

† 6. a. Between 1st and 2nd note
      b. Between 2nd and 3rd note
      c. Between 3rd and 4th note

† 7. a. Between 1st and 2nd note
      b. Between 2nd and 3rd note
      c. Between 3rd and 4th note

8. a. Between 1st and 2nd note
    b. Between 2nd and 3rd note
    c. Between 3rd and 4th note

9. a. Between 1st and 2nd note
    b. Between 2nd and 3rd note
    c. Between 3rd and 4th note

10. a. Between 1st and 2nd note
     b. Between 2nd and 3rd note
     c. Between 3rd and 4th note

Computer Program Disk: Intervals 1, Lesson K

†Indicates examples recorded on the cassettes available for use with this text.

Chapter 9   The Major Triad and the Interval of the Perfect Fifth

The Triad

Three or more different tones sounding together from a *chord*. There are many different kinds of chords, but those that form the basis for the music since the beginning of the fifteenth century are built of thirds.

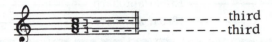

A chord which consists of three different tones, each a third apart, is called a *triad*.

Triads

Tones of the triad may be arranged in different orders or placed in different octaves, but if the names of the notes are the same the chord preserves its identity. It is always possible to reassemble the notes of the triad in thirds to show its construction. This arrangement of the notes of the triad is called the **simple position of the triad.**

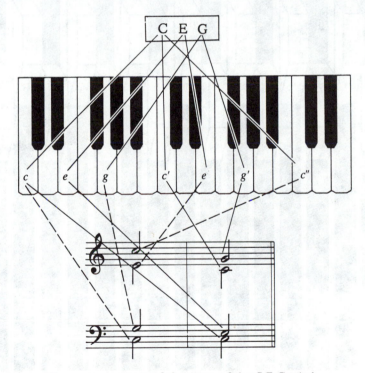

Two arrangements of the notes of the C E G triad

Simple position of the C E G triad

An easy instrument to play chords on is the autoharp. Press the C Major bar and that chord will sound. Autoharps have 12 or 15 bars across a set of strings. They are set so that when each of these bars is pressed only the notes of the chord whose name is on the bar will sound. It is a very easy way to hear chords and even to accompany singing. Play each of the major triads on an autoharp by pressing each bar labeled with the name of a major chord and strumming the strings of the instrument. Notice how different these chords sound from all the other chords on the instrument.

Maj. is the symbol for a **major triad.**

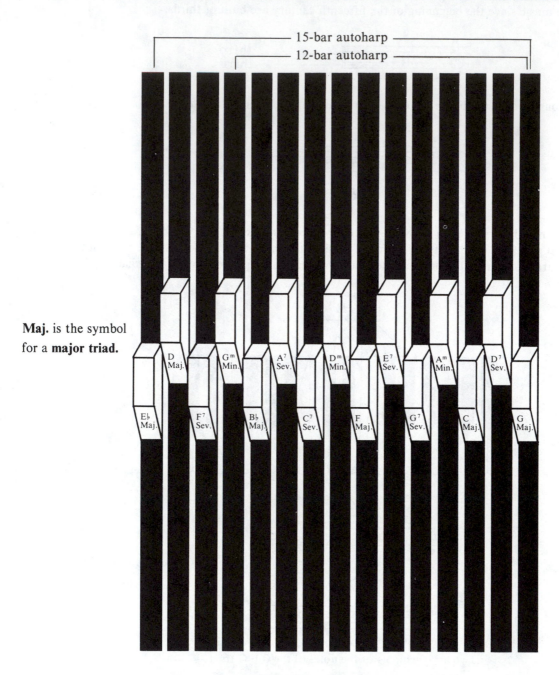

THE CHORD BARS ON AN AUTOHARP

On the autoharp you hear different kinds of chords; you can hear even more variety if you play the following triads on the piano. (They cannot all be played on the autoharp.)

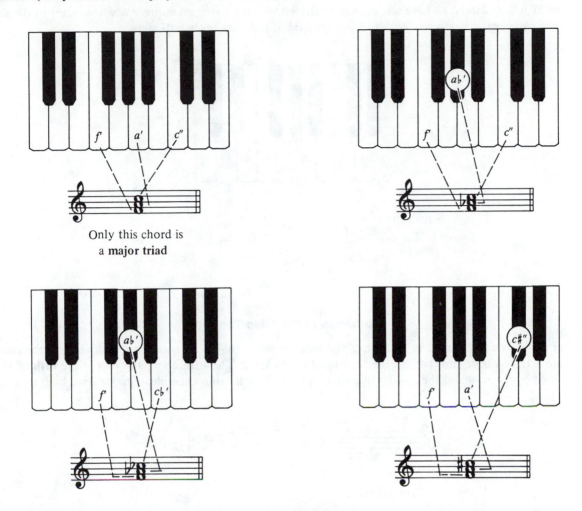

Only this chord is
a **major triad**

The Major Triad

A triad with a major third on the bottom and a minor third on the top is called a *major triad*.

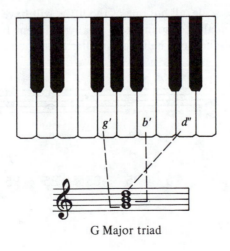

G Major triad

You can also play this major triad on the autoharp.

The Perfect Fifth

The interval between the bottom and top notes of a triad is a **fifth**. In the major triad, the fifth always contains seven half steps. The fifth is an interval whose size cannot be altered without giving an entirely new character to the sound, so it belongs to the category of *perfect intervals*. A *perfect fifth* always has *seven* half steps.

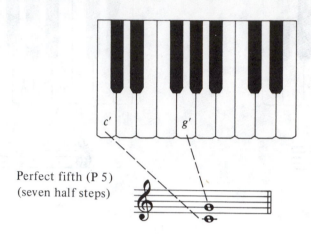

Perfect fifth (P 5)
(seven half steps)

The Names of the Triad Tones

Each member of the triad is named in relation to the tone on which the chord is constructed, which is the **root of the triad.** The note a third above the root is called the **third of the triad.** The fifth above the root is the **fifth of the triad.** Triads are named by the *root* and the *quality* of sound: thus, in the following example, a major triad built on C is called the *C major triad.*

fifth
third — m3 — P 5
root — M3

C major triad

The Diminished Fifth

If a fifth is built on each note of any major scale, all but one of the fifths will have seven half steps (perfect fifths). One fifth, however, has only six half steps. Its quality of sound is so totally different from that of the perfect fifth that it is called **diminished** (the term used for all intervals one half step smaller than the normal size of the interval).

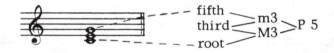

C major								
Scale degree	1	2	3	4	5	6	7	8
Number of half steps	7	7	7	7	7	7	6	7
Name of interval	P5	P5	P5	P5	P5	P5	d5	P5

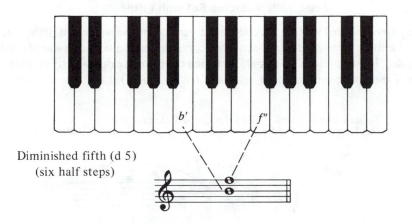

Diminished fifth (d 5)
(six half steps)

How to Write Fifths

The very first harmony in Western European music was based on the interval of the perfect fifth, back in the ninth century. Here is how that music (called **organum**) sounded, in an example from one of the earliest theory textbooks.

Musica Enchiriadis (Musical Handbook) (c. 850)

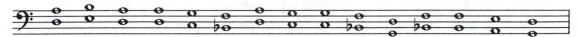

This music was for singers, so sing the example together in class.

In this music, *only perfect intervals could be used,* so it was necessary to alter the fifth between B and F by adding a flat. (Notice that, like Gregorian chant of the same period, this music is nonmetric.)

All fifths on the white keys except the fifth between *B* and *F* are perfect fifths. *B* to *F* has only *six half steps* and is a *diminished fifth.* If either note of any perfect fifth on the white keys is raised or lowered by a sharp or flat, the other must have the same accidental for the interval to remain perfect.

Perfect fifths (P 5)
(seven half steps)

To make a perfect fifth on B, however, an F♯ must be used. B♭ to F is also a perfect fifth. These are the *only* two perfect fifths in which both notes do *not* have the same accidentals.

Perfect fifths (P 5)
(seven half steps)

Music with Melodies Set with Fifths

After the Middle Ages composers avoided writing successions of perfect intervals like the fifths you just sang. However, at the end of the nineteenth century composers like Debussy became fascinated with the sounds of fifths. Play this little passage from his piano prelude "The Engulfed Cathedral," in which the fifths are doubled by octaves (just as the Medieval fifths you sang earlier were if they were sung by both male and female voices).

Claude Debussy (1862–1918), La Cathédrale engloutie
(The Engulfed Cathedral), *Preludes pour Piano*, Book I (1910)

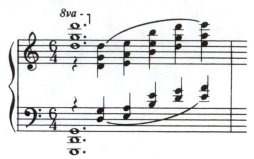

Copyright 1913. Durand et Cie. Used by permission of the publisher, Elkan-Vogel, Inc. Sole Representative U.S.A.

Bartók presents one melody in **parallel fifths** in his *Concerto for Orchestra*. This time the pair of instruments is flutes. If two members of your class play flute, have them play the passage for the class.

Béla Bartók (1881–1945), "Giuoco delle Coppie," ("Game of Pairs"), *Concerto for Orchestra* (1944), Flutes I and II

Copyright 1946 by Hawkes & Son (London) Ltd.; Renewed 1973. Reprinted by permission of Boosey & Hawkes, Inc.

Does Bartók use both sizes of fifths in this passage?

The Major Triads in the Major Scale

If a triad is constructed on each note of the C major scale, using only the notes of the scale, there will be three major triads in the series, on the first, fourth, and fifth degrees of the scale (C, F, and G).

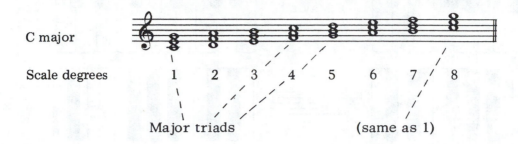

How to Construct a Major Triad

These are the only three major triads consisting entirely of white keys. These three triads are the *C major* triad, the *F major* triad, and the *G major* triad. Find these three triads on the piano and play them, listening carefully to the sound.

To construct all other major triads, sharps and flats must be used to make a major third and perfect fifth above the root of the triad.

Major triad = M3 + P 5 above the root

Common fingerings for playing many of the major triads on the guitar are given in Appendix 7. Those with guitars can find these fingerings and play the major triads given there. Listen carefully to all the sounds played. The common symbol for a major triad is the name of the root of the chord written as a capital letter. Thus C means to play a C major chord on the guitar.

Keyboard Harmony

Following are all the major triads in simple position. First the position on the keyboard is shown, and then the proper notation on the music staff. Learn to find these major triads in *all* octaves of the regular piano keyboard. The shading on the keyboard shows you which notes to play.

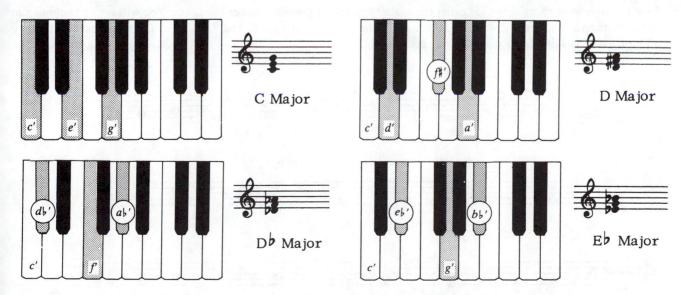

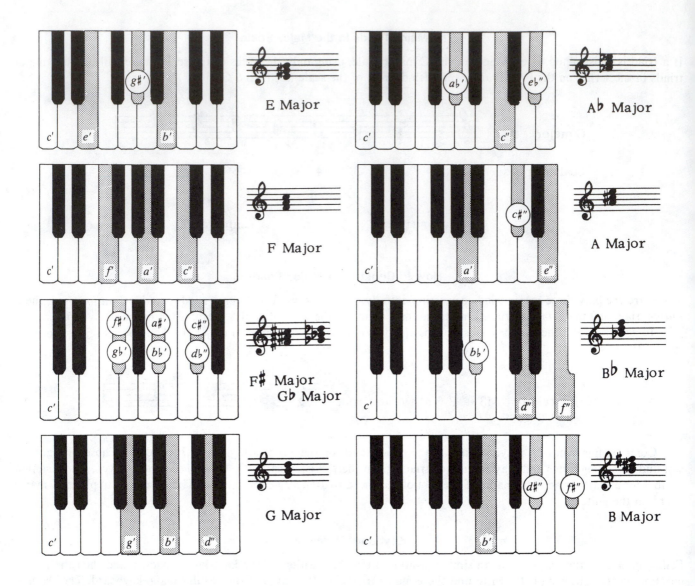

E Major

A♭ Major

F Major

A Major

F♯ Major
G♭ Major

B♭ Major

G Major

B Major

Sight Singing Assignment

A. Sing the following short melodies using the scale numbers as provided under the notes. You will notice the melodic use of the triad. Exercises 2, 4, 6, and 8 are the same as exercises 1, 3, 5, and 7, but they are **transposed** to the key of F major. Use syllables if your teacher prefers.

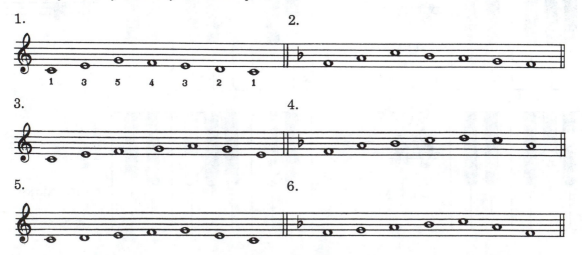

1.

  1   3   5   4   3   2   1

2.

3.

4.

5.

6.

7.   8.

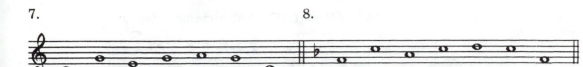

B. Sing the following short melodies, providing the correct scale numbers or syllables as you sing.

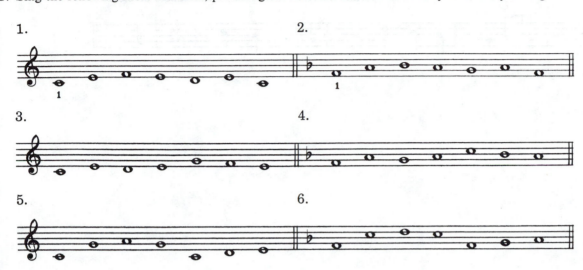

C. In this set of exercises only the numbers are indicated. The number 1 refers to the tonic (first note) of a major scale, and so on. Choose any beginning pitch you wish and sing these just as you sang the exercises in the two previous sets of Sight Singing Assignments.

1.	1	3	5	6	5	4	3	2	1
2.	1	3	3	4	5	1	3	2	1
3.	1	7	1	1	2	3	5	3	1
4.	1	3	3	4	5	6	7	8	1

Computer Program Disk: Intervals 1, Lesson J

D. Sing the following melodies with scale numbers, syllables, or letter names.

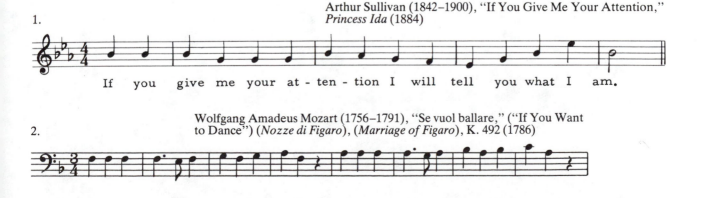

1.   Arthur Sullivan (1842–1900), "If You Give Me Your Attention," *Princess Ida* (1884)

If   you   give   me   your   at - ten - tion   I   will   tell   you   what   I   am.

2.   Wolfgang Amadeus Mozart (1756–1791), "Se vuol ballare," ("If You Want to Dance") (*Nozze di Figaro*), (*Marriage of Figaro*), K. 492 (1786)

3.

Michael Haydn (1737–1806), hymn tune, "Salzburg"

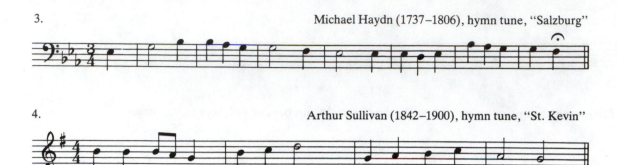

4.

Arthur Sullivan (1842–1900), hymn tune, "St. Kevin"

Computer Program Disk: Intervals 1, Lesson K

Written Assignment

A. *Recognition of Triads by Sight*. Following is a series of chords. Some are triads, and some are not. Circle the chords that *are* triads. In this group of exercises, the root of each chord is the lowest (bottom) note.

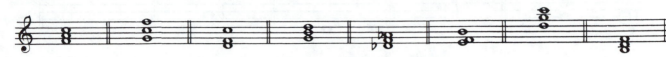

B. *Rearranging Triads into Simple Root Position*. All of the chords in these exercises are triads, but the triad notes are not arranged in *simple root position* (with the root as the lowest note). Rearrange the notes of each exercise into simple root position. The example is worked correctly for you.

EXAMPLE:

1. Triad notes   Triad in simple root position   2. Triad notes   Triad in simple root position

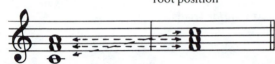

3.   4.

5.   6.

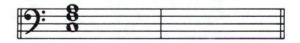

7.   8.

9.   10.

C. *Drill in Writing Perfect Fifths on the Music Staff.* Write a perfect fifth *above* each given note. The example is worked correctly for you.

D. *Recognition by Sight of Major Triads.* Circle only the triads that are *major* triads.

Written Assignment (cont.)

E. *Placing Triads on the Keyboard*. Using letter names with octave designation to mark the right keys, place the following triads on the keyboard. *Play* all the triads you have labeled on the piano. The example is worked correctly for you. Guitar fingerings for many of these triads will be found in Appendix 7, Fingerboard Harmony for Guitar.

After labeling the diagrams and playing the triads, write each triad in bass clef in the space provided.

EXAMPLE:

1. G MAJOR TRIAD

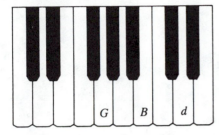

5. A♭ MAJOR TRIAD

2. E♭ MAJOR TRIAD

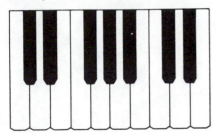
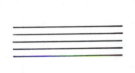

6. E MAJOR TRIAD

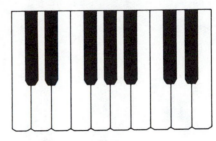

3. F MAJOR TRIAD

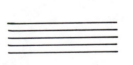

7. C♯ MAJOR TRIAD

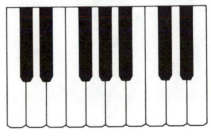

4. D MAJOR TRIAD

8. D♭ MAJOR TRIAD

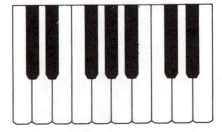

9. A MAJOR TRIAD

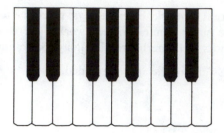

10. Gb MAJOR TRIAD

Ear Training Assignment

A. *Major Triads in Simple Position.* In each of the following exercises one of the four triads played will be a major triad. Circle the letter that represents the major triad.

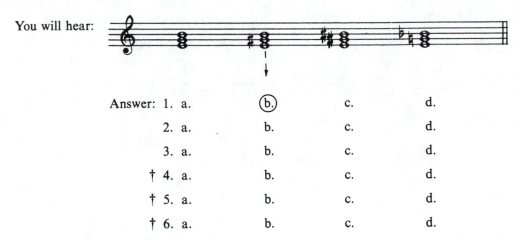

You will hear:

Answer: 1. a.   (b.)   c.   d.

   2. a.   b.   c.   d.

   3. a.   b.   c.   d.

† 4. a.   b.   c.   d.

† 5. a.   b.   c.   d.

† 6. a.   b.   c.   d.

Computer Program Disk: Harmony 1, Lesson A

B. *Major Triads in Four-Part Harmony.* In each of the following exercises one of the three triads (this time in four-part harmony) is a major triad. Circle the letter that represents the major triad.

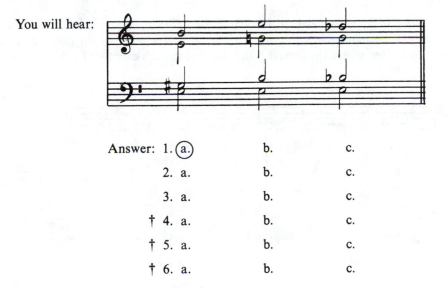

You will hear:

Answer: 1. (a.)   b.   c.

   2. a.   b.   c.

   3. a.   b.   c.

† 4. a.   b.   c.

† 5. a.   b.   c.

† 6. a.   b.   c.

Computer Program: Disk: Harmony 1, Lesson B

C. *Recognition of the Perfect Octave, Perfect Fifth, and Major Third.* In each exercise you will hear three harmonic intervals.

1. One will be a perfect fifth (P 5).
2. One will be a perfect octave (P 8).
3. One will be a major third (M3).

Mark each interval you hear with the proper symbol. Each exercise will be played twice.

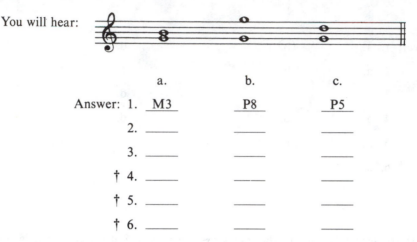

You will hear:

	a.	b.	c.
Answer: 1.	M3	P8	P5
2.	_____	_____	_____
3.	_____	_____	_____
† 4.	_____	_____	_____
† 5.	_____	_____	_____
† 6.	_____	_____	_____

Computer Program Disk: Intervals 2, Lesson E

D. *Recognition of the Perfect Fifth in Melodic Context.* In each of the following exercises you will hear four notes of a melody. Somewhere in each of these melodies you will hear the leap of a *perfect fifth* (between adjacent tones). Underline the phrase which describes where the perfect fifth is located in each exercise. Each exercise will be played twice.

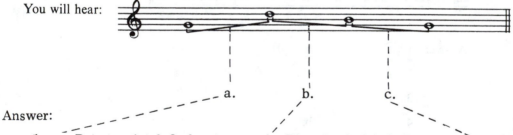

You will hear:

Answer:

1. a. Between 1st & 2nd note   b. Between 2nd & 3rd note   c. Between 3rd & 4th note
2. a. Between 1st & 2nd note   b. Between 2nd & 3rd note   c. Between 3rd & 4th note
3. a. Between 1st & 2nd note   b. Between 2nd & 3rd note   c. Between 3rd & 4th note
† 4. a. Between 1st & 2nd note   b. Between 2nd & 3rd note   c. Between 3rd & 4th note
† 5. a. Between 1st & 2nd note   b. Between 2nd & 3rd note   c. Between 3rd & 4th note
† 6. a. Between 1st & 2nd note   b. Between 2nd & 3rd note   c. Between 3rd & 4th note

Computer Program Disk: Intervals 2, Lesson E

Chapter 10   The Circle of Fifths and the Key Signatures of the Major Scales

The Pattern of the Major Scale

When major scales begin on notes other than C, sharps or flats must be used to produce the correct pattern of whole steps and half steps—half steps between the third and fourth and the seventh and eighth degrees.

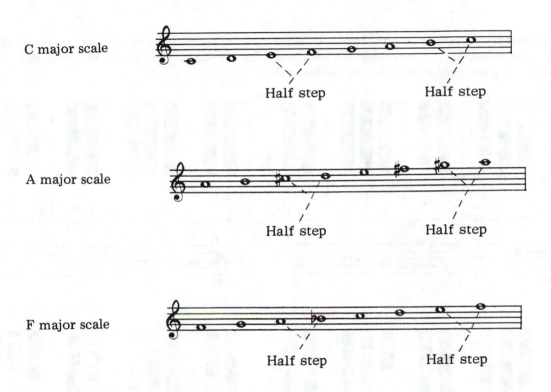

The Keys with Sharps

The only scale among the major keys with no sharps or flats is C major. If a scale begins a perfect fifth higher than C (on G), it will have one sharp on its seventh degree (F sharp).

To find the next scale, begin a fifth above G on the note D. This scale will keep the F♯ of the preceding scale and add one more sharp (on *its* seventh degree). Thus, it has two sharps, F♯ and C♯.

D major scale

Half step   Half step

This process may be continued until all the notes of the scale are sharped. The order of the scales with sharps follows. The first few scales are written out completely, but space is left for you to complete the rest. Play the scales you have written, using the piano and/or any other instrument or instruments you play.

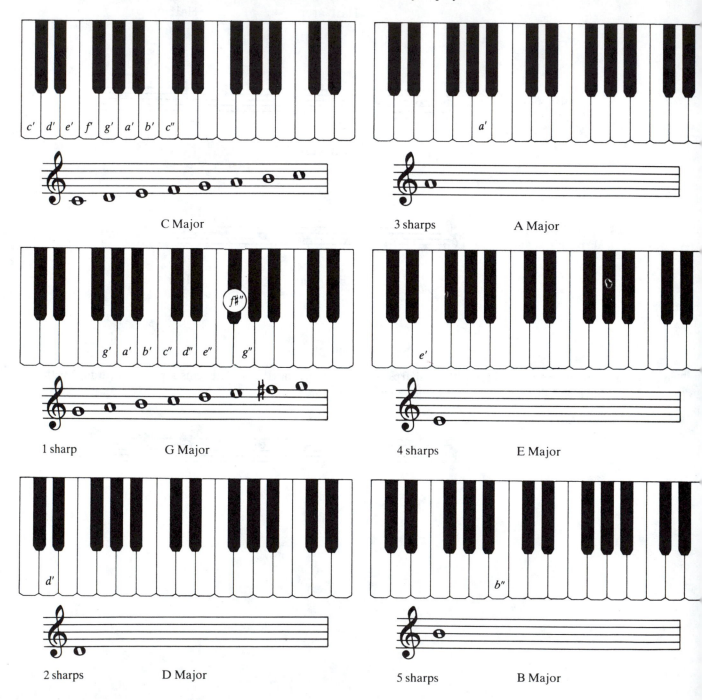

C Major

3 sharps   A Major

1 sharp   G Major

4 sharps   E Major

2 sharps   D Major

5 sharps   B Major

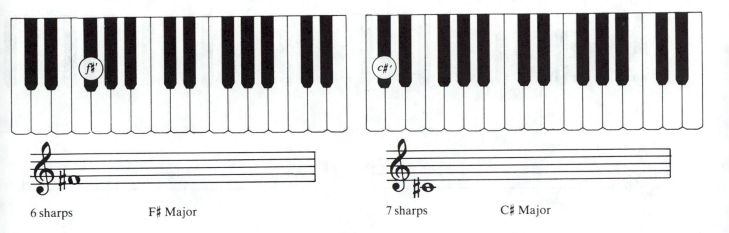

6 sharps   F♯ Major   7 sharps   C♯ Major

The Keys with Flats

The major flat scales are found by beginning each scale a fifth lower than the preceding scale, beginning with the fifth below the C major scale.

F major scale

Half step   Half step

This process is continued until all the notes of the scale are flats.

C♭ major scale

Half step   Half step

The order of the scales is given here. The first two scales are written out completely. Space is left for you to complete the rest.

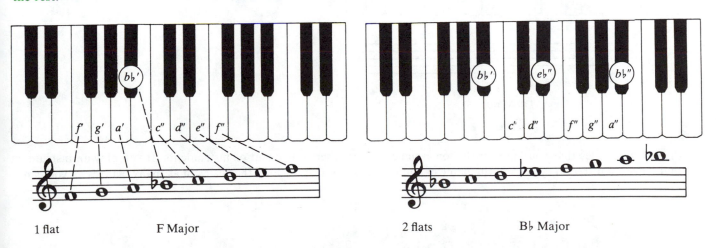

1 flat   F Major   2 flats   B♭ Major

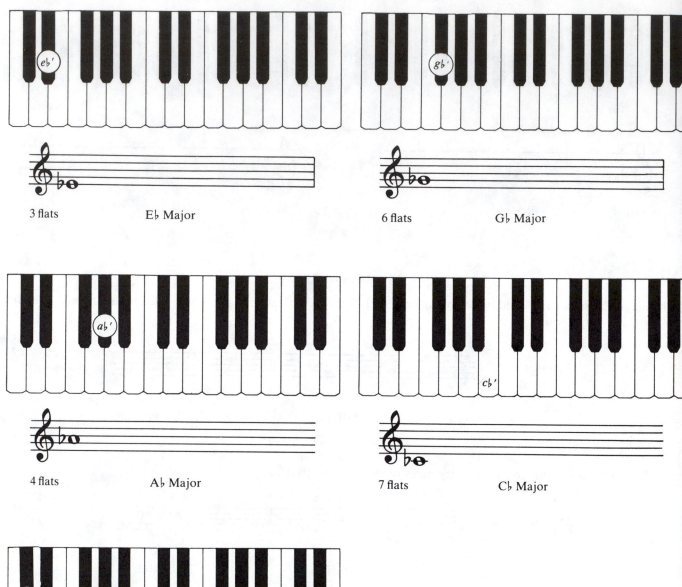

3 flats   E♭ Major

6 flats   G♭ Major

4 flats   A♭ Major

7 flats   C♭ Major

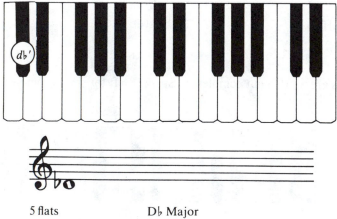

5 flats   D♭ Major

Play all the scales that you have written on a piano and/or other instrument or instruments. If you play an instrument that leaves you free to do so, say the name of each note as you play it. Play the scales in as many octaves as you can.

The Circle of Fifths

The order of all the sharp and flat scales can be shown by a circle, since by moving in either direction in perfect fifths, you eventually return to the starting key. The **circle of fifths** here illustrates this return.

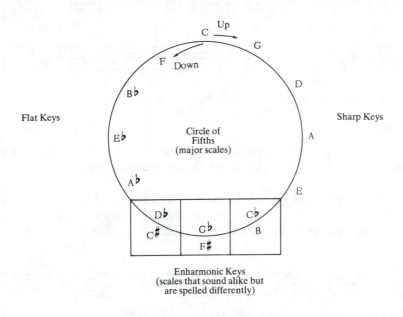

Enharmonic Keys
(scales that sound alike but
are spelled differently)

The Key Signature

Music using the notes of a particular scale is said to be *in the key of the first note of that scale.*

Anonymous (formerly attributed to Henry Carey), "My Country Tis of Thee" (As "God Save the King," this tune dates back to about 1744); also known as "America"

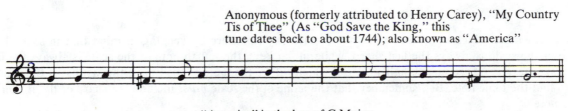

"America" in the key of G Major

When a composer writes music in keys that have sharps or flats, it would be quite cumbersome to have to write a sharp or flat sign in front of every affected note, so a **key signature** (sharps or flats showing the notes of the key) is used at the beginning of every staff to show which sharps or flats are in the key. In effect, the F lines and spaces are made into F♯ lines and spaces by the G major key signature. The sharp or flat need appear only once in the signature to affect all octaves.

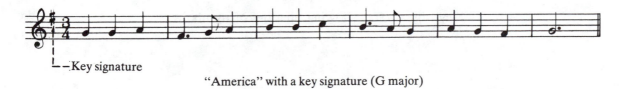

└─Key signature

"America" with a key signature (G major)

The conventional pattern of arrangement of sharps or flats in the key signature shows the order of introduction of the sharps or flats. Since the pattern never varies, it is easy to tell at a glance what the sharps or flats of the key will be.

Key signatures of the sharp keys in treble and bass clef

To remember the order of the sharps, memorize the signature for C♯ major. To find the signature for the other keys, subtract the proper number of sharps from the right side of the key signature to find which sharps are left in the key you need.

The order of the flats in the key signature follows the order of introduction of the flats in the circle of fifths. As with the sharps, it is easy to memorize the key signature of C♭ major, which contains all the flats, and subtract from the right side the proper number to find the flats remaining in the key desired.

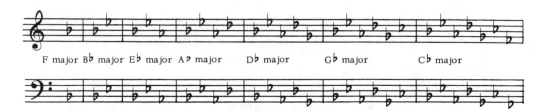

Key signatures of the flat keys in treble and bass clef.

You can remember which major scale belongs to each key signature by keeping in mind that in sharp keys, the seventh note of the scale is always the last sharp, while in flat keys, the fourth note of the scale is always the last flat. Thus, if the last sharp is A♯, go up one half step to B which will be the tonic of the key; if the last flat is E♭, count down four notes to find the tonic note, B♭. Remember that the name of the scale *must* include the sharp or flat if there is one on the tonic note.

When you notate key signatures, allow sufficient space so that none of the sharps or flats is directly above or below another, and the proper order is kept clear.

Key signatures showing spacing of symbols

Accidentals

When sharps, flats, or naturals that are not part of the key signature are used, they are placed to the left of the note which they affect. They are called **accidentals.** When an accidental occurs, it affects all notes of that pitch that follow it in the same measure. The effect of an accidental is canceled by the bar line. If a sharp or flat has been used at the beginning of a measure, and a note without accidental is needed later in the measure, a natural sign must be used.

G sharp, from previous accidental   G natural   natural sign required to cancel sharp within the bar

Sight Singing Assignment

A. *Singing Scales and Intervals above the Tonic Note.* Sing the following exercise in all the major sharp scales using scale step numbers first and then letter names of the notes. The example is given in C major. It may be *transposed* (that is, *exactly duplicated beginning on a different pitch*) to all the other major sharp keys. It is very useful to sing *each* scale with the names of the notes as well as with numbers or syllables. Use the scales you have written out in this lesson.

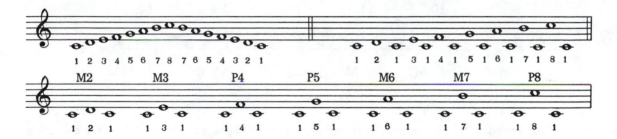

Sing the intervals in all major scales, using the names of the notes.

B. The more you practice *singing* intervals the easier they will be to hear. When you hear the white note, respond by singing the black notes.

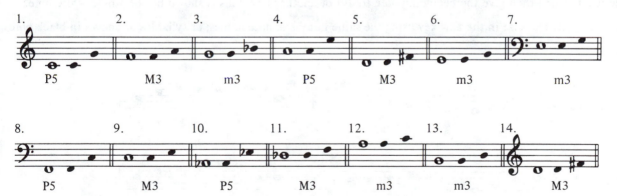

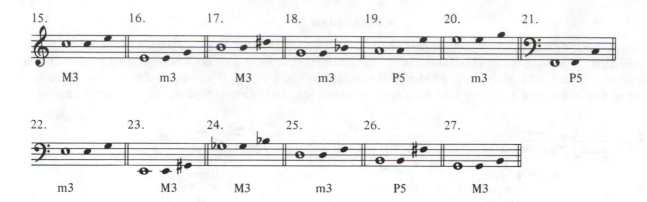

15.   16.   17.   18.   19.   20.   21.

M3   m3   M3   m3   P5   m3   P5

22.   23.   24.   25.   26.   27.

m3   M3   M3   m3   P5   M3

C. Here the intervals are *descending* instead of *ascending*.

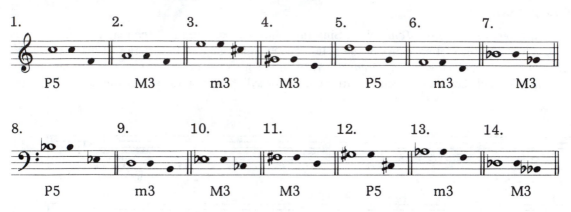

1.   2.   3.   4.   5.   6.   7.

P5   M3   m3   M3   P5   m3   M3

8.   9.   10.   11.   12.   13.   14.

P5   m3   M3   M3   P5   m3   M3

D. Do you know any melodies that begin with thirds or fifths (ascending or descending)? Make a collection in your class of such melodies to help you remember the sounds of the intervals.

E. Close your books for this exercise.

    1. Your teacher will play the exercise on the piano—as shown in whole (white) notes.

    2. Then you sing the exercise back using scale numbers, note names, or syllables.

    3. The teacher will then give the beginning note (only) of another key. This is shown by the single white note.

    4. Sing the same exercise in the new key using the same numbers, note names, or syllables as shown in black notes.

1.

    1   2   3   4   5   3   1   1   2   3   4   5   3   1

2.

3.

4.

5.

6.

F. The following exercises are for rhythm. Sing or say the regular meter beat (as indicated), and at the same time clap the note values as shown.

1.

Clap: 1 2   4   2 3 4   1 2   4   2 3 4   1 2   4   1   3   1

Say or sing: 1 2 3 4   1 2 3 4   1 2 3 4   1 2 3 4   1 2 3 4   1 2 3 4   1234

2.

3.

G. Sing the following melodies with the syllables, scale numbers, or texts where these are given.

1.
                                           Spiritual, "Michael, Row de Boat Ashore" +

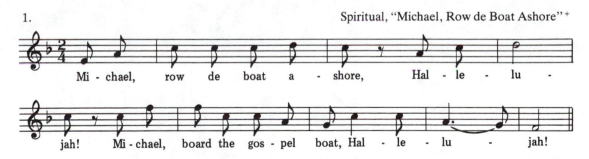

Mi - chael,   row   de   boat   a - shore,   Hal - le - lu -

jah!   Mi - chael,   board   the   gos - pel   boat, Hal - le - lu - jah!

2.

John Frederik Peter (1746–1813), "Glory be to Him" [+]

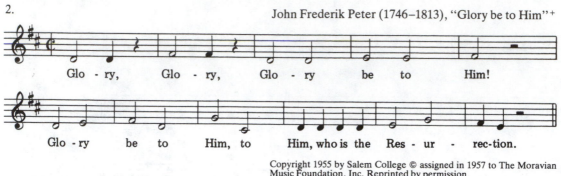

Glo - ry, Glo - ry, Glo - ry be to Him!

Glo - ry be to Him, to Him, who is the Res - ur - rec - tion.

Copyright 1955 by Salem College © assigned in 1957 to The Moravian
Music Foundation, Inc. Reprinted by permission.

3.

Giuseppe Verdi (1813–1901), Anvil Chorus,
Il Trovatore (*The Troubadour*) (1853)

Who has made beautiful the day for the gypsies?

4.

Vincent Persichetti (1915–   ), March, *Divertimento for Band* (1951) [+]

Copyright 1951, Oliver Ditson Company. Used by permission.

Written Assignment Quiz

It is very important to *memorize* the scales and key signatures, that is, to be able to write each scale from memory and to write the key signature for each major key, with the sharps or flats in the correct order. The best way to be sure you can do this is for your teacher to give you a quiz on them.

+Denotes American composer.

Ear Training Assignment

A. *Further Drill on Major and Minor Thirds and Major and Minor Seconds*. In each exercise you will hear a series of four harmonic intervals. Two intervals will be seconds (major or minor); two intervals will be thirds (major or minor). Mark the correct symbol in the space provided, using M3 for major third, m3 for minor third, M2 for major second, and m2 for minor second. The example is worked correctly for you.

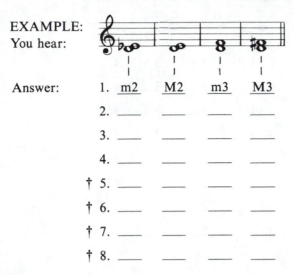

EXAMPLE:
You hear:

Answer:
1. <u>m2</u>   <u>M2</u>   <u>m3</u>   <u>M3</u>
2. ___   ___   ___   ___
3. ___   ___   ___   ___
4. ___   ___   ___   ___
† 5. ___   ___   ___   ___
† 6. ___   ___   ___   ___
† 7. ___   ___   ___   ___
† 8. ___   ___   ___   ___

Computer Program Disk: Intervals 2, Lesson C

B. *Recognition of Major Triads*. In each of the following exercises, one of the three triads played will be a *major triad*. Circle the letter that represents the major triad. The example is worked correctly for you.

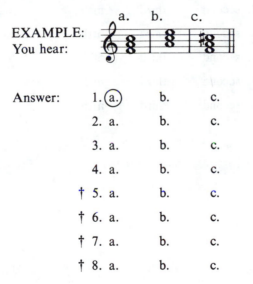

EXAMPLE:
You hear:

Answer:
1. (a.)   b.   c.
2. a.   b.   c.
3. a.   b.   c.
4. a.   b.   c.
† 5. a.   b.   c.
† 6. a.   b.   c.
† 7. a.   b.   c.
† 8. a.   b.   c.

Computer Program Disk: Harmony 1, Lesson C

C. *Recognition of Major and Minor Thirds and Perfect Fifths in Melodies.* In each of the following exercises you will hear four notes of a melody. The only intervals used in the melodies will be major and minor thirds and perfect fifths. Each melody may contain *any combination* of these intervals. Label each interval in the space provided, using M3 for a major third, m3 for a minor third, and P5 for a perfect fifth.

EXAMPLE:

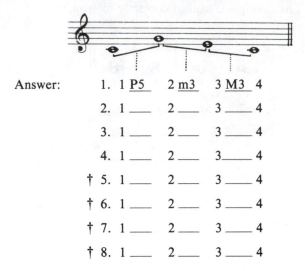

Answer: 1. 1 <u>P5</u>   2 <u>m3</u>   3 <u>M3</u> 4

     2. 1 ___   2 ___   3 ___ 4

     3. 1 ___   2 ___   3 ___ 4

     4. 1 ___   2 ___   3 ___ 4

    † 5. 1 ___   2 ___   3 ___ 4

    † 6. 1 ___   2 ___   3 ___ 4

    † 7. 1 ___   2 ___   3 ___ 4

    † 8. 1 ___   2 ___   3 ___ 4

Computer Program Disk: Intervals 2, Lesson G

D. *Recognition of parallel lines in thirds, seconds, and fifths.* In each exercise you will hear a short melody. It will be set with a parallel line a second, a third, or a fifth away. Underline the correct interval.

     1. second third fifth

     2. second third fifth

     3. second third fifth

    † 4. second third fifth

    † 5. second third fifth

    † 6. second third fifth

Chapter 11   The Natural Minor Scale

The Minor Scale

The scales studied so far have been major scales, which have half steps between the *third and fourth* and *seventh and eighth* degrees of the scale. When the arrangement of half steps and whole steps is changed, the aesthetic effect of the music is profoundly altered. For example, if a familiar tune like "My Country 'Tis of Thee" has the third degree of the scale lowered one half step, a completely new tonal feeling results.

Lowering the third degree in this manner produces a *minor third* between the first and third degrees of the scale. Many scales have this characteristic interval between the first and third degrees, but by far the most common one is the **minor scale,** which has half steps between the *second and third* and *fifth and sixth* degrees of the scale.

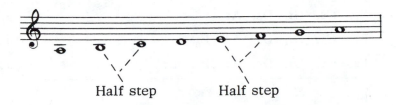

Half step   Half step

The A minor scale

This scale is often altered by accidentals, but the basic form shown above is called the **natural** or **pure** minor scale.

The Circle of Fifths for Minor Scales

The order of sharps and flats in minor key signatures is the same as for major scales. Like the major scales, minor keys follow the circle of fifths, with *a minor,* rather than *C major,* as the starting point.

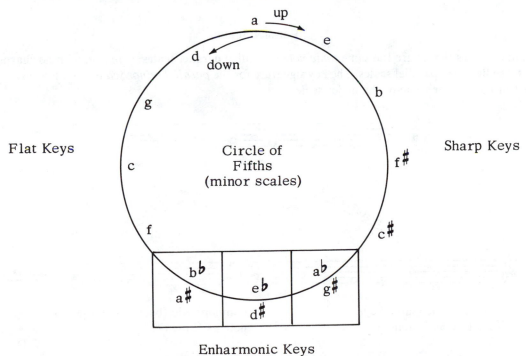

Enharmonic Keys

Relative Scales

Major and minor scales that share the same key signature are called **relative scales.** G major and e minor both have a key signature of one sharp (F-sharp); therefore, G major is the *relative major* of e minor, and e minor is the *relative minor* of G major. The relative minor scale always begins a *minor third* below the major scale with the same key signature.

TABLE OF SCALES

MAJOR	KEY SIGNATURE							RELATIVE MINOR
C major	No sharps or flats							a minor
G major	F♯							e minor
D major	F♯,	C♯						b minor
A major	F♯,	C♯,	G♯					f♯ minor
E major	F♯,	C♯,	G♯,	D♯				c♯ minor
B major	F♯,	C♯,	G♯,	D♯,	A♯			g♯ minor
F♯ major	F♯,	C♯,	G♯,	D♯,	A♯,	E♯		d♯ minor
C♯ major	F♯,	C♯,	G♯,	D♯,	A♯,	E♯,	B♯	a♯ minor
F major	B♭							d minor
B♭ major	B♭,	E♭						g minor
E♭ major	B♭,	E♭,	A♭					c minor
A♭ major	B♭,	E♭,	A♭,	D♭				f minor
D♭ major	B♭,	E♭,	A♭,	D♭,	G♭			b♭ minor
G♭ major	B♭,	E♭,	A♭,	D♭,	G♭,	C♭		e♭ minor
C♭ major	B♭,	E♭,	A♭,	D♭,	G♭,	C♭,	F♭	a♭ minor

Parallel Scales

Major and minor scales that share the same *tonic note* are called **parallel scales.** *C major,* with no sharps or flats, and *c minor,* with three flats, are parallel scales. The key signature for the *parallel minor scale* is the same as that of the major key a minor third above the tonic of the major scale.

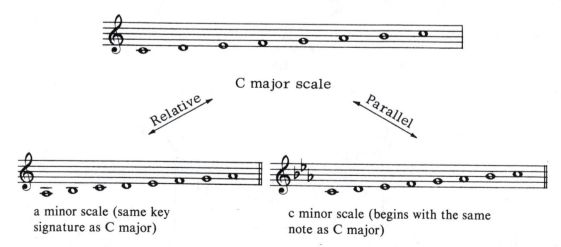

C major scale

a minor scale (same key signature as C major)

c minor scale (begins with the same note as C major)

Sight Singing Assignment

A. *Natural Minor*. Sing the following short melodies in the natural minor mode. Use syllables or scale numbers on all exercises.

   1. The scale numbers are provided for you in the first two exercises.

   2. In the other six exercises figure out the scale numbers or syllables for yourselves.

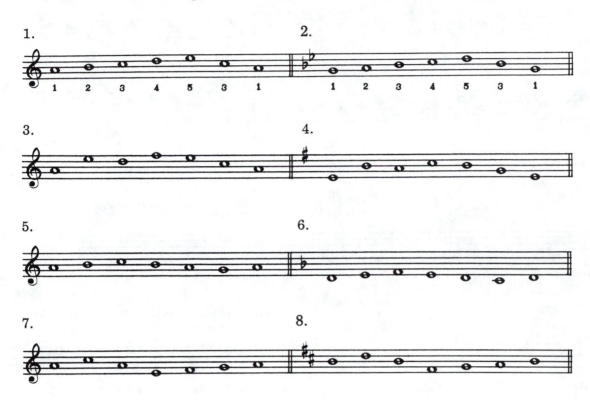

B. *Natural Minor*. In this set of exercises only the numbers are indicated. The number "1" refers to the tonic (first note) of the natural minor scale. Choose any beginning pitch you wish and sing these just as you sang the previous exercises.

(a) 1 3 5 6 4 5 3 1   (c) 1 5 6 7 8 6 4 1   (e) 1 3 2 4 2 3 1 7 1

(b) 1 2 3 4 3 8 7 8   (d) 1 4 3 5 2 4 7 8   (f) 1 5 3 1 7 1 3 2 1

C. *Close your books for this exercise.*

   a. The instructor plays the exercise on the piano—as shown in whole (white) notes.

   b. The student then sings the exercise back to the instructor using scale numbers. This is shown in black notes.

   c. The instructor gives the first note of a new key, and the student sings the same exercise using the same scale numbers.

D. *Melodies to Sing.* Sing the melodies below with syllables, scale step numbers, or with the texts.

1.

Gabriel Fauré, (1845–1924), "Libera me" (Set Me Free), *Requiem (Mass for the Dead)* (1877)

From death e - ter - nal, O set me free, Lord my God.

2.

John H. Hopkins, Jr. (1820–1891), "We Three Kings of Orient Are" (1857)[+]

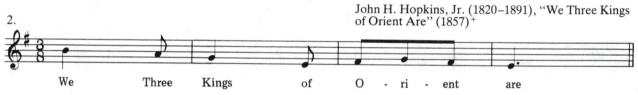

We Three Kings of O - ri - ent are

3.

Béla Bartók, (1881–1945), "New Hungarian Folk Song," *Mikrokosmos (Little Universe)*, Vol. V (1940)

Oh, how high, green for - est, spread your high - est tree?

Copyright 1940 by Hawkes & Son (London) Ltd.; Renewed 1967. Reprinted by permission of Boosey & Hawkes, Inc.

4.

Antonin Dvořák (1841–1904), First Movement, *Symphony No. 9 in E Minor (from the New World)* (1893)

5.

Traditional Irish Hymn, "St. Patrick"

6.

Carol based on Gregorian Chant, "O Come, O Come Emmanuel"

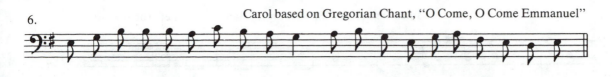

7.

Russian Folk Song, "The Birch Tree"

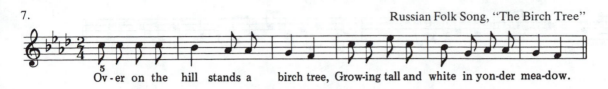

Ov-er on the hill stands a birch tree, Grow-ing tall and white in yon-der mea-dow.

The Russian composer Tchaikovsky used the melody you just sang as the basis for a theme and variations in his fourth symphony (1877). You might like to hear how he treated this old folk tune.

8.

John Merbecke (circa 1505–1585), "Agnus Dei" (1550) ("Lamb of God"), *The Book of Common Prayer Noted*

Notice that this example, like those from Gregorian chant, is nonmetric. Read the rhythm carefully and sing it smoothly without accent.

9.

Anne L. Miller (20th century) "Give Peace, O God, the Nations Cry" (1941)[+]

E. The preceding melodies all used the natural minor scale. Sing the following three melodies, which are in major, using scale step numbers, syllables or texts if they are given.

1.

Johannes Brahms (1833–1897), "Vergebliches Ständchen" "False Serenade" (1882)

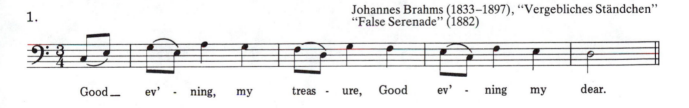

Good ___ ev' - ning, my treas - ure, Good ev' - ning my dear.

2.

Dutch Folk Song, "We Gather Together"

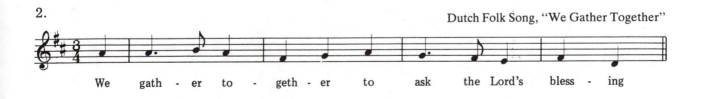

We gath - er to - geth - er to ask the Lord's bless - ing

3.

F. The following melody is a dance tune that was always accompanied by a repeated drum-beat pattern. Sing the melody with scale step numbers, syllables, or the text while tapping the drum-beat pattern or playing it on a drum. The piece is a **pavan,** a popular Renaissance dance.

Thoinot Arbeau (circa 1519–1595), "Pavan," *Orchesographie* (1588)

Beau - ty, who has my heart cap - tive with - in your eyes,
Whose love - ly smiles will teach se - crets of Pa - ra - dise.

Drum

Come, quick - ly give me hope; with - out it I'll sure - ly die.

Drum

Although this piece is in g minor, it is not natural minor. What makes it different? You will learn more about this in a later chapter!

Written Assignment

Placing Minor Scales in Position on the Keyboard. Place the following natural minor scales on the keyboard by writing the letter names of the notes on the proper keys. Then place the proper key signature on the staff at right. Then, indicate the relative major key in the space provided. The example is worked correctly for you. After writing out the scales and giving the name of the relative major, write the name and signature for the parallel major.

1. EXAMPLE: Scale of E natural minor

Key Signature   Relative Major

G

What is the *parallel* major scale and signature?

E Major

Parallel Major

2. Scale of D natural minor

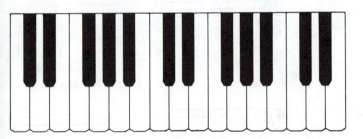

Key Signature   Relative Major

_____

Parallel major scale name and signature

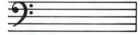

_____

3. Scale of C♯ natural minor

Key Signature   Relative Major

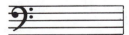

_____

Parallel major scale name and signature

_____

4. Scale of G natural minor

Key Signature   Relative Major

_____

Parallel major scale name and signature

_____

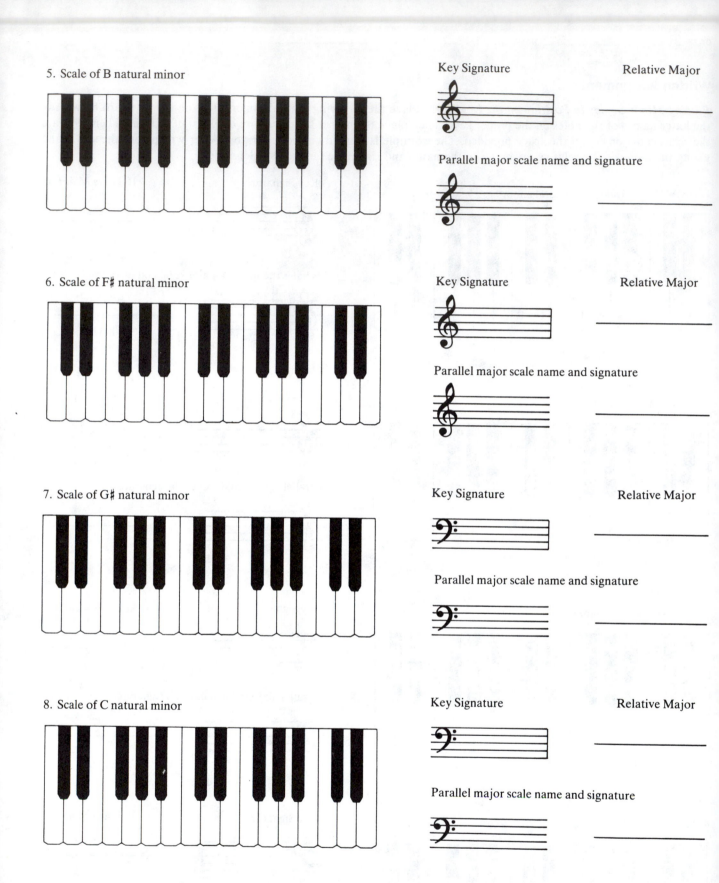

5. Scale of B natural minor

Key Signature

Relative Major

_____

Parallel major scale name and signature

_____

6. Scale of F♯ natural minor

Key Signature

Relative Major

_____

Parallel major scale name and signature

_____

7. Scale of G♯ natural minor

Key Signature

Relative Major

_____

Parallel major scale name and signature

_____

8. Scale of C natural minor

Key Signature

Relative Major

_____

Parallel major scale name and signature

_____

Play all the scales you have written on the piano and/or any other instrument.

Ear Training Assignment

A. *Melodies Using the Minor Scale.* In each of the following exercises you will hear six notes of a melody in the minor mode. The first three notes of the melody are written on the staff for you. Write the other notes of the melody on the staff in whole notes. Each melody will be played twice. See the example.

1. EXAMPLE:

Given   Completed

2.

3.

†4.

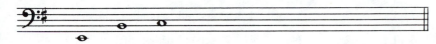

†5.

†6.

B. *Hearing Major and Minor Modes in Musical Examples.* You will hear six phrases of music. Some will be in major and some will be in minor mode. Underline the correct mode for each example.

   1. Major   Minor

   2. Major   Minor

   3. Major   Minor

† 4. Major   Minor

† 5. Major   Minor

† 6. Major   Minor

Computer Program Disk: Scales and Keys, Lesson I

C. *Recognition of Major and Minor Thirds, Major and Minor Seconds, and Perfect Fifths.* In each of the following exercises you will hear four notes of a melody. The intervals used in the melodies will be major and minor thirds, major and minor seconds, and perfect fifths. In each exercise you will be told whether the intervals will include thirds, seconds, or fifths. You are to determine how many of each are used and whether the thirds and seconds are major or minor. Label each interval in the space provided, using *M3* for major thirds, *m3* for minor thirds, *M2* for major seconds, *m2* for minor seconds, and *P5* for perfect fifths. The example is worked correctly for you. Each exercise will be played twice.

EXAMPLE: Instructor plays:

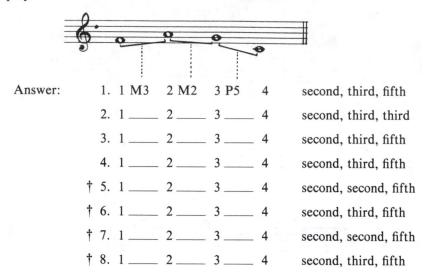

Answer:
1. 1 M3 2 M2 3 P5 4   second, third, fifth
2. 1 ____ 2 ____ 3 ____ 4   second, third, third
3. 1 ____ 2 ____ 3 ____ 4   second, third, fifth
4. 1 ____ 2 ____ 3 ____ 4   second, third, fifth
† 5. 1 ____ 2 ____ 3 ____ 4   second, second, fifth
† 6. 1 ____ 2 ____ 3 ____ 4   second, third, fifth
† 7. 1 ____ 2 ____ 3 ____ 4   second, second, fifth
† 8. 1 ____ 2 ____ 3 ____ 4   second, third, fifth

D. *More Drill on Major Triad Patterns in a Melodic Context.* A group of three triad patterns will be played as broken chords. One triad pattern will be a major triad. Circle the letter that indicates the major triad. The example is worked correctly for you. Each exercise will be played twice.

EXAMPLE: Instructor plays:

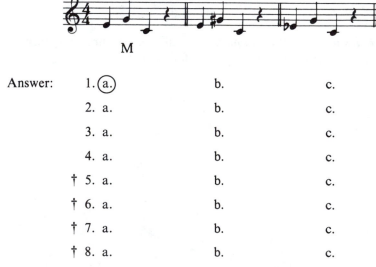

M

Answer:
1. (a.)   b.   c.
2. a.   b.   c.
3. a.   b.   c.
4. a.   b.   c.
† 5. a.   b.   c.
† 6. a.   b.   c.
† 7. a.   b.   c.
† 8. a.   b.   c.

Computer Program Disk: Harmony 1, Lesson D

Chapter 12   Intervals: Fourths, Fifths, and the Tritone

The Perfect Fourth

The perfect intervals studied so far include: the perfect unison (no half steps), the perfect octave (twelve half steps), and the perfect fifth (seven half steps). There is one other perfect interval: the *perfect fourth,* which has five half steps. Following is a perfect fourth on the keyboard. The strings on the guitar are tuned in perfect fourths (except for the major third you found in Chapter 8), as you see on the tablature.

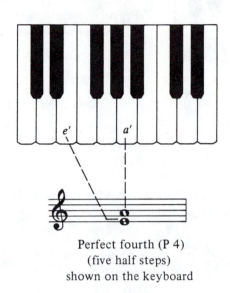

Perfect fourth (P 4)
(five half steps)
shown on the keyboard

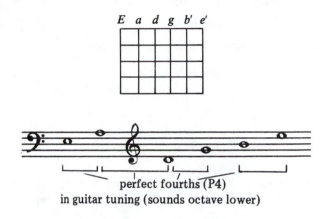

perfect fourths (P4)
in guitar tuning (sounds octave lower)

The Fourths in Major

When all the fourths of the major scale are arranged in order, all but one are perfect fourths.

	1	2	3	4	5	6	7	8
Scale degree	1	2	3	4	5	6	7	8
Number of half steps	5	5	5	6	5	5	5	5
Size of interval	P4	P4	P4		P4	P4	P4	P4

C major

The Augmented Fourth (The Tritone)

Since the fourth built on the fourth degree of the major scale is one half step larger than a perfect fourth, it is called an **augmented fourth.** Since the six half steps equal *three whole steps,* it is called the **tritone** (meaning "three tones"). In the Medieval era, when harmonies were all based on perfect fourths or perfect fifths, the tritone was a forbidden interval. The old name for it was *diabolus in musica*—"the devil in music!"—because it had such a restless sound.

The augmented fourth between F and B is the only augmented fourth composed only of white keys. All other fourths on the white keys are perfect fourths. If one note of any fourth (other than that between F and B) is sharped or flatted, the other note must have the same accidental to be a perfect fourth.

Augmented fourth (A 4)

Tritone

(six half steps or three whole steps)

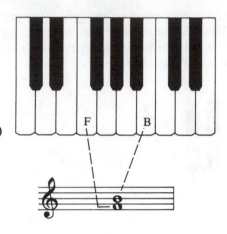

F-B, the only augmented fourth using only white keys

To make the augmented fourth F to B a perfect fourth, either sharp the F or flat the B. Play the intervals below on a keyboard instrument and/or any other instruments played by members of the class.

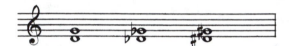

Both natural Both flats Both sharps

Perfect fourths (P 4)

Perfect fourths (P 4)

The Diminished Fifth (Also a Tritone!)

The interval of the augmented fourth contains the same number of half steps as the **diminished fifth**. On the piano, they have an identical sound and are distinguished by the context in which they are used. Unlike the perfect fourth and perfect fifth, the augmented fourth and diminished fifth have a restless, unstable quality of sound and are classed as **dissonant** intervals. A4 is the abbreviation for an augmented fourth—d5 is the symbol for a diminished fifth. Both are the tritone (three whole steps) sound.

Ways of writing the tritone sound

When you hear the interval *G to C♯* (*D♭*) in isolation, you may hear it either as an augmented fourth (G to C♯) or as a diminished fifth (G to D♭). For this reason, both intervals are referred to as the *tritone* (that is, the interval with three whole tones) in the ear training drills.

Ancient Harmony Using Fourths

Harmony back in the ninth century was based on the interval of the fourth, so if you sing the following example in class you will be hearing a use of the fourth that is eleven centuries old:

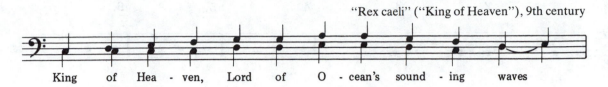

"Rex caeli" ("King of Heaven"), 9th century

King of Hea - ven, Lord of O - cean's sound - ing waves

Modern Music Using Fourths

At the beginning of this century, composers again became fascinated by the sound of melodies set with the perfect intervals—fourths, fifths, and octaves. Play the following passage on the piano and listen to the fourths with an occasional third!

Claude Debussy (1862–1918), "La fille aux cheveux de Lin" ("The Girl with the Flaxen Hair"), *Préludes pour Piano*, Book I (1910)

Twentieth century composers have also been interested in the way fourths can be used to build melodies. This example is from the opening of Bartók's *Concerto for Orchestra* and is played by the low strings of the orchestra—violas, cellos, and string basses.

Béla Bartók (1881–1945), Introduzione, *Concerto for Orchestra* (1944)

Andante non troppo

Copyright 1946 by Hawkes & Son (London) Ltd.; Renewed 1973. Reprinted by permission of Boosey & Hawkes, Inc.

Compare the sound of this melody built of *melodic fourths* with Beethoven's similarly-shaped melody based on a *chord built of thirds (triad)* written a century and a half ago.

Ludwig van Beethoven (1770–1827), Third Movement, *Symphony No. 5 in C Minor* (1807–1808)

Allegro

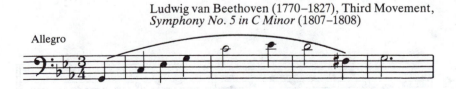

Sight Singing Assignment

A. By practicing the interval of the fourth you will learn to hear it better and to use it in singing melodies. Play the whole note and sing the black notes.

B. "Here Comes the Bride" (Bridal Chorus from *Lohengrin* by Wagner) begins with a *perfect fourth* up. Can you think of some more tunes you know that begin with a perfect fourth up or down? Collect a list of the tunes your class knows that could help you remember the sound of the perfect fourth.

C. *Close your book for this exercise,* which uses many intervals you have learned.

1. The instructor plays the exercise on the piano—as shown in whole notes.

2. Then sing the exercise back to the instructor using the scale numbers. This is shown by the black notes.

3. The instructor gives the first note of a new key (the whole note shown), and the student sings the same exercise using the same scale numbers.

1.

2.

3.

4.

5.

6.

D. *Melodies That Use Fourths*. These melodies can be sung with words, syllables, or scale step numbers.

Engelbert Humperdinck (1854–1921), "Children's Prayer"
Hansel and Gretel (1893) (the *original* musician by this name!)

1.

When at night I go to sleep Four-teen an - gels watch do keep.

English Folk Song, "The Foggy, Foggy Dew"

2.

When I was a bach -'lor I lived by my-self and worked at the weav - er's trade.

Written and Keyboard Assignment

(Play all the examples on the keyboard after writing them):

A. *Recognition of the P4, P5, A4, and d5.* Each exercise contains four intervals, one each of the following:

Interval	Abbreviation Symbol	Half Steps	Whole Steps
Perfect fourth	P4	5	2½
Perfect fifth	P5	7	3½
Augmented fourth	A4	6	3
Diminished fifth	d5	6	3

Name the intervals in each exercise and place the answers in the blanks beneath the staff. The example has been worked correctly for you. Remember, each exercise will contain one each of the four intervals listed above. Keep in mind that accidentals occurring in a measure retain the alteration until the bar line unless altered again. Be able to play these intervals.

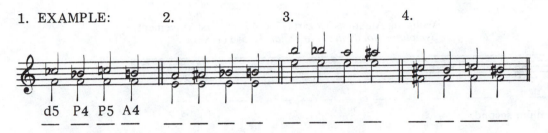

1. EXAMPLE: 2.   3.   4.

d5 P4 P5 A4

5.   6.   7.   8.

B. *Placement of Intervals on the Music Staff.* In each exercise place the interval on the staff above the given note as directed, and then play it. See the example.

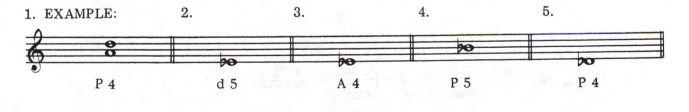

1. EXAMPLE: 2.   3.   4.   5.

P 4   d 5   A 4   P 5   P 4

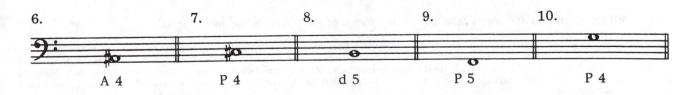

6.   7.   8.   9.   10.

A 4   P 4   d 5   P 5   P 4

C. *Recognition of Melodic Intervals.* Each exercise consists of a short melody. Name the intervals between the successive notes of the melody and write them in the blanks provided. The example is begun for you. Use these abbreviations:

Perfect octave	P8	Major third	M3		
Perfect unison	P1	Minor third	m3	Augmented fourth	A4
Major second	M2	Perfect fourth	P4	Diminished fifth	d5
Minor second	m2	Perfect fifth	P5		

EXAMPLE:

1.

John Phillip Sousa (1854–1932),
"Semper Fidelis March" (1888)[+]

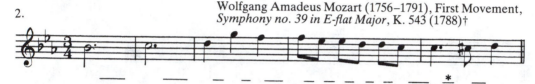

2.

Wolfgang Amadeus Mozart (1756–1791), First Movement,
Symphony no. 39 in E-flat Major, K. 543 (1788)[†]

*Half step, *not* a minor second.

3.

Modest Mussorgsky (1839–1881), "Promenade
Theme," from *Pictures at an Exhibition* (1874)

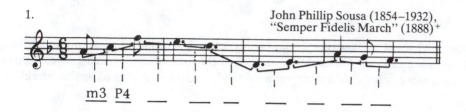

Felix Mendelssohn (1809–1847), Second Movement, *Symphony
No. 4 in A Major,* (Italian) (1833) (Note that not all movements
of the symphony may be in the main key of the work.
This then is in d minor!)

4.

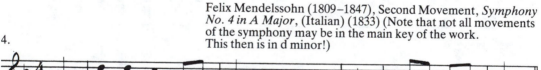

5.

Johann Sebastian Bach (1685–1750),
Third Movement, *Sonata for Violin
and Continuo* (about 1720)**

Play all the examples and listen carefully to the sounds of the intervals you have named.

[†]Not all composers marked their works with *opus numbers.* Mozart's works were put in chronological order after his death by a man named Köchel, so we refer to Mozart's compositions by *K. numbers* that show the order in which it is thought they were composed. Thus the example on p. 268 in this text, *K. 2,* was a very early work, written when this astonishing composer was only five years old; the symphony quoted here, *K. 543,* was written late in his life—just three years before his death. Many of you may have seen the movie *Amadeus* about this composer's life and wondered why Wolfgang Mozart is referred to in the title as *Amadeus!* It is because that was his *middle* name and means "beloved of God."

**The numbering system used for Bach's works is indicated by the abbreviation BWV, for *Bach Werke-Verzeichnis,* the German words for *Bach's Works Index.*

Ear Training Assignment

A. *Recognition of Tritone, P4, P5, P8, M3, and M2.* In each exercise you will hear three harmonic intervals played. The *order of playing* of these intervals will be different from the order which you see. Rearrange the order (as given) so that the intervals are in the order played. The example is illustrated and is worked correctly for you. Each exercise will be played twice.

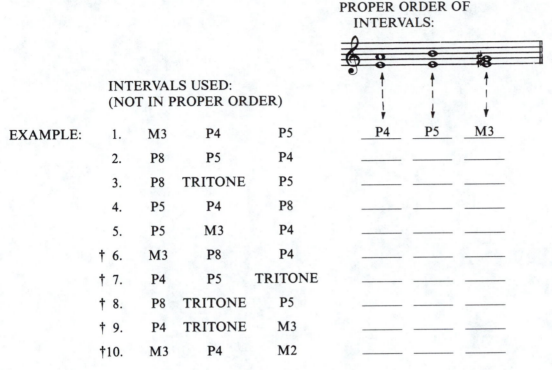

PROPER ORDER OF
INTERVALS:

INTERVALS USED:
(NOT IN PROPER ORDER)

					P4	P5	M3
EXAMPLE:	1.	M3	P4	P5			
	2.	P8	P5	P4			
	3.	P8	TRITONE	P5			
	4.	P5	P4	P8			
	5.	P5	M3	P4			
† 6.		M3	P8	P4			
† 7.		P4	P5	TRITONE			
† 8.		P8	TRITONE	P5			
† 9.		P4	TRITONE	M3			
†10.		M3	P4	M2			

Computer Program Disk: Intervals, Lesson I

B. *Recognition of the Tritone in a Melody.* In each exercise a six note melody will be played. Some of the melodies include a tritone; others do not. Underline the proper answer. The example is illustrated and worked correctly for you. Each melody will be played twice.

EXAMPLE:

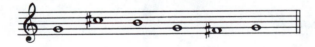

Answer: 1. a. <u>Includes tritone</u>   b. No tritone

2. a. Includes tritone   b. No tritone

3. a. Includes tritone   b. No tritone

† 4. a. Includes tritone   b. No tritone

† 5. a. Includes tritone   b. No tritone

† 6. a. Includes tritone   b. No tritone

Chapter 13   The Minor Triad

Introduction to the Minor Triad

The triad with a perfect fifth between the root and fifth and a minor third between the root and third is called a **minor triad.** In the minor triad, the interval between the third and fifth is a major third.

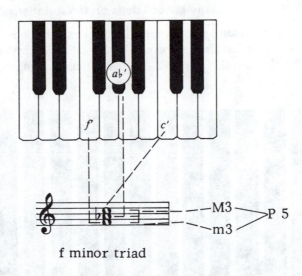

f minor triad

Minor Triads in the Major Scale

There are three minor triads in the major scale.

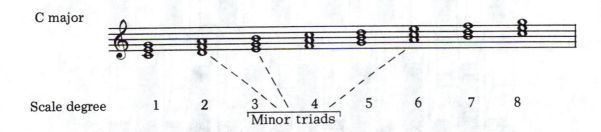

Minor Triads in the Minor Scale

In the natural minor scale, there are minor triads on the first, fourth, and fifth degrees. Since these are the most important chords in the key, the predominance of minor triads imparts a characteristic color to minor harmonies.

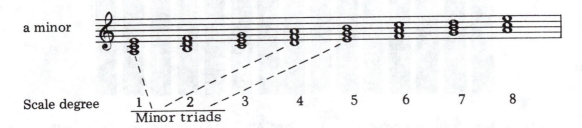

The Minor Triads on the White Keys

There are only three minor triads that consist entirely of white keys. These three triads are *a minor* triad, the *d minor* triad, and the *e minor* triad. Find these three triads on the piano and play them, listening carefully to the sound.

To construct all other minor triads, use sharps or flats to make a minor third and a perfect fifth above the root of the triad.

The Minor Triads on the Autoharp

The chords on the autoharp include some minor triads. Find the minor triads and strum them. Because there are only a few (12 or 15) chord bars on this instrument it can only play in a few keys. Play the G Minor chord and then the G Major chord and listen to the difference! If you have a 15-bar autoharp, compare the sounds of the D Major and D minor triads.

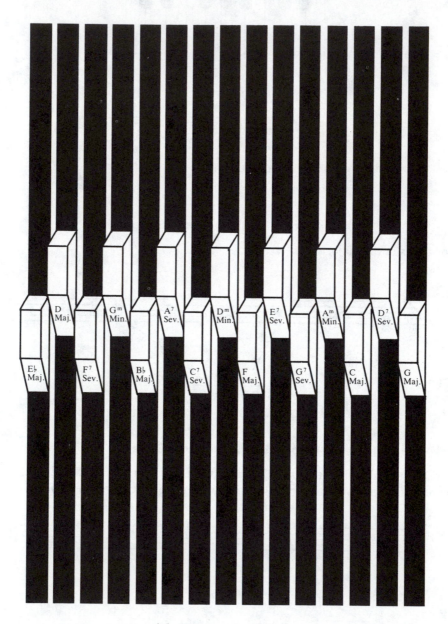

The minor chords are shown with the symbols $G^m_{Min.}$, $D^m_{Min.}$, and $A^m_{Min.}$. The remaining bars are *seventh chords* that you will study in a later chapter. Their abbreviation on the autoharp is the $\frac{\text{root name}^7}{\text{sev.}}$.

Guitar Chords

Common fingerings for playing many of the minor triads on the guitar are given in appendix 7. Those with guitars can find these fingerings and play the minor triads given there. Listen carefully to all the sounds you play. The common symbol for a minor triad is the name of the root (capitalized) followed by the letters "m" or "mi." Thus, *Cmi* or *Cm* means a *c minor* triad on the guitar. In this book "m" is used for minor triads on the guitar.

Sight Singing Assignment

A. *Minor Triad Drill*. Sing the black notes after hearing the whole note. You may give yourself the first note or it may be played for you by your teacher.

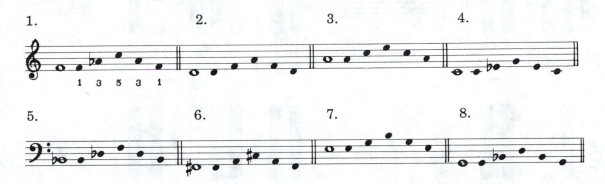

B. *Minor Triad Drill*. You will hear the whole note played, then sing the broken chords from the fifth or the third.

Keyboard Assignment

Following are all of the minor triads in simple position. First the position on the keyboard is shown, and then the proper notation on the music staff. Learn to find these minor triads on *all* octaves of the keyboard.

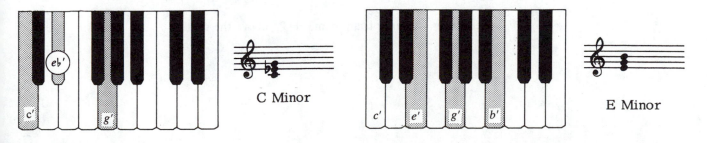

C Minor

E Minor

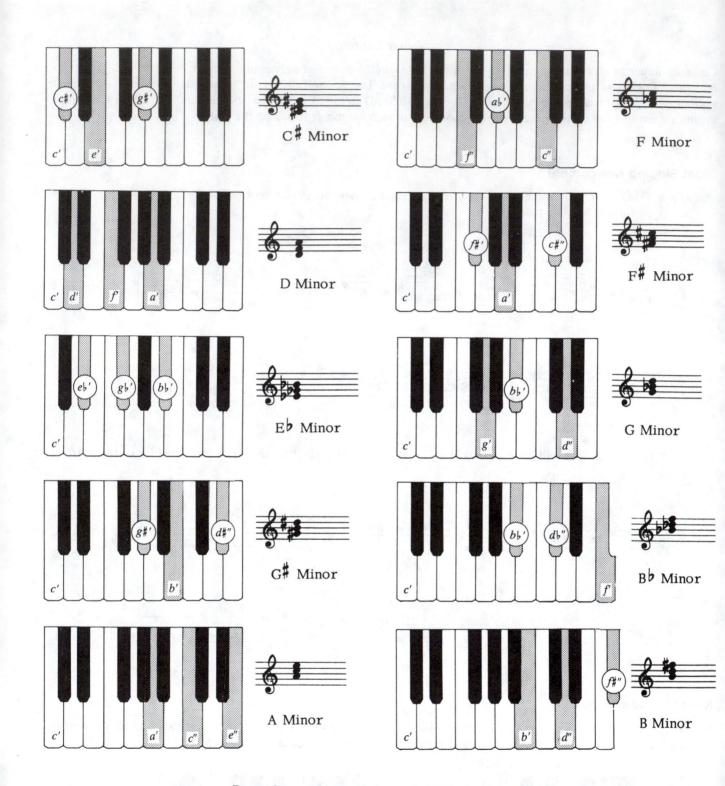

Remember → minor triad = m3 + P5 above the root!

Ear Training Assignment

A. *Recognition of the Major and Minor Triads.* In each exercise you will hear four chords. Of the four, one will be a *minor triad,* and one will be a *major triad.* The other two will be chord formations not yet studied. Mark the *major triad* with an "M," the *minor triad* with an "m," and leave the other chords blank. See the example. Each exercise will be played twice.

EXAMPLE: You will hear:

	a.	b.	c.	d.
Answer: 1.	M	m	_____	_____
2.	_____	_____	_____	_____
3.	_____	_____	_____	_____
† 4.	_____	_____	_____	_____
† 5.	_____	_____	_____	_____
† 6.	_____	_____	_____	_____

Computer Program Disk: Harmony 1, Lesson K

B. *Recognition of Minor Triads in a Phrase of Music.* A chord progression will be played in each exercise; it will include one or more minor triads. Place an "X" in the blank for each minor triad. Leave the other spaces blank. See example. Each exercise will be played twice.

EXAMPLE: You will hear:

1.	X	X	_	_	X	_	X

2.	_	_	_	_	_	_	_
3.	_	_	_	_	_	_	_
† 4.	_	_	_	_	_	_	_
† 5.	_	_	_	_	_	_	_
† 6.	_	_	_	_	_	_	_

Computer Program Disk: Harmony 1, Lesson J

Chapter 14 More Intervals: Major and Minor Sixths and Sevenths, and More Augmented and Diminished Intervals

Sixths and Sevenths

Sixths and **sevenths** come in two normal sizes. Sixths contain either eight or nine half steps. A sixth with *nine* half steps (4½ whole steps) is a *major sixth* (M6); with *eight* half steps (4 whole steps), a *minor sixth* (m6).

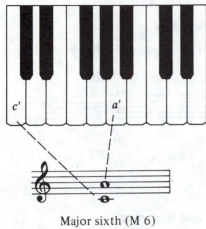

Major sixth (M 6)
(nine half steps)

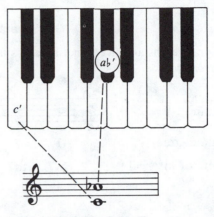

Minor sixth (m 6)
(eight half steps)

Major sevenths have eleven half steps (5½ whole steps), just one half step less than an octave. The symbol for this interval is M7. *Minor sevenths* (m7) have ten half steps (5 whole steps), one whole step less than an octave.

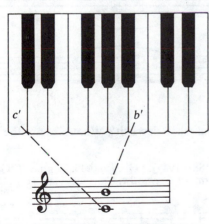

Major seventh (M 7)
(eleven half steps)

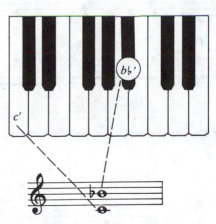

Minor seventh (m 7)
(ten half steps)

The Sixths in a Major Key

There are four major sixths, and three minor sixths in a major scale. Major and minor sixths have a bland, smooth quality, like thirds, and are *consonances*.

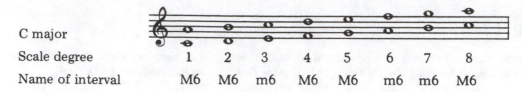

	1	2	3	4	5	6	7	8
C major								
Scale degree	1	2	3	4	5	6	7	8
Name of interval	M6	M6	m6	M6	M6	m6	m6	M6

The Sevenths in a Major Key

There are two major sevenths and five minor sevenths in the major scale. Sevenths, like seconds, have a harsh, restless quality and are *dissonances*.

	1	2	3	4	5	6	7	8
C major								
Scale degree	1	2	3	4	5	6	7	8
Name of interval	M7	m7	m7	M7	m7	m7	m7	M7

Melodies Set with Sixths and Sevenths

The Bartók movement previously used to find examples of melodies set with various other intervals also contains themes set in sixths and sevenths.

Béla Bartók (1881–1945), "Giuoco della Coppie," ("Game of Pairs"), *Concerto for Orchestra,* (1944), Bassoons I and II

One sixth is not the same size as the rest. Which one is it, and what size is it? What size are the rest?

Béla Bartók (1881–1945), "Giuoco della Coppie" ("Game of Pairs") *Concerto for Orchestra*, Clarinets I and II

Are all these sevenths the same size?

Now listen to a recording of the whole movement to see how these themes are used, and in what order they appear. Listen carefully to the interval sounds in the pairs of instruments.

All the Interval Sounds

The following table summarizes the intervals.

CONSONANT		CONSONANT		DISSONANT		DISSONANT	
Perfect Intervals	Half steps	Major and Minor Intervals	Half steps	Major and Minor Intervals	Half steps	Augmented and Diminished Intervals	Half steps
UNISON	0	MAJOR THIRD	4	MAJOR SECOND	2	AUGMENTED FOURTH	6
OCTAVE	12	MINOR THIRD	3	MINOR SECOND	1		
FOURTH	5	MAJOR SIXTH	9	MAJOR SEVENTH	11	DIMINISHED FIFTH	6
FIFTH	7	MINOR SIXTH	8	MINOR SEVENTH	10		

Other Augmented and Diminished Intervals

This chart summarizes the *interval sounds* within the octave. There is also a group of intervals that are formed by different spellings of the sounds. Intervals are always named on the basis of the *written* appearance of the interval, which means that f′ to a′, f′ to a ♭′, f′ to a ♯′ and f′ to a 𝄪 are all thirds.

Obviously some of these thirds are neither major nor minor thirds, since they do not all have the proper number of half steps. If a written third is one half step smaller than a minor third, it is called a *diminished third*. If it is a half step larger than a major third, it is an *augmented third*. In the unlikely event that it is a half step larger than an augmented third, it is called a *doubly-augmented third,* and so forth. Doubly-augmented and doubly-diminished intervals are rarely used.

Diminished Augmented Doubly-augmented Doubly-diminished
third   third   third   third

The same principle applies to all other intervals. A *written* sixth, seventh, second, or third that is a half step larger than the major interval is called an *augmented interval*. A *written* second, third, sixth, or seventh that is a half step smaller than a minor interval is called a *diminished interval*. Intervals a half step larger than perfect intervals are also augmented; those a half step smaller than perfect intervals are diminished.

The chart below summarizes the relationship of intervals of various qualities:

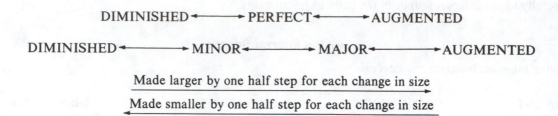

Made larger by one half step for each change in size ⟶
Made smaller by one half step for each change in size ⟵

Sight Singing Assignment

A. *Major Sixth Interval Drill.* The teacher will play the whole note; after hearing it, sing the black notes. (You may play the first note yourself and then sing the black notes.)

B. *Major Sixth Identification Drill.* This simple pattern will help you to identify and sing the major sixth.

C. *Minor Sixth Interval Drill.* The whole note will be played; sing the black notes.

4.　　　　　　　**5.**　　　　　　　**6.**

D. *Minor Sixth Identification Drill.* The first interval in this simple melody is a *minor sixth*. You can use this tune to help you identify and sing the minor sixth easily.

1.　　　　　　　　　　　　　　　　　　Spiritual, "Go Down Moses"[+]

5　　3　3　2　2　　3　3　1　　5　5　7　7　　1

E. *Major Sixth Identification Drill.* The first interval in this well-known melody is a *major sixth*. Thus, it can also be used as a memory device to fix the sound of the major sixth in your mind easily.

Charles Pratt (pseudonym, H. J. Fuller), "My Bonnie Lies
Over the Ocean" (1881)[+]

2.

Perhaps you know some tunes that begin with other intervals. For example, "A Bicycle Built for Two" begins

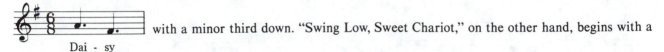

Dai - sy

with a minor third down. "Swing Low, Sweet Chariot," on the other hand, begins with a

major third down. Make a collection for yourself (and to share with the class) of tunes you know well that begin with different intervals and that you could use to help you remember the sound of the interval.

Other Melodies Containing Sixths

Franz Schubert (1797–1828), First Movement, *Sonata in A Minor
for Arpeggione and Piano* (1824)

3.

Wolfgang Amadeus Mozart, First Movement, Symphony No. 40
in G Minor, K. 550 (1788)

4.

F. *Melody Using the Tritone.* Before singing the melody, sing the following pattern of whole steps that uses the scale on which the melody is based. This will help you to fix the sound of the tritone in your ear. Note that the melody is not major or minor but uses another, more exotic sounding scale!

L - - - - - - - Lydian scale - - - - - - - J

Béla Bartók (1881–1945), Ostinato, *Mikrokosmos*, Vol. VI. (1940)

G. *Continued Practice of Intervals Already Studied.* By continuing to practice intervals you have already learned, your facility in singing all intervals will improve. When you hear the whole note played, sing back the black notes to review the intervals you studied in previous chapters.

Sing up.
Uses Notes of C Major

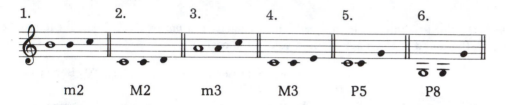

Uses Notes of D Major

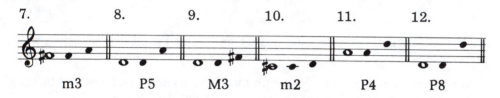

Sing down.
Uses Notes of A Major

Sing up.
Uses Notes of D Major

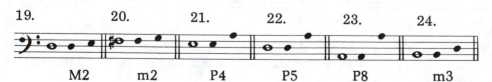

Written and Keyboard Assignment

A. *Writing Sixths and Sevenths.* Below are several intervals of sixths or sevenths. Some are major and some are minor. Label each interval. Then, if it is major write the minor form of the interval in the space provided. If the given interval is minor, write the major form of the interval in the space. Play all of the intervals you have written.

B. *Placing the M6, m6, M7, and m7 on the Keyboard and Music Staff.* Using the letter names of the notes, write the intervals requested on the keyboard; then, place the same interval on the staff at the right of the keyboard. Play all of the intervals on the piano (or on any other instrument you play).

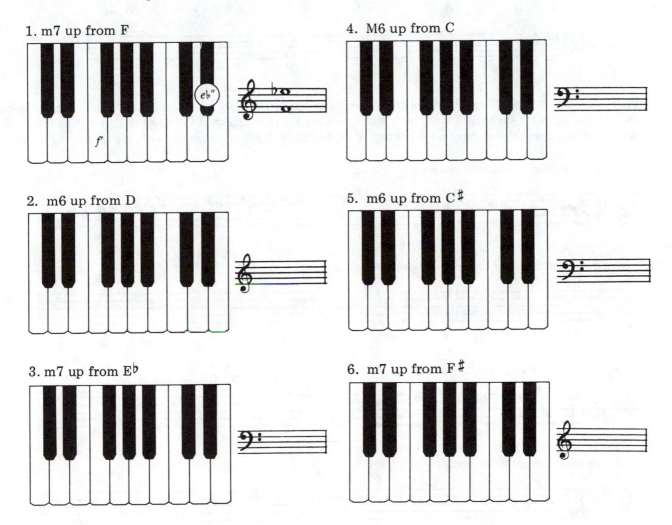

1. m7 up from F

2. m6 up from D

3. m7 up from E♭

4. M6 up from C

5. m6 up from C♯

6. m7 up from F♯

C. *Changing Perfect Intervals to Diminished and Augmented Intervals.* In each of the following eight exercises you are to change the perfect interval by altering the upper note so that: (1) the interval is augmented, and (2) the interval is diminished. The example is worked correctly for you.

EXAMPLE:

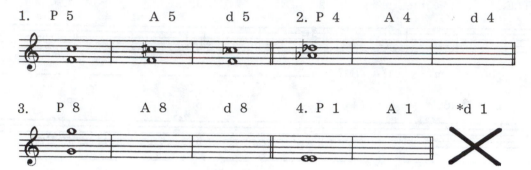

*The diminished unison cannot exist, as an interval with less than no half steps is impossible!

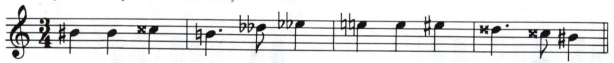

D. *Drill in Enharmonic Spelling.* Following are two very familiar tunes. They are difficult to read and sing because of the way the notes are spelled. Beneath each melody rewrite the tune and spell the notes so they can be read easily in the key suggested. *Remember that the sound of the melody will not be changed—only the spelling of the notes.*

1. Melody with notes spelled enharmonically:

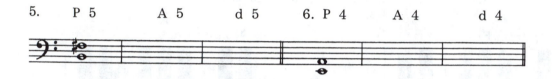

1. Melody with notes spelled correctly in the key of C major:

2. Melody with notes spelled enharmonically.

2. Melody with notes spelled correctly in the key of D major.

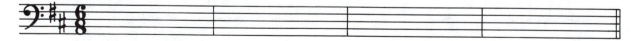

What are the names of the tunes?

Ear Training Assignment

A. *Recognition of All Intervals.* In each exercise you will hear a melody of four notes. The intervals used between the notes of the melody are listed in incorrect order in a column at the left. After listening to the melody, rearrange the intervals in the order in which they are heard in the melody. The example is illustrated and is worked correctly for you. Each melody will be played twice.

PROPER ORDER
OF INTERVALS:
1. Instructor plays:

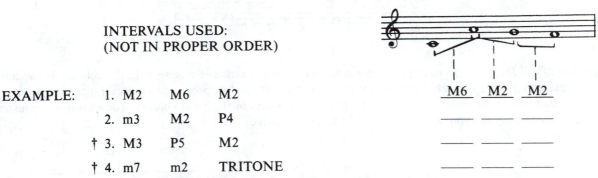

INTERVALS USED:
(NOT IN PROPER ORDER)

EXAMPLE:	1. M2	M6	M2
	2. m3	M2	P4
† 3.	M3	P5	M2
† 4.	m7	m2	TRITONE

M6   M2   M2

____ ____ ____

____ ____ ____

____ ____ ____

Now a similar melody of four notes will be played. See if you can identify the intervals you hear and place the interval name in the space provided. Each melody will be played twice.

5. ____ ____ ____

6. ____ ____ ____

7. ____ ____ ____

8. ____ ____ ____

† 9. ____ ____ ____

†10. ____ ____ ____

Computer Program Disk: Intervals 3, Lesson I

B. *Recognition of Errors in Simple Melodies.* In each of the following exercises you will hear and see a melody of four notes. Three of the written notes are correct as played, but *one* is incorrect in each exercise. Circle the note that is written incorrectly. The example is worked correctly for you. Each melody will be played twice.

1. EXAMPLE:

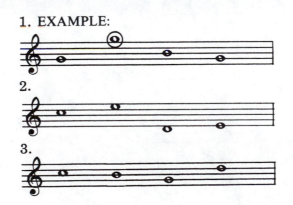

† 4.

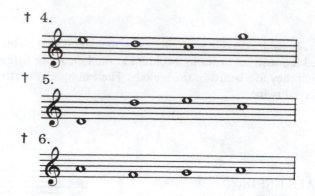

† 5.

† 6.

C. *Recognition of All Intervals*. In each exercise you will hear three harmonic intervals. In the column at the left are listed the intervals played in each exericse, but they are not arranged in proper order. Rearrange the order of the intervals to conform to the order you hear and write your answers in the right column. The example is illustrated and is worked correctly for you. Each exercise will be played twice.

Instructor plays:

EXAMPLE:	1. M3	m7	P5	P5	m7	M3
	2. P4	M6	M2	___	___	___
	3. M6	m7	P8	___	___	___
	4. P4	A4	M3	___	___	___

In the following exercises you will again hear three harmonic intervals in each exercise, but the names of the intervals to be played will not be given you. See if you can identify the intervals you hear and place the interval name in the space provided. Each exercise will be played twice.

5. _____ _____ _____

6. _____ _____ _____

7. _____ _____ _____

8. _____ _____ _____

† 9. _____ _____ _____

†10. _____ _____ _____

†11. _____ _____ _____

†12. _____ _____ _____

Computer Program Disk: Intervals 3, Lesson H

Chapter 15   Harmonic and Melodic Minor Scales

In addition to *natural minor,* two other forms of the minor scale are in common use. These scales use sharps, flats and naturals that are not part of the key signature (*accidentals*) to change the interval structure of the scale.

The Harmonic Minor Scale

The **harmonic minor scale** contains one accidental, the raised seventh degree. This makes a half step between the seventh note (called the **leading tone**) and the **tonic.** This half step increases the tendency of the seventh note of the scale to move toward the tonic, thereby strengthening the feeling of the tonal center.

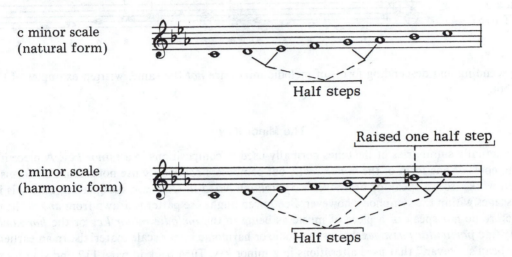

This accidental not only changes the interval between the seventh and eighth degrees of the scale, but it also creates a new interval between the sixth and seventh degrees. This interval, which had been a major second, is now one and one-half steps. Thus, it has become an *augmented second.* The harmonic minor scale has *three half steps,* between the second and third, fifth and sixth, and seventh and eighth degrees of the scale; *one augmented second* between the sixth and seventh degrees of the scale; and *three whole steps,* between the first and second, third and fourth, and fourth and fifth degrees of the scale.

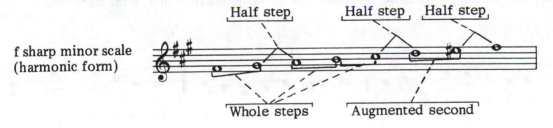

The Melodic Minor Scale

The **melodic minor scale** uses one more accidental to smooth out the "awkward" interval of the augmented second and *raises both the sixth and seventh degrees one half step. Harmonic minor scales are the same both ascending and descending.* In melodic minor, however, the alterations are used in the *ascending scale only,* and the *descending scale is like natural minor.*

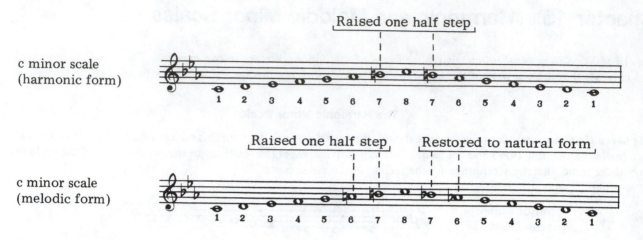

c minor scale (harmonic form) — Raised one half step

c minor scale (melodic form) — Raised one half step — Restored to natural form

Since the ascending and descending forms of melodic minor are *not* the same, written examples of the scale must always include both.

The Minor Key

These scales are actually summaries of the tones normally used in compositions in a *minor key*. A piece in a minor key may use only the notes of one form of the *minor scale,* but composers *commonly* use notes from *all* forms of the minor scale in extended works, so we speak of Beethoven's *Symphony No. 5 in C Minor,* designating that it is in that *minor key.* In some passages within the symphony, however, Beethoven might use patterns drawn from *any* of the normal minor scales. We therefore do *not* speak of a piece of music as being in the *melodic minor key* or the *harmonic minor key,* although we may find *particular passages* that use melodic or harmonic minor scale materials. In an earlier chapter, you sang Thoinot Arbeau's "Pavan" that used alterations in a minor key. Turn back to page 112 and sing it again.

Musicians practice scales in all these forms in order to develop facility on their instruments and in order to train their ears to hear and play these patterns accurately. Learn to play all the scales that you have learned both on your own instrument and on the keyboard.

Sight Singing Assignment

A. *Harmonic and Melodic Minor Drill.* When you hear the white note respond with the black notes.

10. **11.** **12.**

B. *Compositions Using the Notes of the Minor Scales.*

1.

Johann Sebastian Bach (1685–1750), "Schwing' dich zu deinen Gott" ("Soar Upwards to Thy God") (1713)

2.

Traditional melody, arr. Sam Cohen, "Hatikvah" (1888)

3.

Edward Grieg (1843–1907), *Peer Gynt* (1876)

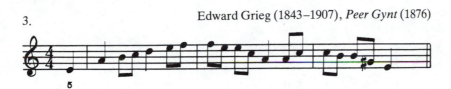

4.

Fanny Mendelssohn Hensel (1805–1847), Finale, *Trio in D Minor*, Op. 11 (1847)

5.

Felix Mendelssohn, (1809–1847), Third Movement, *Concerto in E Minor for Violin and Orchestra*, Op. 64 (1844)

6.

7.

Clara Schumann (1819–1896), First Movement, *Trio in G Minor*, Op. 17 (1847)

8.

Winfred Douglas (1867–1944), hymn tune "Sohren" (1938)⁺

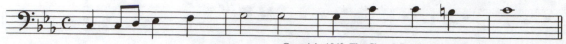

9.

Wolfgang Amadeus Mozart (1756–1791), Third Movement,
Symphony No. 40 in G Minor, K. 550 (1788)

Written Assignment

A. *Writing Harmonic and Melodic Minor Scales.* Write the scale called for in each exercise. Use the proper key signature for each scale. Play all the scales you have written both from your book and from memory.

1. D Melodic Minor

2. E Harmonic Minor

3. F sharp Harmonic Minor

4. G Melodic Minor

5. C sharp Harmonic Minor

6. F Harmonic Minor

7. B Melodic Minor

8. A Harmonic Minor

9. C Melodic Minor

10. G sharp Harmonic Minor

11. A flat Melodic Minor

12. B flat Harmonic Minor

B. On a separate piece of paper write the relative and parallel major scales of each of the minor scales just shown. Play all the scales you have written.

Ear Training Assignment

A. *Recognition of the Major, Natural Minor, Harmonic Minor, and Melodic Minor Scales.* In each exercise you will hear three scales (*ascending only*). The scales used are listed in the left column but are not in the proper order. Rearrange the names of the scales into the order in which they are played. The example is illustrated and is worked correctly for you. Each exercise will be played twice.

Instructor plays.

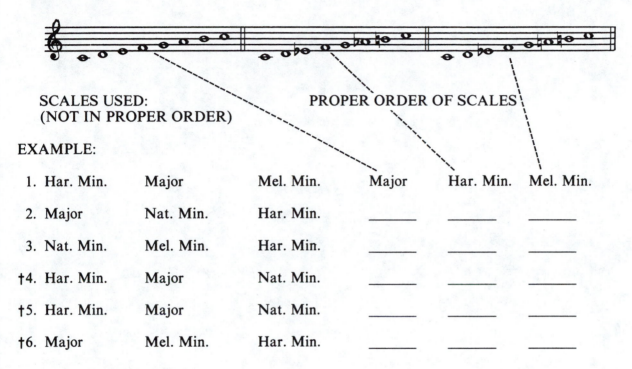

SCALES USED:
(NOT IN PROPER ORDER)

PROPER ORDER OF SCALES

EXAMPLE:

1. Har. Min.	Major	Mel. Min.	Major	Har. Min.	Mel. Min.
2. Major	Nat. Min.	Har. Min.	_____	_____	_____
3. Nat. Min.	Mel. Min.	Har. Min.	_____	_____	_____
†4. Har. Min.	Major	Nat. Min.	_____	_____	_____
†5. Har. Min.	Major	Nat. Min.	_____	_____	_____
†6. Major	Mel. Min.	Har. Min.	_____	_____	_____

Computer Program Disk: Scales and Keys, Lesson G

Chapter 16   Augmented and Diminished Triads; The Whole Tone Scale

Review of Major and Minor Triads

Major and minor triads both contain the interval of a perfect fifth and differ from each other only in the arrangement of their major and minor thirds.

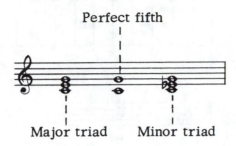

Diminished and Augmented Triads

There are two triads that do not contain the interval of the perfect fifth: the diminished triad, which contains a diminished fifth, and the augmented triad, which contains an augmented fifth.

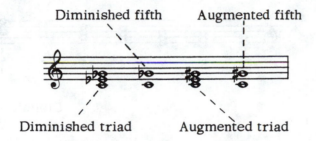

In the diminished triad both the thirds are minor thirds.

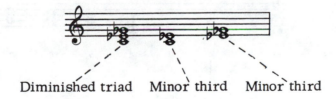

In the augmented triad both thirds are major thirds.

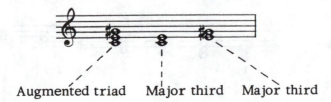

There is only one diminished triad using only white keys on the piano, since there is only one diminished fifth on the white keys.

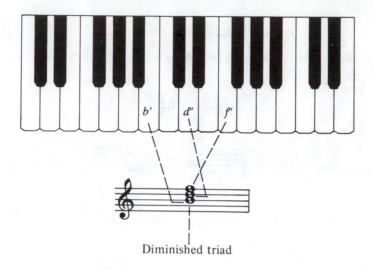

Diminished triad

The Diminished Triad in a Major Key

The triad on the seventh degree of the major scale is the only diminished triad in major.

C major

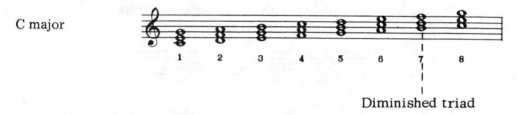

1   2   3   4   5   6   7   8

Diminished triad

The Diminished Triad in the Minor Scales

In natural minor there is a diminished triad on the second degree of the scale.

a minor
(natural)

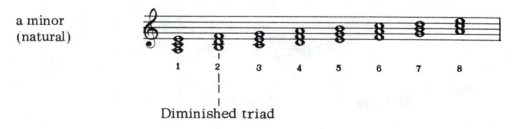

1   2   3   4   5   6   7   8

Diminished triad

In harmonic minor, there are diminished triads on the second and seventh degrees.

a minor
(harmonic)

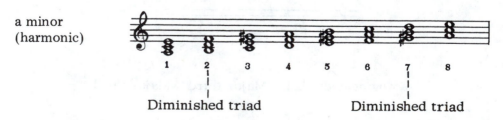

1   2   3   4   5   6   7   8

Diminished triad   Diminished triad

In the ascending form of the melodic minor scale there are two diminished triads on the sixth and seventh degrees of the scale.

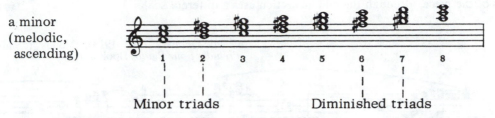

The Augmented Triad in Minor Scales

The augmented triad does *not exist* in the *major scale* or in *natural minor*. The *only* scales in which it can be found are *harmonic and ascending melodic minor,* in both of which there is an augmented triad on the third degree of each scale. The augmented triad *cannot* be played with white keys alone.

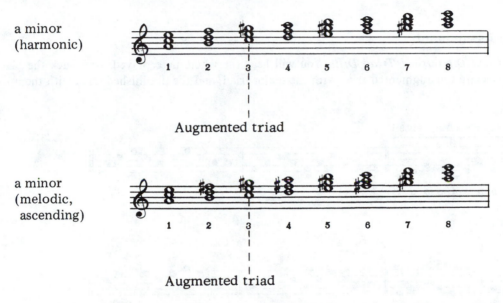

Augmented triads in harmonic and melodic minor scales

The Scale That Has Only Augmented Triads!

There is one twentieth century scale that can produce *only* augmented triads. It is called the **whole tone scale** and is made up entirely of whole tones. There are only two possible groups of pitches on the keyboard that can produce a whole tone scale.

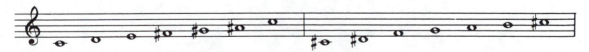

The two whole tone scales

Most composers who use this scale use it only for portions of larger compositions. One of the most famous examples of use of the whole tone scale is the Debussy piano **prelude** "Voiles" ("Sails"). The whole tone scale is used in the first and last sections of the piece, although the middle section uses a different scale.

Claude Debussy (1862–1918), "Voiles" ("Sails"),
Préludes pour Piano, Book I (1910)

Sight Singing Assignment

A. *Augmented and Diminished Triad Drill*. You will hear the whole note played; sing back the black notes. These exercises associate the augmented triad with the major triad, and the diminished triad with the minor triad.

B. *Compositions Using the Notes of the Minor Scale.*

1.

Antonin Dvořák (1841–1904), theme from *Dimitri*, Op. 64 (1894–5)

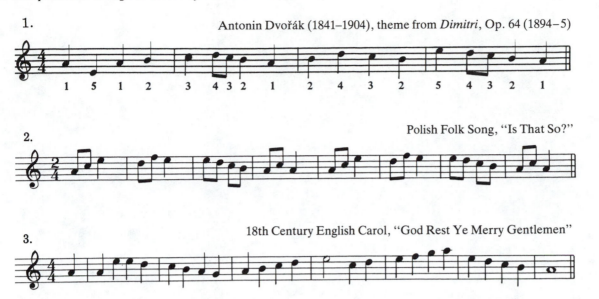

1 5 1 2 3 4 3 2 1 2 4 3 2 5 4 3 2 1

2.

Polish Folk Song, "Is That So?"

3.

18th Century English Carol, "God Rest Ye Merry Gentlemen"

C. *Melodies Using Diminished and Augmented Triads.*

1.

Franz Schubert (1797–1828) *Octet* (1824)

2.

3.

Written Assignment

Placing Augmented and Diminished Triads on the Keyboard and on the Music Staff. Using the letter names of the notes to mark the proper keys of the keyboard, write the augmented and diminished triads requested. Write the same triads on the music staff at the right of each printed keyboard. See the example.

EXAMPLE:

1. Augmented Triad on D

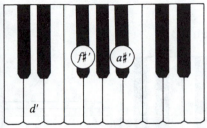

Diminished Triad on D

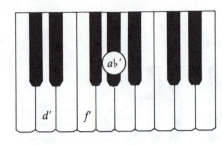

2. Augmented Triad on A♭

Diminished Triad on A♭

3. Augmented Triad on F♯

Diminished Triad on F♯

4. Augmented Triad on C

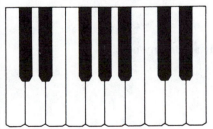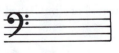

Diminished Triad on C

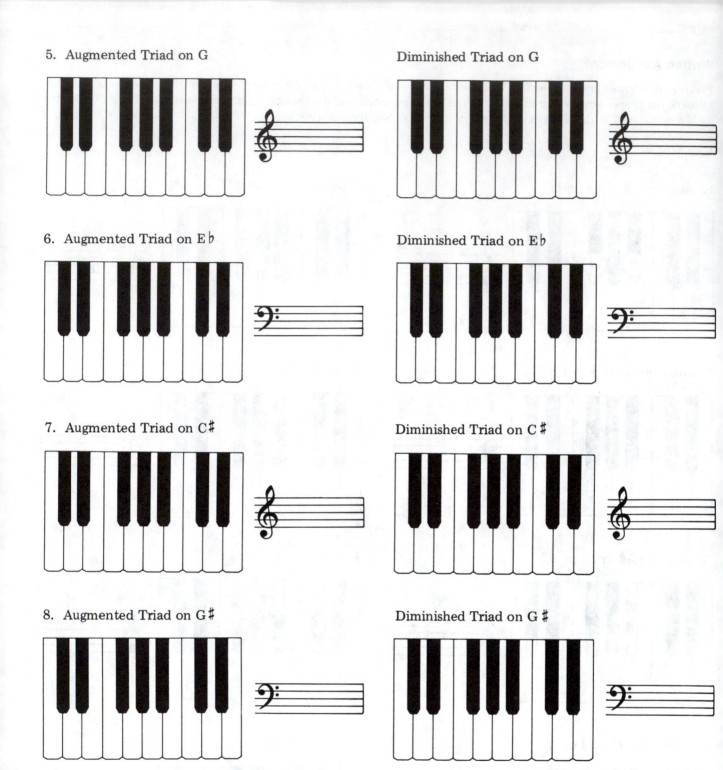

5. Augmented Triad on G

Diminished Triad on G

6. Augmented Triad on E♭

Diminished Triad on E♭

7. Augmented Triad on C♯

Diminished Triad on C♯

8. Augmented Triad on G♯

Diminished Triad on G♯

Play all the triads you have written. Be able to play an augmented or diminished triad on any note!

Ear Training Assignment

A. *Recognition of Major, Minor, Diminished, and Augmented Triads.* In each of the following exercises you will hear three triads played in simple position. The species of triads used in each exercise is found in the left column, but the order of playing is not correct. Place the proper symbol showing the order of the triads in the column at the right. You will hear each exercise twice.

TRIAD SPECIES	SYMBOL FOR IDENTIFICATION
Major Triad	M
Minor Triad	m
Diminished Triad	d
Augmented Triad	A

The example is illustrated and is worked correctly for you.

THESE TRIAD SPECIES
ARE USED:
(not in proper order)

REARRANGE IN
PROPER ORDER
HERE:

EXAMPLE: 1. m   M   A   __M__ __A__ __m__

2. m   A   M   ____ ____ ____

3. A   m   M   ____ ____ ____

4. d   M   m   ____ ____ ____

The remaining exercises will be similar, except that you will not be given the names of the triad species used. Place the names of the triads (using the abbreviations above) in the blanks. You will hear each exercise twice.

5. ____ ____ ____   † 9. ____ ____ ____

6. ____ ____ ____   †10. ____ ____ ____

7. ____ ____ ____   †11. ____ ____ ____

8. ____ ____ ____   †12. ____ ____ ____

Computer Program Disk: Harmony 2, Lesson I

B. *Recognition of Scale Numbers*. In each exercise you will hear a four note melody. Four possible combinations of scale numbers are given for each four note melody. Only one answer is correct. Underline this answer. The example is illustrated and is worked correctly for you. Each exercise will be played twice.

EXAMPLE: 1. Instructor plays:

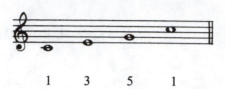

                                        1   3   5   1

Answer:

1.	a.	<u>1</u>	<u>3</u>	<u>5</u>	<u>1</u>	b.	1	2	3	4	c.	1	2	4	1	d.	1	4	3	2
2.	a.	1	4	3	2	b.	1	5	6	7	c.	1	5	4	3	d.	1	6	5	4
3.	a.	1	5	3	1	b.	1	6	4	2	c.	1	5	2	1	d.	1	4	5	1
4.	a.	1	3	4	4	b.	1	4	5	5	c.	1	2	3	4	d.	1	2	3	3
† 5.	a.	1	5	5	1	b.	1	4	4	1	c.	1	4	5	6	d.	1	6	6	4
† 6.	a.	1	7	6	7	b.	1	5	3	5	c.	1	4	2	1	d.	1	6	4	6
† 7.	a.	1	2	3	4	b.	1	3	5	1	c.	1	7	6	5	d.	1	3	4	5
† 8.	a.	1	1	5	3	b.	1	1	2	3	c.	1	1	7	6	d.	1	1	5	1

Computer Program Disk: Melody and Texture, Lessons B and C

Chapter 17   Inversion of Intervals; Compound Intervals

Inversion of Intervals

If the lower note of an interval is raised an octave or the upper note lowered an octave, the new interval formed is called the **inversion** of the first interval.

Some intervals and their inversions

When any interval is inverted, the sum of the interval and its inversion will always be *nine*. This is due to the fact that in combining the two intervals, one note within the octave is counted twice.

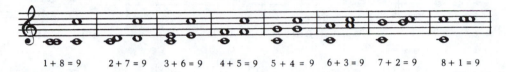

1 + 8 = 9   2 + 7 = 9   3 + 6 = 9   4 + 5 = 9   5 + 4 = 9   6 + 3 = 9   7 + 2 = 9   8 + 1 = 9

Every *major* interval inverts to a *minor* interval; every *minor* interval becomes *major;* every *diminished* interval becomes *augmented;* every *augmented* interval becomes *diminished. Perfect intervals* alone do not change their quality in inversion and *remain perfect.*

Major→minor   Minor→major   Perfect→perfect   Augmented→ diminished   Diminished→ augmented

Simple and Compound Intervals

Intervals that encompass more than an octave are called **compound intervals,** those of an octave or less, **simple intervals.**

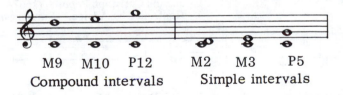

M9   M10   P12   M2   M3   P5
Compound intervals   Simple intervals

Compound intervals can be described in terms of their actual size, such as *tenth, eleventh, twelfth,* and so forth, but for most purposes it is more convenient to reduce them to the octave span and make them equivalent to the simple interval with the same letter names for some types of analysis. However, in *chords* which involve more notes than a triad, the compound names of intervals like ninth, eleventh, and thirteenth are used.

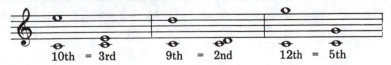

10th = 3rd   9th = 2nd   12th = 5th

Sight Singing Assignment

A. *Interval Inversion Drill.* These exercises may be done two different ways:

1. *For the classroom:* The teacher plays the whole notes, and the student immediately sings the black notes.

2. *For individual drill:* Play the whole notes (outside class) and immediately sing the black notes. Play the black notes on the piano *after* singing them. This acts as a final check on the accuracy of singing.

B. *Melodies for sight-singing.* Sing all melodies in the octave register comfortable for your own voice range.

Johann Christoph Pepusch (1667–1752), "Can Love be Controlled by Advice," *The Beggar's Opera* (1728)

William Clayton (19th Century), "Come, Come, Ye Saints" +

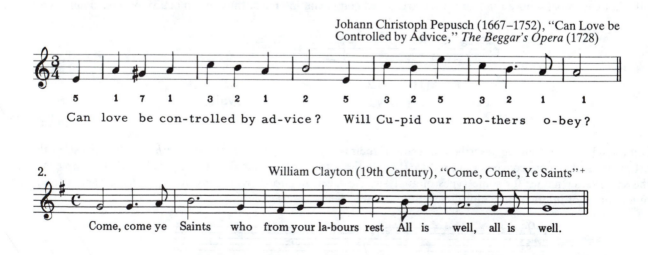

4. Joseph Haydn (1732–1809), Minuet, *String Quartet in D Minor*, Op. 76, No. 2 (1797)

5. Johann Sebastian Bach (1685–1750), "Liebster Herr Jesu, wo bleibst Du?" ("Dear Lord Jesus, Where art Thou?")

6. "Sumer is Icumen In" (c. 1240)

Sum-mer is a - com - in' in,___ Loud -ly sing cuck - oo. Grow-eth seed, and blow -eth mead-ows, woods are grow - ing new. Sing cuck - oo, Ewes are bleat -ing at their lambs, at calf the cow doth moo. Bull-ock leap-ing, Bucks are run-ning, Mer-ry sing cuck- oo, Cuck - oo, cuck - oo, well sing-est thou cuck-oo, Who sor-row nev-er knew.

(English text has been modernized)

This is the oldest known **round,** and can be sung like "Row, Row, Row Your Boat." * marks the spot where the new voice enters.

Written Assignment

Interval Inversion. Find the interval asked for on the keyboard diagram and mark the notes with "X." Write "O" on the notes for the inversion of that interval. Then write both intervals on the staff and name each inverted interval. See the example.

1. P 4 above *c'*

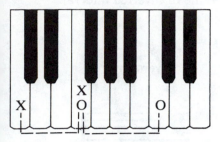

P 4 above *c'*

Inversion

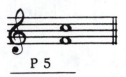

P 5
_____

Name of inverted interval

2. m 6 above *c*

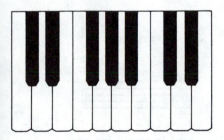

m 6 above *c*

Inversion

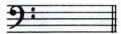

_____

Name of inverted interval

3. M 7 above *d'*

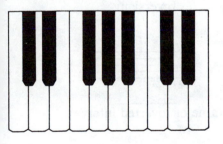

M 7 above *d'*

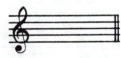

Inversion

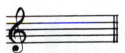

_____

Name of inverted interval

4. m 3 above *C♯*

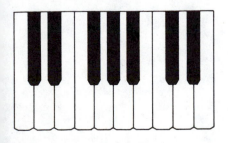

m 3 above *C♯*

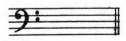

Inversion

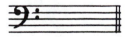

_____

Name of inverted interval

5. P 5 above *e"*

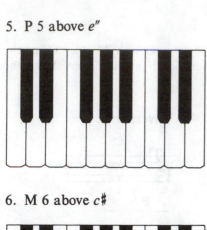

P 5 above *e"*

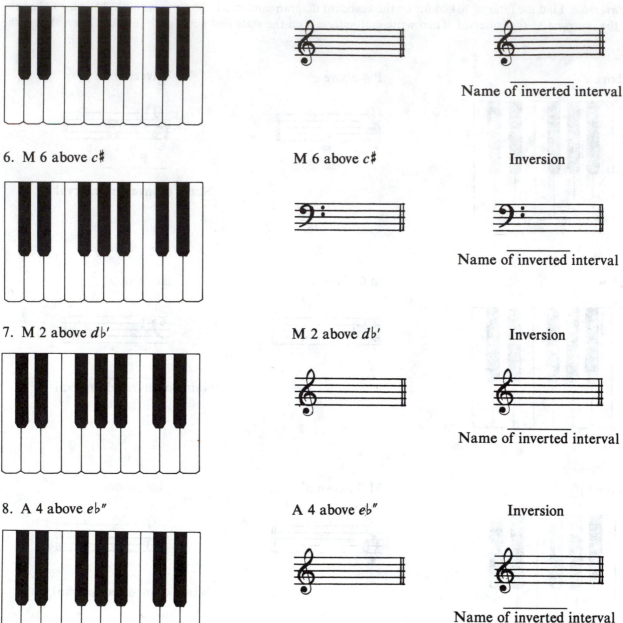

Inversion

Name of inverted interval

6. M 6 above *c♯*

M 6 above *c♯*

Inversion

Name of inverted interval

7. M 2 above *d♭'*

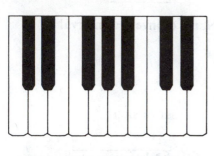

M 2 above *d♭'*

Inversion

Name of inverted interval

8. A 4 above *e♭"*

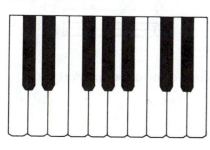

A 4 above *e♭"*

Inversion

Name of inverted interval

Play and sing all intervals you have written.

Ear Training Assignment

A. *Recognition of All Simple Intervals*. In each exercise you will hear four harmonic intervals. In the answers given three are correct, but one interval is not the same as the interval you hear. Circle the incorrect interval in each exercise. Each exercise will be played twice. See the example.

EXAMPLE:　　　　　　　1.　Instructor plays:

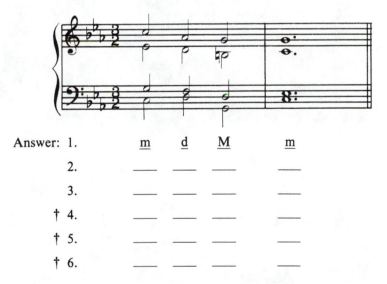

Answer:	1.	M 6	P 4	(M 2)	M 3
	2.	P 8	M 2	m 6	m 3
	3.	M 3	P 5	P 4	A 4
	4.	M 6	M 2	M 3	M 7
†	5.	P 8	M 6	P 8	P 5
†	6.	m 3	P 5	M 2	M 6
†	7.	m 6	P 5	m 6	P 4
†	8.	M 3	P 5	m 3	m 2

Computer Program Disk: Intervals 3, Lesson H

B. *Recognition of Triads in Chord Progressions*. In each exercise you will hear a chord progression of four chords. The progressions will use all four types of triads: major (M), minor (m), diminished (d), and augmented (A), although all four may not occur in every exercise. Put the abbreviation for the triad you hear in each of the spaces provided. Each progression will be played three times. See the example.

EXAMPLE:

Answer:	1.	m	d	M	m
	2.	___	___	___	___
	3.	___	___	___	___
†	4.	___	___	___	___
†	5.	___	___	___	___
†	6.	___	___	___	___

Computer Program Disk: Harmony 3, Lesson A

Preface to Parts III, IV, and V: Rhythm and Meter, Melody, and Harmony

In Part I of this book you learned to recognize (by sight and sound), to write, and to sing the basic musical building materials. You learned how pitch, rhythm, and other musical qualities are organized and notated and how they are related to the keyboard and guitar. You also had experience in hearing them, performing simple rhythms, and singing short patterns.

In Part II you saw how these basic elements could be combined to create a tonal center and to produce intervals, triads, and scales. You also learned to listen to these basic combinations. You sang some melodies that displayed the qualities of the intervals and scales and learned how to write these basic combinations on the staff.

Now you are ready for more lengthy and complicated combinations of rhythms together with systematic practice in using different meters. You can also now see how **melody** is created from the two dimensions of movement—*movement from pitch to pitch* and *movement in time*. And you now have the materials to consider how to relate chords to each other—the study of **harmony**.

Suggested Order of Study of These Parts

Parts III through V of the book can be studied just in the order they appear in the text, or you can study a chapter of each part and then move on to the next chapter in each part. The advantage of the second approach is that you will continue to sing and practice rhythms even when you are working with chords. Likewise, when you are studying melody, you will have in mind its relation to harmony and rhythm. Keep in mind that these aspects of music are all interrelated!

Rhythm and Meter   Part III

Chapter 18   Simple Duple, Triple, and Quadruple Meters

Duple Meter

In duple meters the musical pulse is grouped in *twos*. The first pulse is somewhat *accented* and serves as a point of arrival in the measure. The second pulse has less stress. The conductor beats all duple meters by moving the baton down for the first beat (the **downbeat**) and up for the second beat (the **upbeat**).

Various note values may serve as the note which receives the beat (the *beat unit*). As you remember, the value of the beat unit is shown by the bottom number of the time signature. In **simple time,** the beat unit is a note value that normally subdivides into two parts. Common simple duple meters are:

Half note beat unit

Quarter note beat unit

Although the preceding examples look quite different in notation, the sound of both is identical, since the beat is the same tempo for each line. *The tempo must always be set on the basis of the tempo markings rather than from the appearance of the note values,* since *tempo* is determined by the *speed of the beat* and not by the notation of the beat unit.

Triple Meter

In triple meters the musical pulse is grouped in *threes*. Simple triple meters have beat units subdivided into two parts.

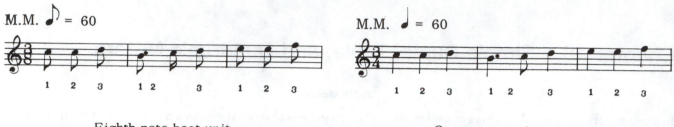

| Eighth note beat unit | Quarter note beat unit |

Although these examples look quite different, they sound exactly alike, since it is the *tempo marking* and not the appearance of the note values which determines the speed.

The conductor's beat for triple meters is:

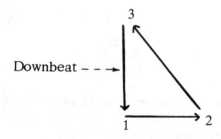

Downbeat – – →

In triple meter the first beat is the stressed beat:

$$>$$
1   2   3

Quadruple Meter

Quadruple meter is a combination of two duple groups in one measure. The first beat receives the primary accent and the third beat receives a secondary accent:

$$> \qquad >$$
1   2   3   4

The conductor's beat pattern for quadruple meter is:

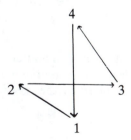

Note that 1 is a downbeat in every meter. Quadruple meters use the same beat unit values as duple meters.

$\frac{4}{4}$ meter is also called **common time** and sometimes has the sign $\mathbf{C}$ in place of $\frac{4}{4}$ as a time signature.

If a vertical line is drawn through the $\mathbf{C}$, the time becomes **alla breve** $\mathbf{\Phi}$, which means that the half note becomes the beat unit. This is actually the equivalent of the $\frac{2}{2}$ time signature.

Divisions within the Beat in Simple Meters

In $\frac{2}{4}$, $\frac{3}{4}$, and $\frac{4}{4}$ time, for which the beat unit is a quarter note, the half-beat note value is an eighth note. In the following examples, the beats are divided into half beat values, with two notes per beat.

Ludwig van Beethoven (1770–1827), Second Movement,
Symphony No. 7 in A Major, Op. 9 (1816)*

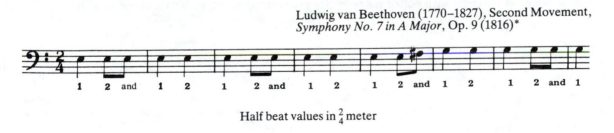

Half beat values in $\frac{2}{4}$ meter

Eighth notes are counted as shown:

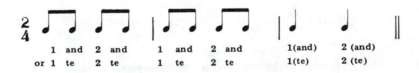

When you count half-beat values, it is very important to keep the tempo of the beat *steady* and to divide the beats *evenly*. In the following examples, the half-beat values are counted with *rhythmic syllables* (*1 and 2 and* or *1 te 2 te*).

Russian Folk Tune, "Song of the Volga Boatmen"

*Note that some movements of the symphony may be in keys that contrast with the main key of the work.

In $\frac{2}{8}$, $\frac{3}{8}$, and $\frac{4}{8}$ time, the half-beat value is a sixteenth note. The same syllables are used for counting sixteenth notes in these meters as for eighth notes in meters with a quarter note beat unit.

Felix Mendelssohn (1809–1847), Scherzo,
Midsummer Night's Dream (1842)

In $\frac{2}{2}$, $\mathbf{\math0}$, $\frac{3}{2}$, and $\frac{4}{2}$ time, the half-beat value is a quarter note.

Johannes Brahms (1833–1897), First Movement, *Trio for Violin, Cello, and Piano in B Major*, Op. 8 (1853–54)

Half-beat values in rhythms with dotted notes or ties are notated in the various meters:

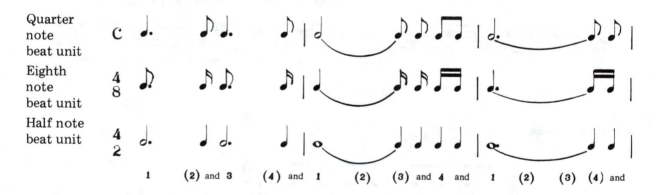

The most common dotted note pattern is the one used in the examples:

Johannes Brahms (1833–1897), *Liebeslieder Waltzes*, (Love-Song Waltzes) Op. 52, No. 11 (1868–69)

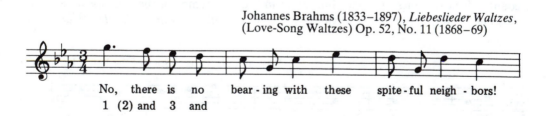

No,   there   is   no   bear - ing with   these   spite - ful neigh - bors!
1 (2) and   3   and

The same kind of pattern could be notated with ties.

Georges Bizet (1838–1875), "Fate Motive,"
from *Carmen* (1873–74)

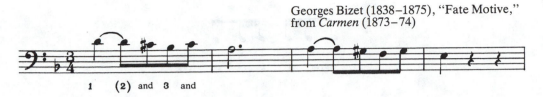

1 (2) and 3 and

Half-beat values for rests produce rhythms similar to dotted notes or ties when the rest is used on the first half of the beat.

John Phillip Sousa (1854–1932), "The Stars and Stripes
Forever" (1896)[+]

1 (2)and 3 4

Half Beat Value Rests on the First Half of the Beat

When a rest is used on the second half of the beat, the effect is like *staccato,* except that the exact duration of the note is shown. The following melody was originally notated with rests, but a second version has been added using staccato marks instead. The sound of the two notations is very similar, although the staccato marks do not show exactly how detached the notes should be, while the rests call for a precise amount of silence between the notes.

Robert Schumann (1810–1856), "Soldier's March,"
Album für die Jugend (*Album for the Young*) (1848)

Half beat value rests on the second half of the beat

(rewritten to show alternate notation)

Eighth notes and rests replaced by quarter notes with staccato marks

In meters with a quarter note beat unit ($\frac{2}{4}$, $\frac{3}{4}$, and $\frac{4}{4}$), division of the beat into four equal parts produces sixteenth notes. When the beat is divided into four equal parts, the following syllables shown are used in counting:

1 a and du   2 a an du
or 1 ta te ta   2 ta te ta

+Denotes American composer.

Two sixteenths can combine with an eighth note to produce two normal patterns within beats.

1 (a) an du   2 a   an (du)
or 1 (ta)te   ta   2 ta te (ta)

One sixteenth note is needed to fill the beat following a dotted eighth note.

1 (a an) du 2 (a an)du

Reversing the pattern and placing the short note on the first quarter beat produces a lively rhythm called the "Scotch Snap." It is used in some Scotch folk dances (hence the name), jazz, Hungarian folk tunes, and other music. The short note is usually accented strongly. It often occurs in connection with a language pattern, reflecting the emphatic rhythm of the words.

American Folk Tune, "Hello, Girls!"

Hel-lo Girls! . . .

Scotch Snap

In meters which have a half note for the beat unit ($\frac{2}{2}$, ¢, $\frac{3}{2}$, and $\frac{4}{2}$), the four equal parts of the beat are eighth notes.

1 a an du 2 a an du   1(a) an du   2 a   an (du)   1   a (an)du   2

Typical quarter beat value patterns with a half note beat unit

Meters with eighth note beat units have thirty-second notes as quarter-beat values.

1 a an du   2 a an du   1 (a) an du   2   a   an (du)   1   a(an)du   2

Typical quarter beat value patterns with eighth note beat units

Sight Singing Assignment

A. *Duple and Quadruple Meter Drill.* Sing or say the regular meter beat (1, 2 or 1, 2, 3, 4), and at the same time clap the note values as shown. You may conduct while you sing instead of clapping. Both ways of doing sight singing should be practiced.

B. *Triple Meter Drill.* Sing or say the regular meter beat (1, 2, 3) and at the same time clap the note values as shown.

C. *Half Beat Values in Simple Time.* Each exercise is taken from a well-known melody. Perhaps you will be able to recognize the tune from the rhythm alone as given here. Practice these values as you did for A and B.

1.

2.

3.

4.

D. *Rhythm Drill. Exercises in Accents.* The following four exercises show each melody in $\frac{2}{4}$, $\frac{3}{4}$, and $\frac{4}{4}$ meter. Practice singing these exercises in each of the three different meters listed. In some meters the melodies sound natural; in others they sound awkward. Try to sing the melodies accurately in all meters given.

1.

Clap: 1   3   4   1   2   3   2   3   4   1   2   3

Sing or say: 1 2 3 4   1 2 3 4   1 2 3 4   1 2 3 4

2.

E. *Quarter Beat Values in Simple Time.* Do these exercises in the same manner as for A, B, and C. You can also sing all these exercises up and down major or minor scales.

1.

2.

3.

4.

Written Assignment

A. *Completion of Measures in Duple and Quadruple Meters.* Following is a series of short exercises in which each measure of the exercise is incomplete rhythmically. Complete each measure with *only one note* of the proper value. The example is worked correctly.

1. EXAMPLE (with incomplete measures):   EXAMPLE (with measures completed correctly):

2.

3.

4.

B. *Unit Value Drill.* Following is a series of short melodies. Each one is written out using a certain value of note per beat. Beneath each melody rewrite the melody using the new time signature provided. You will need to use a new note value for the beat in each case. The example is worked correctly.

1. EXAMPLE (melody as given):   EXAMPLE (melody with new note values):

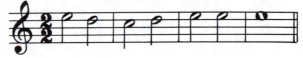

2.

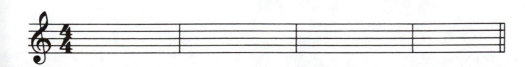

3.

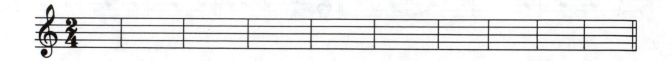

Ear Training Assignment

A. In each exercise you will hear a short melody with the same rhythm in each measure. Circle the letter indicating the correct rhythm. The first exercise is worked correctly for you.

EXAMPLE (instructor plays this):

Answer:

1. a.   b.   ⓒ.   d.

2. a.   b.   c.   d.

3. a.   b.   c.   d.

† 4. a.   b.   c.   d.

† 5. a.   b.   c.   d.

† 6. a.   b.   c.   d.

Computer Program Disk: Rhythm, Lesson C

†Indicates examples recorded on the cassettes available for use with this text.

B. *Simple Rhythmic Patterns in Duple and Quadruple Meters.* In each exercise you will hear a rhythmic pattern of one measure length repeated several times in a melodic context. Three possible rhythmic patterns are given. Choose from among these the one which is played. Circle the letter indicating the correct rhythmic pattern played.

Computer Program Disk: Rhythm, Lessons B and C

C. *Simple Rhythmic Patterns in Triple Meter.* In each exercise you will hear a rhythmic pattern of one measure length repeated several times in a melodic context. Three possible rhythmic patterns are given. Choose from among these the one which is played. Circle the letter indicating the correct rhythmic pattern played.

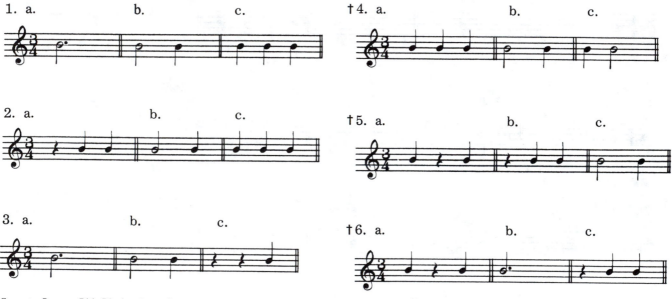

Computer Program Disk: Rhythm, Lesson D

D. *Dictation of Half Beat Rhythmic Values in Simple Times.* Following is a series of incomplete rhythmic exercises. You will hear the exercises in their completed form. Write in the missing rhythmic values on a neutral pitch—disregard the pitches in this series of exercises. The example is illustrated and has been worked correctly for you. Each exercise will be played twice.

EXAMPLE:

1. Example completed correctly:

2.

3.

†4.

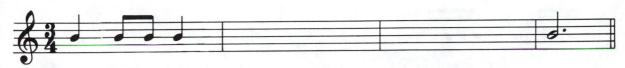

†5.

†6.

Computer Program Disk: Lessons C and D

E. *Dictation of Quarter Beat Values in Simple Time.* Following is a series of incomplete rhythmic exercises. You will hear the exercises in their completed form. Write in the missing rhythmic values on a neutral pitch—disregard the pitches in this series of exercises. The example is illustrated and has been worked correctly for you. Each exercise will be played twice.

EXAMPLE:

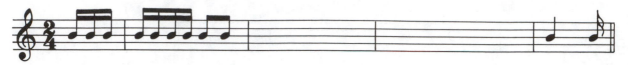

1. Example completed correctly:

2.

3.

†4.

†5.

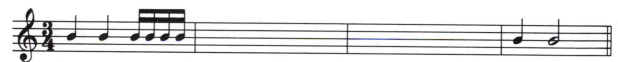

†6.

Computer Program Disk: Rhythm, Lessons C and D

Chapter 19   Syncopation

When the accent in music is shifted so that the stress falls on a weak beat instead of on the expected strong beat, the effect is called **syncopation.** There are three ways to emphasize a weak beat: (1) by beginning a note on a weak beat and tying it to a strong beat, (2) by placing rests on the strong beats so that the only notes heard are on weak beats, or (3) by placing dynamic accents on weak beats instead of strong beats.

Examples of Syncopations

In the following phrase, the syncopated note begins on the weak second beat and is held through the strong third beat of the measure. The exciting effect of this rhythm comes from the suppression of the expected accent on the third beat and the unexpected stress on the second beat, due to its position in the rhythmic pattern, even though it receives no special dynamic accent. When the rhythm returns to the normal accent pattern in the second measure, there is a great release of tension as a result. Play all the musical examples, counting them aloud. Sing the examples too!

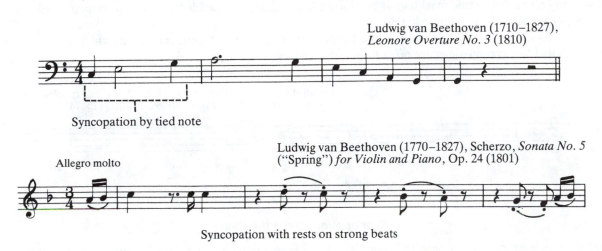

Ludwig van Beethoven (1710–1827),
Leonore Overture No. 3 (1810)

Syncopation by tied note

Allegro molto

Ludwig van Beethoven (1770–1827), Scherzo, *Sonata No. 5* ("Spring") *for Violin and Piano*, Op. 24 (1801)

Syncopation with rests on strong beats

The rests on the first beats of this example delay the beginning of the staccato melodic fragments until the second beat. This gives a breathless, jesting quality to the rhythm, made more pronounced by the rapid tempo. Beethoven loved to use syncopation and other surprising rhythmic effects in his Scherzo ("Joke") movements!

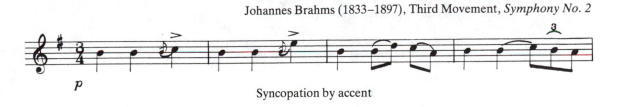

Johannes Brahms (1833–1897), Third Movement, *Symphony No. 2*

Syncopation by accent

The preceding example uses both a dynamic *accent* and a *grace note* to the emphasize the third beat. A grace note is a note printed in small type which takes part of the time normally alloted to an adjacent note. A small line running diagonally through the stem indicates that the note comes slightly before the beat and is very rapid. Grace notes give a melodic decoration to the note and add rhythmic stress and spice to the beat.

Ludwig van Beethoven (1770–1827), Scherzo, *Sonata No. 10 for Violin and Piano*, Op. 96 (1812)

Syncopation by accents in another Beethoven Scherzo

Syncopation by accent often requires vivid contrasts between the stressed and unstressed notes of the pattern. It is not unusual to find such extreme markings as *fp* (*forte piano*—loud, then suddenly soft), (*sfortzando*—strong accent), or even *sfp* (strong accent, then immediately soft).

Not all syncopation involves strong accents. In much music of the sixteenth century in which a very smooth performance is called for, syncopations are often found in cadences.

Giovanni Pierluigi da Palestrina (1525–1594), "Kyrie eleison" ("Lord, Have Mercy"), *Pope Marcellus Mass* (1567)

Syncopation within the Beat

Syncopation, emphasis on a weak beat and suppression of a strong beat, is also used with subbeat values.

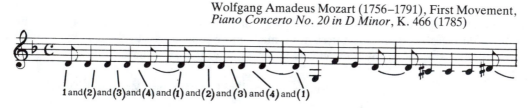

Wolfgang Amadeus Mozart (1756–1791), First Movement, *Piano Concerto No. 20 in D Minor*, K. 466 (1785)

Syncopation with every note beginning on the weak half of the beat after the first eighth note.

This kind of syncopation may continue for a long time. It may be used for a melody, as above, or as an accompaniment pattern.

Syncopation with rests produces a detached version of the same rhythm.

Rests on the first half beat and eighth notes
on the second half beat.

Folk tunes, spirituals, and jazz often use syncopation with half beats or even smaller values. In jazz, it is an important means of making the tune "swing." The most common type of syncopation in jazz style is the type with the beginning of the syncopation anticipating the next beat of the tune. The note to which the short note is tied is sometimes very long.

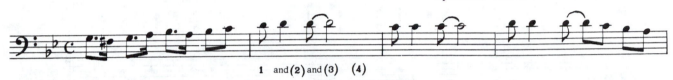

By putting one eighth note between two sixteenth notes, a syncopated pattern at a lower subbeat level is created.

Syncopation at the *sixteenth note level* is the characteristic syncopation of **ragtime.** It derives part of its effect from the contrast between the syncopated right hand of the piano and the regular eighth note striding bass in the left. Ragtime was intended to be played in a *slow march tempo* (often the tempo indication in Scott Joplin's **rags**), so the syncopations could be savoured fully. As Joplin said in many of his publications "It is never right to play 'Ragtime' fast."

Sight Singing Assignment

A. *Syncopated Rhythm Drill.*

Sing or say the meter (1, 2; 1, 2, 3; *or* 1, 2, 3, 4), and at the same time, clap the rhythm as notated. You may conduct while you sing instead of clapping. You may also sing major scales with syllables or note names, using the rhythms of the exercises given.

B. *Syncopation with Half-Beat Values.* Sing or say the meter and at the same time clap the notated rhythm. You may conduct while you sing instead of clapping. You may also sing the rhythms using major scales.

1.

2.

3.

4.

C. *Syncopation with Quarter-Beat Values.* These exercises are to be practiced in the same manner as the preceding ones, except that the beat should be tapped with the foot, and the eighth notes tapped with the left hand while the rhythm is said, sung, or tapped with the right hand.

The rhythms in this exercise are those used by Scott Joplin (1868–1917) in his *School of Ragtime* (1908).

1.

2.

Written Assignment

Some exercises should be sung or accompanied with clapping.

A. *Completion of Measure*. Complete the following measures with *one* note of proper value. The example is worked correctly for you.

EXAMPLE:

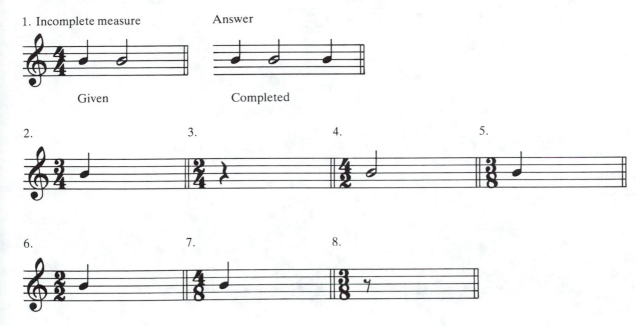

B. *Unit Value Drill*. Rewrite each of the following measures using the new time signature given at the right. The example is worked correctly for you.

EXAMPLE:

C. *Above* the exercises indicate the regular beats of the measure. *Below* the same exercises write the rhythmic syllables for each note (the syllables you would recite in rhythmic reading drill). The first exercise is written correctly for you.

1. EXAMPLE:

Beats:

Rhythmic
syllables:

2.

Beats:

Rhythmic
syllables:

3.

Beats:

Rhythmic
syllables:

4.

Beats:

Rhythmic
syllables:

5.

Beats:

Rhythmic
syllables:

D. Clap or sing on a single pitch all the rhythms in the above exercises, using the rhythmic syllables you have written when you sing. These exercises may also be sung by applying the rhythms to a scale (major or melodic minor).

E. You probably know some tunes that use syncopation. Make a collection of syncopated tunes known by the class.

Ear Training Assignment

A. *Simple Rhythm Patterns with Syncopations.* In each exercise you will hear a rhythmic pattern of one measure in length repeated several times in a melodic context. Four possible rhythmic patterns are given. You are to choose from among these the one which is played. Circle the letter indicating the correct rhythmic pattern played. *Your teacher will beat two measures of meter before beginning each exercise.* Each example will be played twice.

Instructor plays:

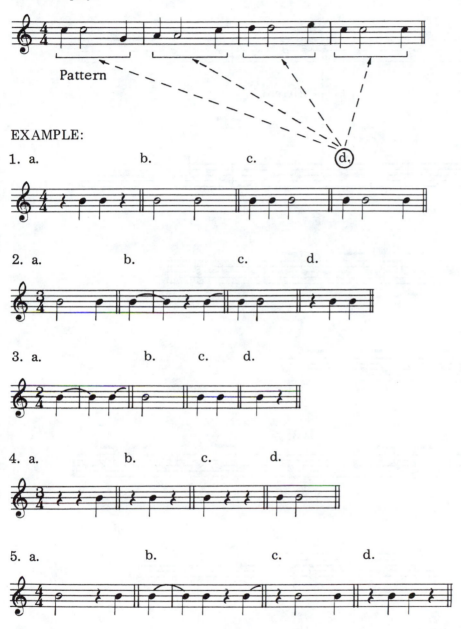

EXAMPLE:

1. a.　　　　　b.　　　　　c.　　　　　ⓓ.

2. a.　　　　　b.　　　　　c.　　　　　d.

3. a.　　　　　b.　　c.　　d.

4. a.　　　　　b.　　　　　c.　　　　　d.

5. a.　　　　　b.　　　　　c.　　　　　d.

6. a.　　　　　　b.　　　　c.　　　d.

Computer Program Disk: Rhythm, Lesson F

B. *Recognition of Errors in Rhythms Using Syncopations with Half-Beat Values.* Following is a series of four measure rhythmic exercises. In each exercise the notation you see agrees with the dictated version you hear *except in one measure*. Determine which measure is played different rhythmically from the notated version and circle the number that represents that measure. Each exercise will be played twice. The example is illustrated and is worked correctly.

EXAMPLE:

Chapter 20 Triplets

What Triplets Are

As you remember, when a group of three equal notes takes the place of two even notes of the same kind, the three notes are called *triplets*. In this chapter we will see more examples of triplet use and more exercises to practice them.

	1 and 2 and	
or	1 te 2 te	1 la li 2 la li (pronounced "lah," "lee")
	Normal division	Triplet division

Cécile Chaminade (1857–1944), First Movement, *Concertino for Flute and Orchestra,* Op. 107 (1902)

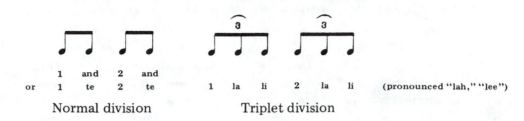

Melody using both normal and triplet division of beats

How to Write Triplets

If the triplets require beams, they are connected so that they show the rhythmic grouping, and the number 3 is placed above or below each triplet group.

Sometimes a slur sign is also used, but people have not been consistent about using it. When used to show a triplet group, a slur does not describe the phrasing, but merely indicates the rhythmic grouping of the notes enclosed by it. It is therefore not usually written with the slur sign close to the note heads, but so that it forms a symbol with the number showing the grouping of the notes.

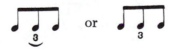

Examples of Triplets in Different Meters

These examples show various triplet groups lasting one beat.

	Unit	Normal division	Triplet
Eighth note beat unit	♪		

Gioachino Rossini (1792–1868), Overture from *William Tell* (1804)

1 (2) la li 3 la li 1 (2) la li 3 la li 1 (2) la li 3 la li 1 (2 3)

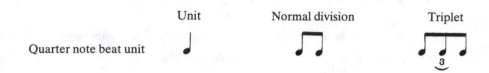

Felix Mendelssohn (1809–1847), Fourth Movement, *Symphony No. 4 in A Major* ("Italian") (1833)

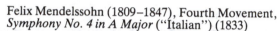

2 la li 3 la li 4 la li 1 la li 2 la li 3 la li 4 la li 1 la li

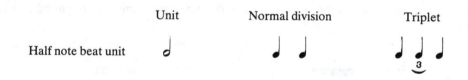

Edward Lalo (1823–1892), First Movement, *Symphonie Espagnole for Violin and Orchestra*, Op. 21 (1875)

1 la li 2 and 1 and (2) la li 1 la li 2 and 1
te te te

The long–short pattern within the triplet group is notated as in this table:

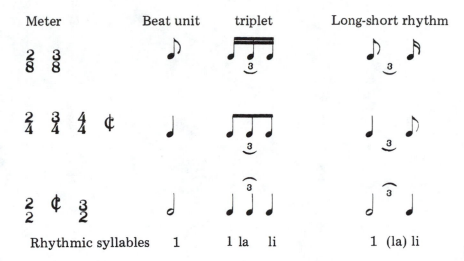

Meter	Beat unit	triplet	Long-short rhythm
$\frac{2}{8}$ $\frac{3}{8}$	♪	(triplet of three eighths) 3	♪ ♪ 3
$\frac{2}{4}$ $\frac{3}{4}$ $\frac{4}{4}$ ¢	♩	(triplet of three quarters) 3	♩ ♪ 3
$\frac{2}{2}$ ¢ $\frac{3}{2}$	♩	3 ♩ ♩ ♩	3 𝅗𝅥 ♩
Rhythmic syllables	1	1 la li	1 (la) li

Sight Singing Assignment

A. *Triplets in Simple Meter*

As you count the meter, clap the notated rhythm. Then do the exercises again, clapping the beat (or using a conductor's beat with your hand) and sing or say the rhythm using the rhythmic syllables you have learned (*1 la li, 2 la li,* and so on).

1.

2.

3.

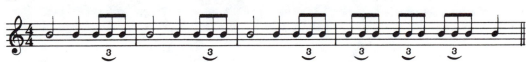

4.

B. Apply the above rhythms to scales you sing or play on an instrument. Use major or one of the three forms of the minor scale.

C. Sing or play all the examples in the text of this lesson.

Written Assignment

A. Rewrite the four sight singing assignments on the preceding pages in the meters indicated.

1.

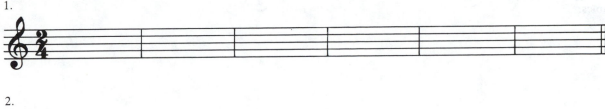

2.

3.

4.

B. Write the correct syllables under each note in the following exercises.

1. EXAMPLE:

Rhythmic
syllables:

2.

Rhythmic
syllables:

3.

Rhythmic
syllables:

4.

Rhythmic
syllables:

Ear Training Assignment

You will hear exercises with triplet figures on various beats of the measure. Circle those beats of the measures where triplets occur. The example is illustrated and worked correctly for you. Each exercise will be played twice.

EXAMPLE:

Instructor plays this:

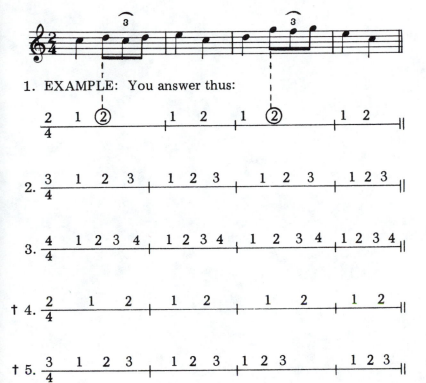

1. EXAMPLE: You answer thus:

$\frac{2}{4}$ 1 ②   1   2   1   ②   1   2 ‖

2. $\frac{3}{4}$ 1 2 3 ┊ 1 2 3 ┊ 1 2 3 ┊ 1 2 3 ‖

3. $\frac{4}{4}$ 1 2 3 4 ┊ 1 2 3 4 ┊ 1 2 3 4 ┊ 1 2 3 4 ‖

† 4. $\frac{2}{4}$ 1   2 ┊ 1   2 ┊ 1   2 ┊ 1   2 ‖

† 5. $\frac{3}{4}$ 1 2 3 ┊ 1 2 3 ┊ 1 2 3 ┊   1 2 3 ‖

† 6. $\frac{4}{4}$ 1 2 3 4 ┊ 1 2 3 4 ┊ 1 2 3 4 ┊ 1 2 3 4 ‖

Chapter 21   Compound Meters

What Is Compound Meter?

In **compound meters** the beat unit has *three* normal subdivisions. The beat unit in compound meter is *always a dotted note*. The effect of compound meter is that of having a triplet on every beat; thus, some melodies could be notated equally well in simple time with triplets or compound time with normal note values.

American Folk Tune, "Down in the Valley" +

Simple time with triplets

The Compound Meters with a Dotted Quarter Note Beat Unit

The most common compound meters are those with a *dotted quarter note* as the beat unit and eighth note divisions of the beat. The time signatures and the method of counting the beats are given here, and the example shows the normal patterns.

Joseph Haydn (1732–1809), First Movement,
Symphony No. 94 in G Major ("Surprise") (1791)

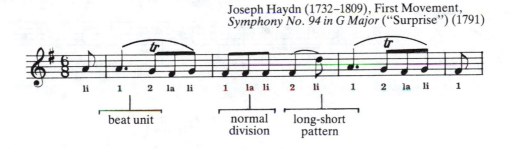

Other Dotted Notes as Beat Units

Compound meters using the dotted half note or the dotted eighth note as the beat unit are often used. They are counted in the same manner.

Counting Subdivisions in Compound Meter

Subdivisions of the beat in compound time are counted as shown here. The syllable *ta* placed between the syllables further divides the beat. Triplets can also be counted *1 ta la ta li ta* if the notes of the triplet are further divided.

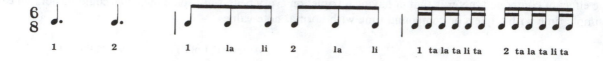

Johannes Brahms (1833–1897), First Movement,
Piano Concerto No. 1 in D Minor, Op. 15 (1854–58)

Fryderyk Chopin (1810–1849), *Nocturne*, Op. 9, No. 1 (1830–31)

Examples of Subdivisions of the Beat in Compound Meters

One of the most common ways to use these values in compound time is in dotted note patterns like these:

Wolfgang Amadeus Mozart (1756–1791), First Movement,
Sonata in A Major for piano, K. 300 (1781–83)

Johann Sebastian Bach (1685–1750), Forlane, *Orchestra Suite No. 1* (about 1720)

Sometimes the third note of the group is divided as well. Syncopation patterns are sometimes used at this level.

Johannes Brahms (1833–1897), Second Movement, *Symphony No. 4*, Op. 98 (1884–85)

The long note in dotted note patterns is usually on the first part of the beat. If it is on the second part of the beat instead, it gives an unusual stress to this part of the rhythm.

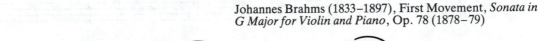

Johannes Brahms (1833–1897), First Movement, *Sonata in G Major for Violin and Piano*, Op. 78 (1878–79)

Another interesting rhythm is produced by tying the beginning of a dotted pattern to the preceding beat.

Ludwig van Beethoven (1770–1827), First Movement, *Symphony No 7 in A Major*, Op. 92 (1811–12)

A Special Rhythm—Hemiola

A very interesting effect can be produced by shifting the accent in a measure with six eighth notes from two groups of three eighth notes (compound duple) to three groups of two eighth notes (simple triple) or the reverse. This effect is called **hemiola.**

Gilles Binchois (circa 1400–60), *De plus en plus* (*More and More*)

Vertical lines show strong beats

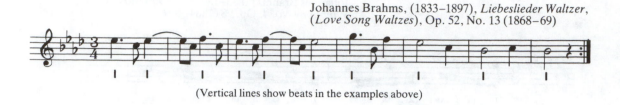

Johannes Brahms, (1833–1897), *Liebeslieder Waltzer*,
(*Love Song Waltzes*), Op. 52, No. 13 (1868–69)

(Vertical lines show beats in the examples above)

The example above could have been barred as follows to show the change in metrical grouping produced by the *hemiola*.

Look for more examples of hemiola in other music you know.

Sight Singing Assignment

A. *Compound Meters*. Count the meter and clap the rhythm. Then clap or beat the meter and sing or say the rhythm, using the rhythmic syllables. Remember that when the beat is divided into three equal parts in compound meter, you use the same syllables as for the triple division of the beat in simple meter.

5.

Syllables:	1	la	ta	li	2		1	la	ta	li	ta	2	li		1	la	ta	li	2		1		li	2
Beat:	1				2		1					2			1				2		1			2

6.

7.

B. *Various Rhythm Patterns in Simple and Compound Time.* Count the meter and clap the rhythm for each of the patterns below, just as you did in the previous exercises, but this time repeat each example *six times continuously.*

Then clap or beat the meter and sing or say the rhythm using rhythmic syllables, again repeating each example *six times continuously.*

Finally, apply the rhythm to scales—major or melodic minor—and repeat the rhythms as many times as are required to sing up and down the scale (one octave).

By the way, for instrumentalists rhythmic scale studies like this are *very useful* ways to practice scales on your instrument, using a metronome to give the beat.

Written Assignment

You can sing or clap these, too!

A. *Above* the exercises below write the regular beats of the measure. Then *below* the same exercises write the proper rhythmic syllables for each note. The example is worked correctly for you.

1. EXAMPLE:

Beats:

Rhythmic syllables:

2.

Beats:

Rhythmic syllables:

3.

Beats:

Rhythmic syllables:

4.

Beats:

Rhythmic syllables:

B. Sing, say, and clap all the examples you have written. Also apply the rhythms to scales you sing or play.

C. Match the column of rhythmic syllables on the right with the notated rhythms on the left. The example is worked correctly for you. Add rest signs between the syllables where rests occur.

1. EXAMPLE: _i_

a. 1 2

b. 1 (2) an du

c. 1 ta la 2 li

d. 1 la li 2 la li

e. 1 ta la ta li ta 2 a an du

f. 1 ta la ta li ta 2 la li ta

g. 2

h. 1 (2) la li ta

i. 1 and 2 la li

j. 1 and 2 an du

k. 1 2 li ta

l. 1 li la

m. 1 ta la ta li ta 2 du

n. 1

o. 1 (2) li ta

2. _____

3. _____

4. _____

5. _____

6. _____

7. _____

8. _____

9. _____

10. _____

D. Play, sing, or clap all the rhythms above, repeating each measure four times. Use a single pitch and then sing or play the rhythms using scales.

Ear Training Assignment

A. *Repeated Compound Rhythm Patterns.* In each exercise you will hear a rhythmic pattern of one measure length repeated several times in a melodic context. Four possible rhythmic patterns are given. Choose the one you hear and circle the letter indicating the correct rhythmic pattern. *Your teacher will beat two measures of meter before beginning each exercise.* Each example will be played twice. See the example.

EXAMPLE:

1.

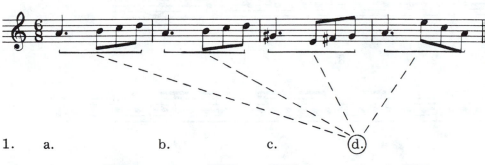

1.   a.   b.   c.   (d.)

2.   a.   b.   c.   d.

3.   a.   b.   c.   d.

† 4.   a.   b.   c.   d.

† 5.   a.   b.   c.   d.

† 6.   a.   b.   c.   d.

Computer Program Disk: Rhythm, Lesson E

B. *Recognition of Errors in Compound Meters Using Sub-Beat Values.* Following is a series of four-measure rhythmic exercises. In each exercise the notation you see agrees with the dictated version *except in one measure*. Determine which measure is rhythmically different from the notated version and circle the number of that measure. Each exercise will be played twice.

Computer Program Disk: Rhythm, Lesson I

C. *Recognition of Simple and Compound Meter.* In each of the exercises you will hear a short melody. Determine whether the melody is in simple or compound time and underline the correct answer. Each exercise will be played twice.

1. SIMPLE	COMPOUND	† 5. SIMPLE	COMPOUND
2. SIMPLE	COMPOUND	† 6. SIMPLE	COMPOUND
3. SIMPLE	COMPOUND	† 7. SIMPLE	COMPOUND
4. SIMPLE	COMPOUND	† 8. SIMPLE	COMPOUND

Melody

Part IV

What Is Melody?

Melody is a series of single musical tones, sounded successively. Since each tone has both pitch and duration, melody has two dimensions of movement: movement in time (*rhythm*) and movement in pitch (**melodic contour**).

Chapter 22:   Movement and Rest in Melody

The Phrase

Melody is divided into **phrases,** which are the "sentences" of musical speech. Phrases may vary greatly in length, but they are usually from two to eight measures long. The normal phrase of music of the eighteenth and nineteenth centuries is four measures.

Johann Crüger (1598–1662), "Jesu, meine Freude" ("Jesus, My Joy") (1653). (This melody was often used by later composers, among them J. S. Bach.)

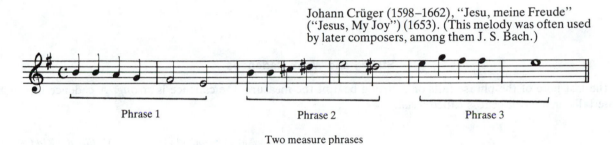

Phrase 1   Phrase 2   Phrase 3

Two measure phrases

Carol based on Gregorian Chant, "O Come, O Come Emmanuel"

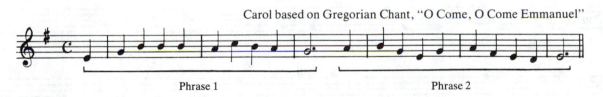

Phrase 1   Phrase 2

Three measure phrases

Lady John Scott, "Annie Laurie" (18th century)

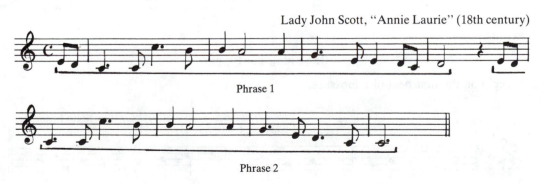

Phrase 1

Phrase 2

Four measure phrases

The Cadence

Every phrase has a beginning, a middle, and an end. Throughout the phrase, the rhythm and the shape of the melodic line (*melodic contour*) combine to create a feeling of movement toward a goal that is a *point of rest*. The moment of arrival, with the melodic progression leading to it, is called the **cadence.**

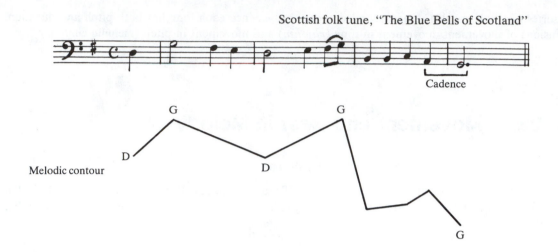

Scottish folk tune, "The Blue Bells of Scotland"

Strong and Weak Cadences

When the last note of the phrase falls on a strong beat of the measure, the cadence is *strong*. A cadence in which the last note falls on a weak beat is called *weak*.

Aaron Copland (1900–   ), *Billy the Kid* (1941)[+]

Copyright 1941 by Aaron Copland. Renewed 1968. Reprinted by permission of Aaron Copland and Boosey & Hawkes, Inc., Sole Licensees.

Beginning the Phrase

A melody may begin on the first beat of a measure.

Joseph Haydn (1732–1809), "Gott, erhalte Franz den Kaiser!" (Austrian Hymn) (1796)

[+]Denotes American composer.

A tune may begin with a melodic movement into the first beat of a measure. The note or notes that move to the first strong beat are called the **anacrusis.** The terms *pick-up* or *up-beat* are sometimes used for describing this type of phrase beginning.

An anacrusis is *not* a measure, but a rhythmic and melodic movement *toward* a measure. In melodies with an anacrusis, the *first measure* is the metric unit with the *first strong beat.*

If the first phrase of a melody begins with an anacrusis, it is likely that the following phrases will also. It is therefore customary for the last measure of a tune with an anacrusis to subtract the beats or portions of beats used in the anacrusis at the beginning from the end of the last measure. This makes it possible to repeat the tune from the beginning without any adjustment between stanzas. This rule is not followed strictly in long, complex works in which many different kinds of phrases may be used.

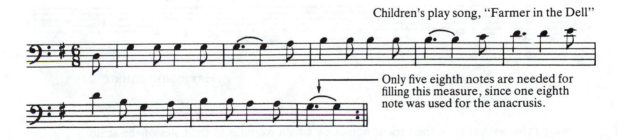

The Names of the Notes in a Scale

Each note of the scale has a name describing its function in melodies and harmonies built from the notes of the scale.

The most important notes of the scale are the *tonic* (tonal center), the **dominant** (the fifth above the tonic), and the **subdominant** (the fifth below the tonic).

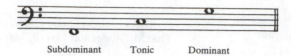

Subdominant Tonic Dominant

Halfway between the tonic and the dominant is the **mediant** (derived from a Latin word meaning *middle*); halfway between the tonic and the subdominant is the **submediant.**

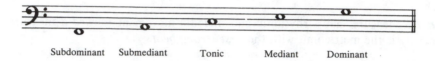

Subdominant Submediant Tonic Mediant Dominant

The two remaining notes of the scale are those just above and below the tonic note—the **supertonic** and *leading tone* respectively. The supertonic, of course, means the note above the tonic. The term *leading tone* describes the tendency of a note a half step below the tonic to move melodically up to the tonic note.

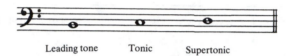

Leading tone Tonic Supertonic

The same names are given to scale steps in minor, except for the seventh degree in natural minor and descending melodic minor. In these forms of the minor scale, the seventh note is a whole step below the tonic, and the term **subtonic** is used. In melodic and harmonic minor, which have a raised seventh degree, the relationship is again a half step, and the raised seventh degree is called a leading tone.

Natural minor Harmonic minor

The following table summarizes the various names by which we refer to the notes of the scale.

Major Scale Function Name	Scale Degree Number	Minor Scale Function Name
TONIC	1	TONIC
SUPERTONIC	2	SUPERTONIC
MEDIANT	3	MEDIANT
SUBDOMINANT	4	SUBDOMINANT
DOMINANT	5	DOMINANT
SUBMEDIANT	6	SUBMEDIANT
	6 (raised)	SUBMEDIANT
LEADING TONE	7	SUBTONIC
	7 (raised)	LEADING TONE
TONIC	8	TONIC

Active and Rest Tones in a Key

Some notes of the scale have a strong tendency to move melodically in predictable directions: the leading tone tends to move toward the tonic, and the raised sixth in melodic minor tends to move to the raised seventh, and from there to the tonic. Tones with a strong feeling of movement toward a goal can be called *active tones*: the notes to which they move, particularly the notes of the tonic chord, can be described as *rest tones*.

Common tendencies of melodic movement in Major and Minor

The most prominent of the active tones is the *leading tone*. When you sing the following melody and stop on the leading tone, you feel a strong urge to continue to the following note—the tonic toward which the leading tone is attracted. This strong sense of direction makes the pattern from the leading tone up to the tonic a strong and important melodic cadence pattern.

William Steffe (19th century), "Battle Hymn of the Republic" (1852) (originally the tune to "John Brown's Body")[+]

In the following tune, the final cadence moves *down* to the tonic from the supertonic, another very common cadence pattern.

Johann Sebastian Bach (1685–1750), "Herr, straf mich nicht" ("Lord, Punish Me Not")

Notice how the raised tones tend to move toward the tonic in this tune in a minor key.

Some Melodic Patterns in Cadences

If a melodic cadence skips to the tonic, it usually moves from the dominant note to the tonic, with either a skip of a fourth or a skip down of a fifth.

Skip from dominant *up* to tonic in the cadence

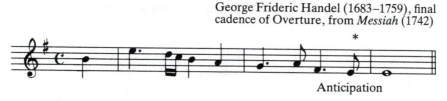

Skip from dominant *down* to tonic in the cadence

A way of decorating at a cadence is to *anticipate* the tonic on the strong beat of the cadence with the tonic note before the bar line.

Tonic approached by supertonic, strong beat anticipated

Some Melodic Patterns in the Anacrusis (Up-beat)

The anacrusis also has several characteristic melodic patterns. Those moving from the dominant to the tonic are very common.

Dominant *up* to tonic

George Frideric Handel (1683–1759),
"O Thou That Tellest Good Tidings,"
Messiah (1742)

Dominant *down* to tonic

The third of the scale may move down to the tonic, or the tonic up to the third. The anacrusis with this pattern often fills in the third with stepwise motion, making a two-note anacrusis.

Interval of the third with stepwise motion

Anacrusis

Irish Folk Tune, "Wearin' of the Green"

The broken triad is another common pattern using more than one note in the anacrusis.

John Stafford Smith (1750–1836),
"The Star-Spangled Banner"

Sight Singing Assignment*

Sing the following melodies in two different ways:

1. Clap the meter and at the same time sing the pitches of the notes in the correct rhythm using scale degree numbers or syllables.

2. Sing the pitches using numbers or syllables without clapping. Learn to maintain a steady tempo without the assistance of clapping.

1.

Johann Sebastian Bach (1685–1750), "Nun ruhen alle Wälder"
("Now Are All the Forests Peaceful")

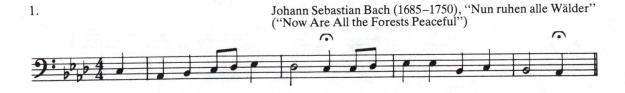

*In addition to the melodies given in the sight singing sections of the lessons on melody, sing *all* the melodies in the text of each lesson, using numbers or syllables as in the sight singing assignments. The greatest value will be derived from these exercises if they are sung while you are reading the text.

This beautiful melody by the American Revolutionary War composer William Billings can be sung as a round, in four parts. Each new voice begins as the first voice begins a new phrase, at the mark of the asterisk (*).

Written Assignment

A. Below is a group of melodies with more than one phrase in each melody. Mark the end of each phrase with a curved bracket as shown in the example, and under each cadence indicate whether the phrase ends on a strong beat or on a weak beat. The example is worked correctly for you.

1.

Ludwig van Beethoven (1770–1827), Second Movement, *Sonatina in G Major for Piano*, Op. 49, No. 2 (1805)

Tempo di minuetto

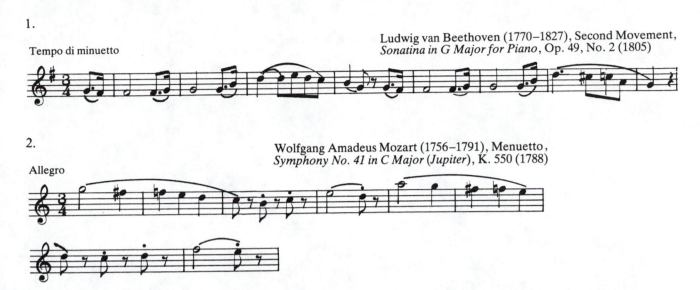

2.

Wolfgang Amadeus Mozart (1756–1791), Menuetto, *Symphony No. 41 in C Major (Jupiter)*, K. 550 (1788)

Allegro

B. The same concern with anacrusis, cadence, and direction is found in melodies of our century whether or not they are based on major and minor scales. Identify the kind of phrase beginnings (with or without anacrusis) and cadences (strong or weak) in the following melodies and mark the phrase endings with a curved bracket as in the preceding exercises. Space is left under each melody for you to draw a chart showing their melodic contour (like the chart for *The Blue Bells of Scotland* earlier in the chapter). Play the melodies.

Paul Hindemith (1895–1963), First Movement, *Piano Sonata No. 2* (1936) (phrase endings are marked)

Contour of Hindemith melody

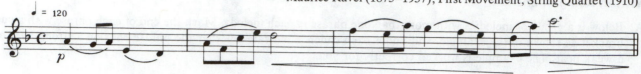

Maurice Ravel (1875–1937), First Movement, String Quartet (1910)

Contour of Ravel melody

Ear Training Assignment

A. *Recognition of the Anacrusis.* In each exercise you will hear a short melody. Some of these melodies begin with an anacrusis and some begin on the first beat of the measure. Underline the answer that applies in each case.

    1. Begins on an anacrusis.   Begins on the first beat of a measure.

    2. Begins on an anacrusis.   Begins on the first beat of a measure.

    3. Begins on an anacrusis.   Begins on the first beat of a measure.

    4. Begins on an anacrusis.   Begins on the first beat of a measure.

† 5. Begins on an anacrusis.   Begins on the first beat of a measure.

† 6. Begins on an anacrusis.   Begins on the first beat of a measure.

† 7. Begins on an anacrusis.   Begins on the first beat of a measure.

† 8. Begins on an anacrusis.   Begins on the first beat of a measure.

B. *Recognition of Active Tones or Tonic at the Phrase End.* In each exercise you will hear a short melody. This melodic phrase will end either on the tonic or an active tone. Underline the proper answer. See example. Each exercise will be played twice.

    1. Active tone.   Tonic.

    2. Active tone.   Tonic.

    3. Active tone.   Tonic.

    4. Active tone.   Tonic.

    5. Active tone.   Tonic.

    6. Active tone.   Tonic.

† 7. Active tone.   Tonic.

† 8. Active tone.   Tonic.

† 9. Active tone.   Tonic.

†10. Active tone.   Tonic.

†11. Active tone.   Tonic.

†12. Active tone.   Tonic.

†Indicates examples recorded on the cassettes available for use with this text.

Chapter 23   Conjunct and Disjunct Motion; Melodic Direction

Conjunct and Disjunct (Smooth and Jagged)

The melodic contour may be smooth, with most intervals whole steps and half steps (**conjunct motion**) or jagged, with leaps of larger intervals (**disjunct motion**).

Johann Crüger (1598–1662), "Nun danket alle Gott"
(Now Thank We All Our God)

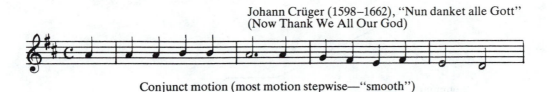

Conjunct motion (most motion stepwise—"smooth")

Ludwig van Beethoven (1770–1827), First Movement,
Piano Sonata in C Minor, Op. 10, No. 1 (1798)

Disjunct motion (most motion by skip—"jagged")

Movement toward a Melodic Climax

A melody is also described in terms of the direction in which it moves. Some melodies move upward to a high note that is the *climax* of the phrase. The climax may be at the very end of the phrase, coinciding with the cadence.

Ludwig van Beethoven (1770–1827), Fourth Movement,
String Quartet, Op. 18, No. 4 (1801)

Climax at the cadence

Beginning

Some melodies reach the high point in the middle of the phrase and then fall back to a cadence at a lower pitch.

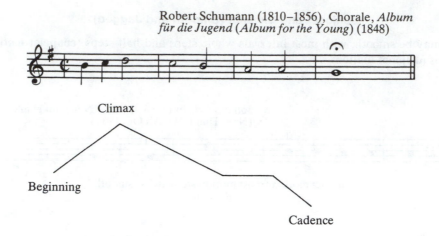

Robert Schumann (1810–1856), Chorale, *Album für die Jugend* (*Album for the Young*) (1848)

Climax

Beginning

Cadence

The melody may sweep downward toward a low point of arrival.

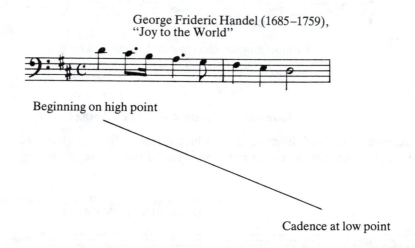

George Frideric Handel (1685–1759), "Joy to the World"

Beginning on high point

Cadence at low point

A melody may even stay on one pitch, building up tension until finally some melodic motion leads to a cadence.

George Frideric Handel (1685–1759), "And the Glory of the Lord," *Messiah* (1842)

These and other contours are found both in conjunct and disjunct motion. Note that in the following melody the motion is conjunct at first but the phrase ends with wide-ranging disjunct motion.

Claude Debussy (1862–1918), *Prélude à l'apres-midi d'un faune*
(*Prelude to the Afternoon of a Faun*) (1892–94)

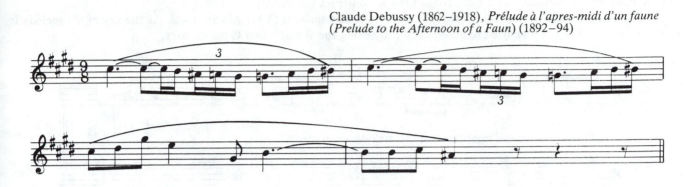

Disjunct Motion in Melodies Outlining Chords

When melodies move with many skips, they often form patterns outlining chords, as in the following example:

Ludwig van Beethoven (1770–1827), First Movement,
Symphony No. 3 in E-Flat Major, Op. 55 (1806)

Triad
E♭ — G — B♭

Chord outline

Melodies can be written using nothing but the notes of the triad built on the first degree of the scale (the *tonic triad*). Bugle calls are built entirely from the notes of the tonic chord.

"Taps"

Triad
F — A — C

Notice that such a disjunct melody still has a strong sense of direction: it rises to a climax and drops back to a more restful cadence. All the melodic contours used in conjunct melodies are also found in disjunct melodies.

Stepwise movement is often combined with disjunct movement in melodies built on chord patterns. Intervals of the triad may be filled in with stepwise movement passing between the notes of the chord without disturbing the essential triadic outline of the melody.

German Folk Song, "Lullaby"

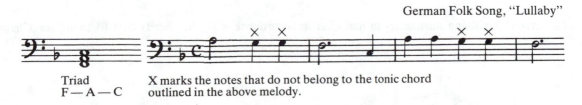

Triad
F — A — C

X marks the notes that do not belong to the tonic chord outlined in the above melody.

Melodies Constructed of Other Triads

Melodies are often constructed of notes of the dominant triad or subdominant triad. In the following two melodies you can see notes of the dominant and tonic triads used to construct the melody.

In the tune "Down in the Valley" only the tonic (I) and dominant (V) triads are used. As the key of the melody is F major, the autoharp can be used to accompany it by using the F major and C major bars.

Notes outlining triads in the melody are circled.

Harmonic
background: F maj.   F maj.   C maj.   C maj.   F maj.

In a minor key the major form of the dominant triad is used so the melody which follows can also be accompanied on the autoharp with the *a minor* (I) bar and the *E major* (V) bar.

Giuseppe Verdi (1813–1901), "Addio del passato" ("Farewell to the Past"), *La Traviata* (*The Lost One*) (1852)

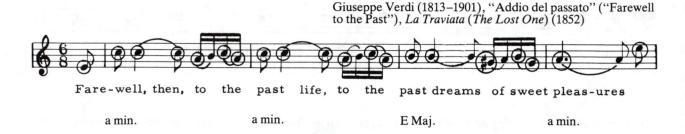

Fare-well, then, to   the   past   life,   to   the   past dreams of sweet pleas-ures

a min.   a min.   E Maj.   a min.

As you see in the example, not all the tones of the triad need to be present in the melody to create the feeling of a change in harmony. Notes that do not belong to the chord may be used to decorate the chord outline without changing the harmony that would be used to accompany the melody at that point. Embellishing notes that do not belong to the harmony are called **nonharmonic tones;** they will be discussed further in chapter 26.

In the next tune, the subdominant triad is part of the melodic structure.

Wolfgang Amadeus Mozart (1756–1791), Menuetto,
Symphony No. 39 in E-flat Major, K. 543 (1788)

I   I   IV   I   IV   IV

For further study of putting harmonies to melodies in accordance with the chords that fit them, see Chapter 26, "Triads in Succession."

Sight Singing Assignment

A. Sing the following melodies in two different ways:
Clap the meter and at the same time sing the pitches of the notes using the scale degree numbers or syllables. Then sing the pitches in the correct rhythm using the numbers or syllables without clapping. Learn to maintain the steady tempo without the assistance of clapping.

1.   Felix Mendelssohn (1809–1847), Scherzo,
     Midsummer Night's Dream (1842)

2.   Antonin Dvořák (1841–1904), Second Movement, *Symphony No. 9
     in E Minor*, Op. 95 (From the *New World*) (1893)

3.   Johann Sebastian Bach (1685–1750), Menuetto,
     Notenbüchlein für Anna Magdalena Bach
     (*Little Notebook for Anna Magdalena Bach*
     —Bach's second wife) (1725)

4.   Johann Strauss, Jr. (1825–1899), "Emperor Waltz"

5.   Dimitry Shostakovich (1906–1975), Second Movement,
     Symphony No. 5 in D Minor (1937)

B. *Sight Singing Exercises Outlining the Tonic Triad.* Sing the following melodies in one or both of these two different ways:

Clap the meter and at the same time sing the pitches of the notes in the correct rhythm using scale degree numbers or syllables. Then sing the pitches using numbers or syllables without clapping. Learn to maintain a steady tempo without the assistance of clapping.

1.

American folk tune, "Clementine"+

Built entirely of tonic triad

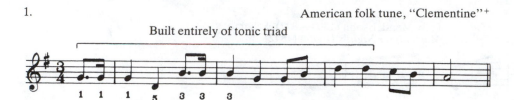

2.

Ludwig van Beethoven (1770–1827), First Movement,
Symphony No. 3 in E-flat Major, Op. 55 (1806)

Built entirely of tonic triad

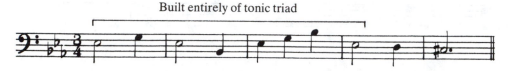

3.

George Frideric Handel (1695–1759),
Music for the Royal Fireworks (1749)

Built entirely of tonic triad except for "×"

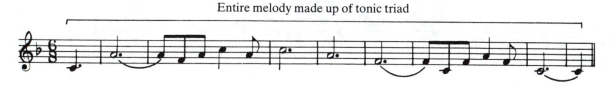

4.

John Phillip Sousa (1854–1932), "Semper Fidelis" (1888)+

Entire melody made up of tonic triad

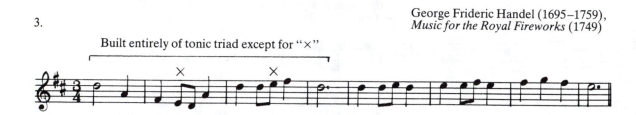

5.

Joseph Haydn (1732–1809), Fourth Movement,
Symphony No. 100 in G Major ("Military") (1793–94)

Allegro

Written Assignment

A. Following is a group of melodies. Find the tonic triads outlined in the melodies and mark the sections of the melody built on the tonic triad with brackets.

1.

Wolfgang Amadeus Mozart (1756–1793), Menuetto,
Symphony No. 40 in G Minor, K. 550 (1788)

2.

Ludwig van Beethoven, Rondo, *Sonata No. 3 in E-flat Major
for Violin and Piano*, Op. 12 (1799)

B. Try your hand at writing some complete melodies, using arpeggiation of the tonic triad as part of the structure of the melody. Write six phrases, each four measures long, in the spaces provided. You may use up-beats or not as you like. Remember that the true test of a melody is how it sounds. Sing or play your examples. There are two aspects of this assignment on which it will be graded: the correctness with which it is notated *and* the melodic beauty or charm of the melody. In these first melodies, make each phrase end on the tonic note or a member of the tonic chord. Be careful to use clear musical handwriting (*calligraphy*).

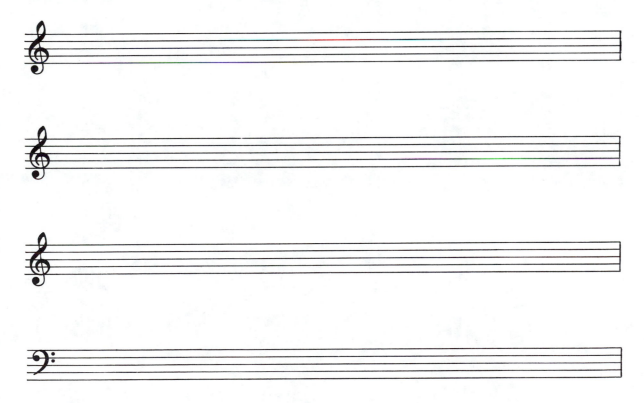

Ear Training Assignment

A. Each of the melodies you will hear is an example of either conjunct or disjunct motion. Underline the term that best describes the melody. See example.

EXAMPLE: You will hear:

1. a. Conjunct Motion   b. <u>Disjunct Motion</u>
2. a. Conjunct Motion   b. Disjunct Motion
3. a. Conjunct Motion   b. Disjunct Motion
4. a. Conjunct Motion   b. Disjunct Motion
5. a. Conjunct Motion   b. Disjunct Motion
† 6. a. Conjunct Motion   b. Disjunct Motion
† 7. a. Conjunct Motion   b. Disjunct Motion
† 8. a. Conjunct Motion   b. Disjunct Motion
† 9. a. Conjunct Motion   b. Disjunct Motion
†10. a. Conjunct Motion   b. Disjunct Motion

Computer Program Disk: Melody and Texture, Lesson G

B. *Dictation of Simple Melodies Outlining the Tonic Triad.* In each exercise you will hear a short four-measure melodic phrase. Determine the correct scale degree numbers for each note and write them in the blanks below. A few numbers have been written to help you. See example. Each exercise will be played twice.

EXAMPLE: 1.

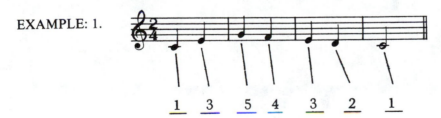

    1   3   5   4   3   2   1

2. ____ ____ ____ __5__ ____ ____ ____
3. __1__ ____ ____ ____ __1__ ____ __5__ ____ ____ ____
† 4. __1__ ____ ____ ____ __1__ ____ ____ ____
† 5. __1__ ____ ____ __2__ ____ ____ ____
† 6. __1__ ____ __1__ ____ ____ __6__ ____ ____ ____

Computer Program Disk: Melody and Texture, Lessons D, E, and F

Chapter 24 Rhythmic and Melodic Motives; Melodic Repetition and Sequence

Motives

Phrases are built from smaller groups of notes called **motives.** A *rhythmic motive* is a short, distinctive rhythmic pattern that may be repeated with different pitch patterns.

George Frideric Handel (1685–1759),
"Hallelujah Chorus," *Messiah* (1742)

A *melodic motive* has a distinctive rhythmic pattern *and* a pattern of pitch relationships.

Wolfgang Amadeus Mozart (1756–1791), First Movement,
Symphony No. 40 in C Major ("Jupiter") (1788)

Motives can be used either without change or with some variation so long as the variation is not so great that their distinctive qualities are lost. A large musical design can be built from a single motive. The first four notes of Beethoven's *Symphony No. 5* form the basis for much of the first movement of the symphony.

Ludwig van Beethoven (1770–1727),
First Movement, *Symphony No. 5*
in C Minor, Op. 67 (1807–8)

Beginning statement of the rhythmic motive

Melodic variation of the motive, both in its
normal position and inverted (upside down)

Another theme beginning with the opening motive

Listen to the whole movement of the symphony to hear how many ways Beethoven uses this motive.

Sequence

A common method of constructing a melody out of a motive is to *repeat it* at various pitch levels. This form of repetition is called a **sequence**.

Felix Mendelssohn (1809–1847), First Movement,
Concerto in E Minor for Violin and Orchestra, Op. 64 (1844)

Sequence of a two-measure motive

When melodic material is repeated with slight changes in some of the intervals or rhythms it is called *modified repetition*. If the pitch level of the restatement is different from that of the first presentation of the motive, and slight changes in intervals or rhythms are used, it is called *modified sequence*.

Antonin Dvořák (1841–1904), Second
Movement, *Symphony No. 9 in E Minor*,
Op. 95 (From the New World) (1893)

Johann Sebastian Bach (1685–1750),
Badinerie, *Orchestra Suite No. 2
in B Minor for Flute and Strings*
(late 1730s)

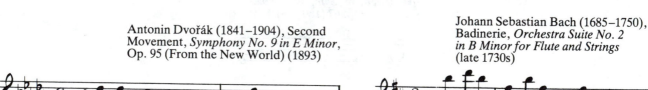

Modified repetition (change of rhythm)

Modified sequence (change of interval)

Sight Singing Assignment

A. *Rhythmic and Melodic Motives, Repetition, and Sequence.* Sing the following melodies using numbers or syllables. Note the instances in which the devices of repetition and sequence have been used.

1.

Henry Purcell (1659–1695), "A New Irish Tune"

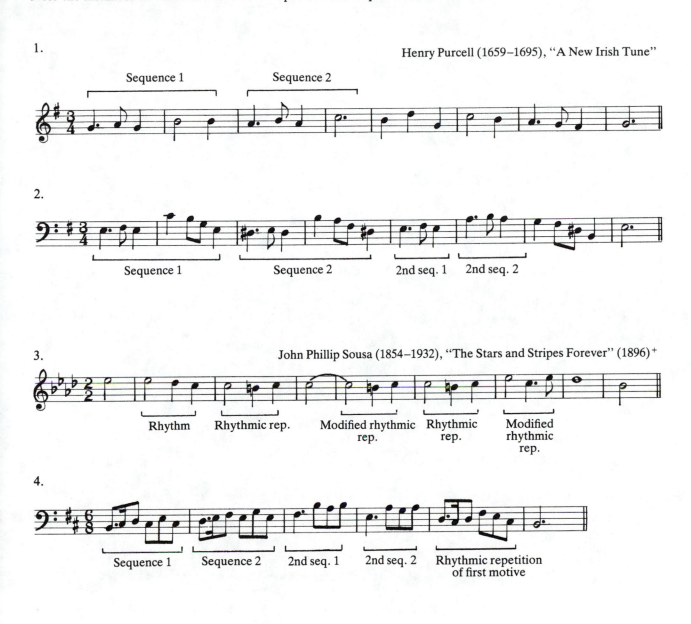

2.

3.

John Phillip Sousa (1854–1932), "The Stars and Stripes Forever" (1896)[+]

4.

5.

Johann Strauss, Jr. (1825–1899), "Wine, Women, and Song Waltz," Op. 333 (1869)

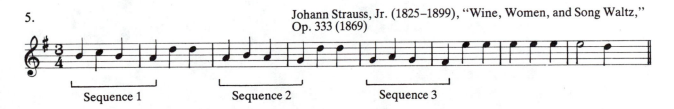

Written Assignment

A. Following are a group of six melodies built from *motives*. These motives are used in:

    a. Melodic and rhythmic repetition.

    b. Rhythmic repetition (but *not* melodic repetition).

    c. Sequence.

Mark each motive in brackets and in the blank supplied at the end of the melody, place the letter "a," "b," or "c" describing the way in which the motives were used. Sing all the melodies after you have analyzed them.

1.

Wolfgang Amadeus Mozart (1756–1791), Second Movement, *Sonata for Violin and Piano*, K. 374e (1781)

2.

Georg Phillip Telemann (1683–1767), *Partia a cembalo solo in G Major* (1728)

3.

Joseph Haydn (1732–1809), Menuetto, *String Quartet*, Op. 64, No. 2 (1790)

Ear Training Assignment

A. *Recognition of Melodic Sequences.* In each exercise you will hear a four-measure melody that uses a sequence. Write the scale numbers in the blanks. Then write the notes on the staff. The example is illustrated and is worked correctly for you. Each exercise will be played twice.

EXAMPLE:

1.

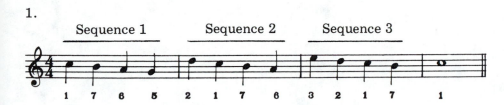

1   7   6   5   2   1   7   6   3   2   1   7   1

2.

1   2   3   5

3.

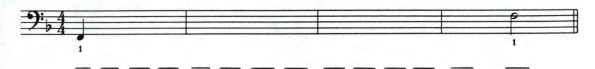

1   1

† 4.

1   1

† 5.

† 6.

1

Computer Program Disk: Melody and Texture, Lessons D, E, and F.

Harmony   Part V

Chapter 25   Triad Arrangements

One could look through a considerable stack of music and not find a single triad that looks like those illustrated so far. What you have seen so far is a "simple" arrangement of triads for easy identification. But, professional composers prefer to weave (arrange) triads into the fabric of music so the vertical (harmonic) and the horizontal (melodic) aspects blend to form a more musically satisfying result. Take, for instance, the first phrase of "A Mighty Fortress Is Our God" as arranged here. The melody (soprano voice) is a **chorale** or hymn tune by Martin Luther, but many composers, including J. S. Bach, have harmonized and arranged the tune according to their own taste.

Martin Luther (1453–1546), "Ein' Feste Burg," ("A Mighty Fortress Is Our God") (1529)

Much can be learned from this short phrase:

1. It is a four-voice (**soprano, alto, tenor, bass**) arrangement intended to be sung, but for the moment you can play it yourself on a piano.
2. If reading all four voices is beyond your capacity, play the soprano (highest) notes together with the block (simple) triads provided on the third staff. You will probably discover also why composers seldom employ triads arranged so simply.
3. For ease in identifying the triads, they are shown in simple arrangement (whole notes) on the bottom staff. This bottom staff is only for convenience and is not a part of the musical composition.
4. Since this arrangement is for four voices and triads contain only three pitches, one must be doubled (appear twice). In all instances the doubled note is the *root* of the triad—a common occurrence in four-voice writing.
5. The bass (lowest voice) contains the root of all triads in the phrase except at No. 3. Here the 3rd (E) is the bass note. When the bass note is *not* the root of the triad, it is said to be "inverted." This will be explained later.
6. It is easy to identify and follow the individual voices in this arrangement:
    a. Soprano voice—treble clef—note stems up
    b. Alto voice—treble clef—note stems down
    c. Tenor voice—bass clef—note stems up
    d. Bass voice—bass clef—note stems down

7. The eighth notes at numbers 5 and 8 are not a part of the existing triads. Observe, in the soprano voice, that note 5 fills in the gap (interval of a third) between notes 4 and 6, while note 8 acts in the same capacity between notes 7 and 9. These fall into a large category known as *nonharmonic tones,* and within that category, they are known more specifically as **passing tones.** See Appendix 2 for a full discussion of nonharmonic tones.

Musicians add Roman numeral **chord symbols** below each triad to show how it relates to the scale, as shown here:

Roman Numeral Analysis

I   ii   iii   IV   V   vi   vii°

Upper case means *major triad.*
Lower case means *minor triad.*
Lower case + degree sign (°) means *diminished triad.*

Triad Positions—Inversions

In almost all of the triads analyzed previously in this chapter, the lowest sounding tone (usually bass) is also the root (that is, the triad is in root position). Here again it would be rare indeed to find a complete composition where all of the triad roots were also the lowest sounding tones. For purposes of smooth voice-leading composers found it musically more expressive to exercise a freedom of choice in selecting triad positions as well as arrangements.

The **position** of a triad is determined entirely by the lowest note:

ROOT POSITION—Lowest note is the *root.*
FIRST INVERSION—Lowest note is the *third.*
SECOND INVERSION—Lowest note is the *fifth.*

So, to arrange (or voice) a triad, C E G for instance, you can change the order of the pitches and add voices: C G E C, C E C G, C G C E C, and so on. But, while arranging the triad, if the lowest note remains the same, the position also remains the same. To change the position while arranging, the lowest note must change to another triad tone:

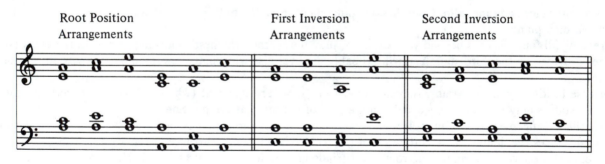

Root Position Arrangements   First Inversion Arrangements   Second Inversion Arrangements

Lowest note is root.   Lowest note is third.   Lowest note is fifth.

Written Assignment

A. The following phrase is similar in type to the illustration on page 245. Play it over several times to get familiar with the sound. If playing all four voices is too much, try playing only the two outer voices (soprano and bass). You'll still get some idea of the composition.

1. On the blank third score reduce the four-voice arrangements to simple triads as shown in the illustration.

2. Circle nonharmonic tones if any.

3. Check to see if the triad roots are doubled—as they are in the illustration, and place a square around each doubled note.

4. Also, place an "X" under any chord where the bass note is *not* the root of the triad (that is, chords in first or second inversion.)

Traditional Welsh Air, "All Through the Night"

Triads Reduced:

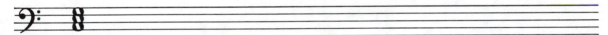

B. This excerpt is similar to the example in Assignment A except that it is written for piano. Observe that all notes in the treble clef are attached to a single stem, meaning that the pianist plays all three notes with the right hand.

Treat Assignment B exactly as you did Assignment A, and follow the four assignment steps.

Fryderyk Chopin (1810–1849), *Nocturne for Piano*, Op. 37, No. 1 (1839)

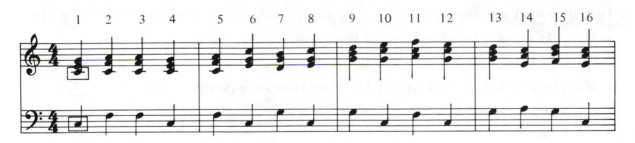

Triads Reduced:

Roman Numeral Analysis

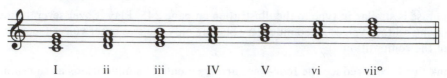

I   ii   iii   IV   V   vi   vii°

C. With the Roman numeral analysis illustration and the music of written assignment B in front of you, write the Roman numeral analysis of each triad. Both the illustration and the assignment are in C major. The following numbers correspond with the numbers of the triads.

EXAMPLE

I
____ ____ ____ ____ ____ ____ ____ ____ ____ ____ ____ ____ ____ ____ ____ ____
1   2   3   4   5   6   7   8   9   10   11   12   13   14   15   16

D. Three illustrations are provided to help you determine the correct procedure for this assignment. Complete each of these four steps for each exercise.

1. Using a black note head, copy the bass note of each arranged triad on the lowest (blank) staff.

2. Using whole notes, copy the remaining two pitches of the triad above or below the black note head. The *simplest* (notes as close together as possible) form of the triad should now be showing on the lowest (third) staff.

3. Determine the *type* (major or minor) of triad, and write either "M" or "m" in the blank beneath the lowest staff.

4. Look at the black note head.

   a. If it is the root of the triad, write "Root" in the blank above the staves.

   b. If it is the third of the triad, write "1st Inv" in the blank above the staves.

   c. If it is the fifth of the triad, write "2nd Inv" in the blank above the staves.

Written Assignment (cont.)

Examples of correct procedure:

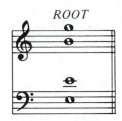

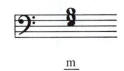

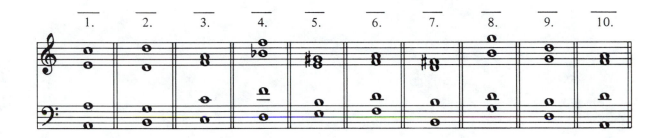

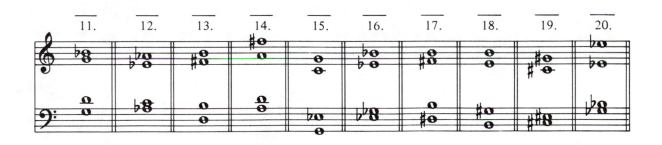

Keyboard Assignment

Playing Major Triads in Various Positions.

1. Play the example in A as written.
2. After observing the four-voice pattern played on the C major triad and then for the F major triad, continue the same pattern on B flat, E flat, and A flat major triads successively.
3. Complete B in the same manner as A. Continue the pattern on with the D, G, and C major triads.

Note in the examples that the soprano and bass both contain the root of the triads. Then, the bass moves up from root to third and then to the fifth. Make sure when you continue on (after the written out patterns) that you maintain the same relationships.

A.

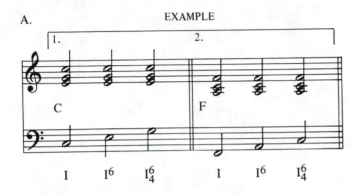

Continue with B♭, E♭, and A♭ major triads

B.

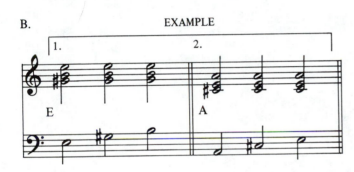

Continue with D, G, and C major triads

Ear Training Assignment

A. This assignment examines four-voice major and minor triads in a chorale setting. Each exercise consists of seven chords (a phrase), and you are to write "M" (for major) or "m" (for minor) triads in the blanks provided. All are either major or minor except the one noted in No. 5.

1. 1. _____ 2. _____ 3. _____ 4. _____ 5. _____ 6. _____ 7. _____

2. 1. _____ 2. _____ 3. _____ 4. _____ 5. _____ 6. _____ 7. _____

3. 1. _____ 2. _____ 3. _____ 4. _____ 5. _____ 6. _____ 7. _____

† 4. 1. _____ 2. _____ 3. _____ 4. _____ 5. _____ 6. _____ 7. _____

† 5. 1. _____ 2. _____ 3. _____ 4. _____ 5. _____ 6. _d_ 7. _____

† 6. 1. _____ 2. _____ 3. _____ 4. _____ 5. _____ 6. _____ 7. _____

Computer Program Disk: Harmony 1, Lessons B and G

B. In the following assignment you are to identify four-voice tonic triads in six or seven chord phrases.

1. Place an "I" in the blanks under the tonic triads.

2. It is not necessary to write in the other blanks.

3. However, if you think you can identify other triads, write their analysis also.

Chord
No. 1   2   3   4   5   6   7   1   2   3   4   5   6   7

1. __   __   __   __   __   __   __   2. __   __   __   __   __   __   __

3. __   __   __   __   __   __   __   † 4. __   __   __   __   __   __   __

† 5. __   __   __   __   __   __   __   † 6. __   __   __   __   __   __   __

Computer Program Disk: Harmony 3, Lessons B and C

C. In the following assignment you are to identify four-voice tonic triads in seven-chord phrases.

1. Place an 'i' (minor tonic) in the blanks representing the tonic triad.

2. It is not necessary to write in the other blanks.

3. However, if you think you can identify other triads, write their analysis also.

Chord Numbers: 1   2   3   4   5   6   7

1.   __   __   __   __   __   __   __

2.   __   __   __   __   __   __   __

3.   __   __   __   __   __   __   __

4.   __   __   __   __   __   __   __

Computer Program Disk: Harmony 3, Lesson D and Harmony 1, Lesson J

†Indicates examples recorded on the cassettes available for use with this text.

D. In this exercise you are to identify *contrary, oblique,* and *similar* motion in two-voice melodic excerpts. The example illustrates correct procedure.

You hear:

EXAMPLE:
1. <u>Contrary</u>   Oblique   Similar   † 4. Contrary   Oblique   Similar

2. Contrary   Oblique   Similar   † 5. Contrary   Oblique   Similar

3. Contrary   Oblique   Similar   † 6. Contrary   Oblique   Similar

Computer Program Disk: Melody and Texture, Lesson H

Chapter 26   Triads in Succession

Progressions—The I, IV, and V Triads

Triads, of course, have a nature of their own. They may be major or minor and built on any degree of any scale, but when composers place them one after another in a composition, they create a **chord progression.** A progression may refer to a succession of only two chords or to a series of any length. Some of the most common progressions in music include the tonic, subdominant, and dominant triads, I, IV, and V.

A very common chord (triad) progression

CM: I   IV   V   I   FM: I   IV   V   I   Gm: i   iv   V   i

Primary Triads and the Circle of Fifths Progression

The chord progression I, IV, V, I is one of the most common in all of music because it is made up entirely of **primary triads** (I, IV, V), and it contains two **circle progressions.** A circle progression occurs when the roots of two adjacent triads lie in a circle of fifths relationship:

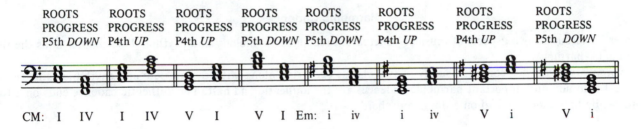

| ROOTS PROGRESS P5th *DOWN* | ROOTS PROGRESS P4th *UP* | ROOTS PROGRESS P4th *UP* | ROOTS PROGRESS P5th *DOWN* | ROOTS PROGRESS P5th *DOWN* | ROOTS PROGRESS P4th *UP* | ROOTS PROGRESS P4th *UP* | ROOTS PROGRESS P5th *DOWN* |

CM: I   IV   I   IV   V   I   V   I   Em: i   iv   i   iv   V   i   V   i

Circle of Fifths Progressions

In a circle of fifths progression (often shortened simply to *circle progression*) the root of the second triad may lie a perfect fifth *below* or a perfect fourth *above* that of the first. If this seems confusing, remember simply that V to I is a circle progression whether the roots go from V *down* to I or V *up* to I. Likewise, I to IV is a circle progression whether I *down* to IV or I *up* to IV.

The circle progression is the single most important shaping force in all of tonal music, whether it is a folk song, popular song, jazz, rock, or concert music in the European tradition.

Nonharmonic Tones

Almost all melodies are a mixture of notes, some of which duplicate accompanying chord factors and others that do not. Those melody pitches that also belong to the chord are of course **chord tones,** and the others are called *nonharmonic tones.* The nonharmonic tones in the first phrase of "Home on the Range" are circled:

American Cowboy Song, "Home on the Range"+

In the above illustration the notes at numbers 1 and 2 are called *passing tones* because they pass from one tone to a different tone. Numbers 3 and 4 are **neighboring tones** because they occur between two tones of the same pitch.

Harmonic Cadences

Chapter 22 discusses two aspects of musical punctuation (cadences)—melody and rhythm. This chapter adds the third ingredient—harmony.

A *harmonic cadence* consists usually of two chords occurring along with the melodic and rhythmic cadence. The two most common and important harmonic cadences are the **authentic** and **half.** The authentic cadence ends on a tonic chord, while half cadences end on a dominant chord.

Authentic cadence = V to I
Half cadence = I to V or IV to V

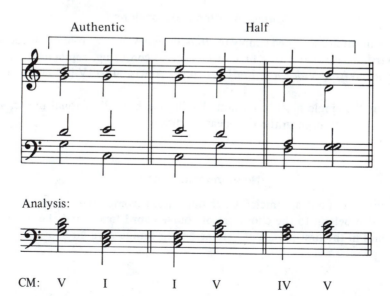

*See Appendix 2 for further discussion of nonharmonic tones.

+Denotes American composer.

The following example illustrates both the half and authentic cadences in the context of a composition:

Half and Authentic Cadences

Robert Schumann (1810–1856), "Wild Rider," *Album für die Jugend (Album for the Young)* (1848)

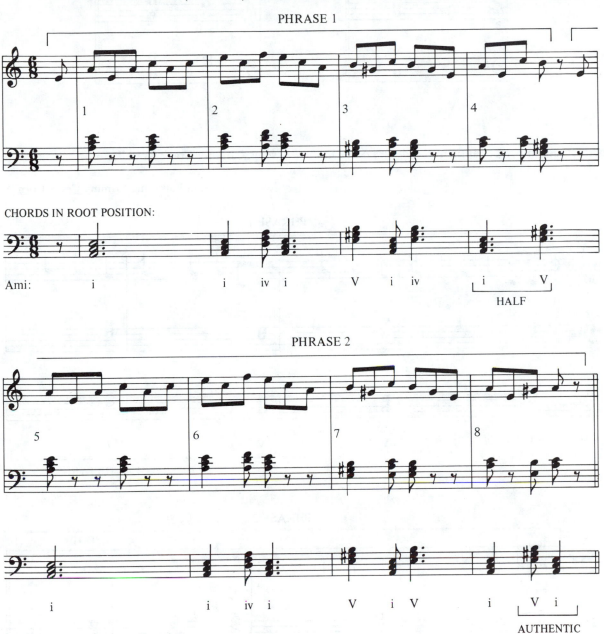

Imperfect and Perfect Authentic Cadences

The authentic cadence is called **perfect** if the melodic phrase ends with the tonic note (root of the tonic triad). When the melody concludes on the third or fifth scale degree (third or fifth of the tonic triad), the cadence is termed **imperfect.**

Perfect Authentic Cadence

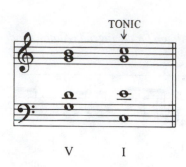

TONIC

V   I

Imperfect Authentic Cadence

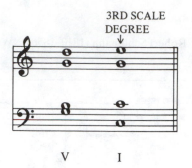

3RD SCALE
DEGREE

V   I

Both perfect and imperfect authentic cadences occur in the folksong, "Jimmy Crack Corn."

American Folksong, "Jimmy Crack Corn"+

PHRASE 1

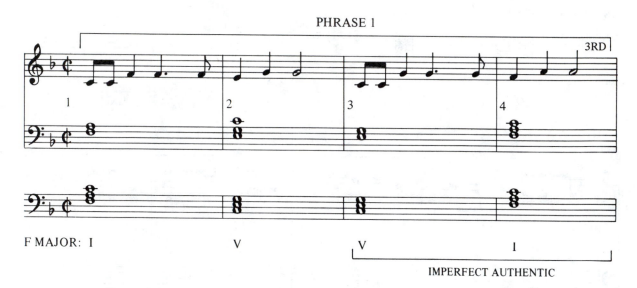

F MAJOR: I   V   V   I

IMPERFECT AUTHENTIC

PHRASE 2

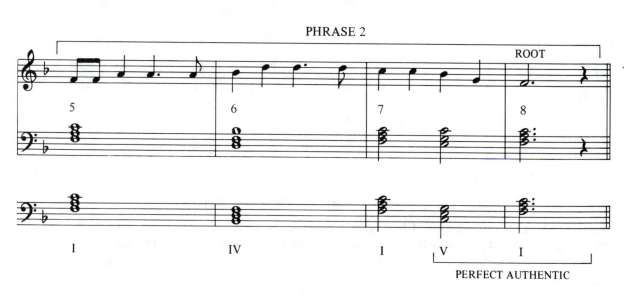

I   IV   I   V   I

PERFECT AUTHENTIC

Written Assignment

In this assignment, you will be writing the I, IV, and V triads.

A. 1. Write the I, IV, V, I progression in each of the keys indicated. The example indicates correct procedure.

    2. If you are working at a piano, play each progression. If not, get out the cardboard keyboard that comes with the book and place the fingers of your left hand over the appropriate keys for each exercise.

    3. Then, go back to the beginning of the assignment and sing (from lowest to highest note) the triads you have written. This will help in recognizing the same triads in the ear training assignments.

The most efficient way to work out this assignment is to:

    a. Write the roots of each triad on the staff first. Be sure your placement of the first root will allow enough lines and spaces for writing the remaining three triads.

    b. When all roots have been located and written, fill in the remaining two factors of all triads.

EXAMPLE:

1.

B♭M: I   IV   V   I

2.

GM: _____ _____ _____ _____

3.

Em: _____ _____ _____ _____

4.

FM: _____ _____ _____ _____

5.

Dm: _____ _____ _____ _____

6.

Gm: _____ _____ _____ _____

7.

DM: _____ _____ _____ _____

8.

Bm: _____ _____ _____ _____

9.

E♭M: _____ _____ _____ _____

10.

Cm: _____ _____ _____ _____

11.

AM: _____ _____ _____ _____

12.

F♯m: _____ _____ _____ _____

13.

A♭M: _____ _____ _____ _____

14.

Fm: _____ _____ _____ _____

15.

EM: _____ _____ _____ _____

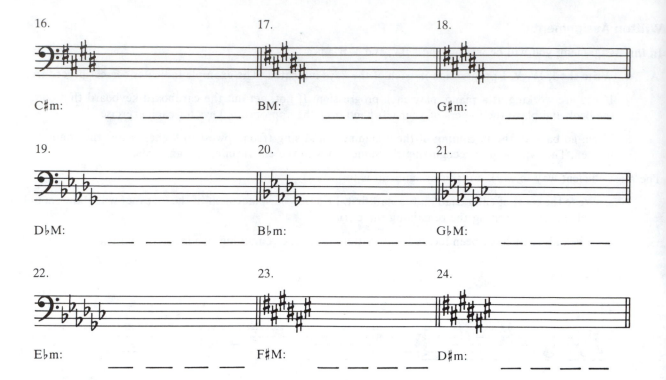

16. C#m: __ __ __ __

17. BM: __ __ __ __

18. G#m: __ __ __ __

19. DbM: __ __ __ __

20. Bbm: __ __ __ __

21. GbM: __ __ __ __

22. Ebm: __ __ __ __

23. F#M: __ __ __ __

24. D#m: __ __ __ __

In this assignment, you will be identifying circle progressions.

B. Each exercise consists of Roman numeral analysis symbols for a set of progressions. Add slurs (⌣) to connect all circle of fifth progressions.

EXAMPLE

1. V I   IV I   V I   2. I IV V I   V I   3. V V I I IV I
4. IV I I IV IV V   5. V I   V I I IV   6. V I IV V I IV
7. V IV I I   V IV   8 I IV V I IV V   9. V V I IV I IV

C. This is the same as assignment B except that the triads are written out. The lowest note is always the root.

1. First, analyze the triads and write the Roman numeral analysis in the blanks.

2. Then, add the slurs to connect the circle progressions.

The example indicates correct procedure.

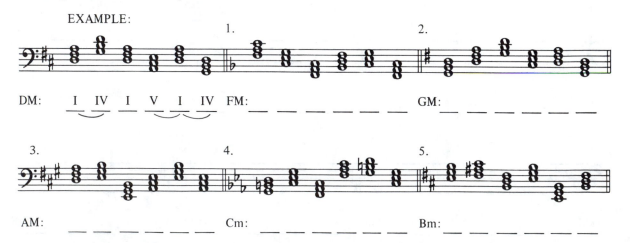

EXAMPLE:

DM: I IV I V I IV   FM: __ __ __ __ __ __   GM: __ __ __ __ __ __

1.

2.

3. AM: __ __ __ __ __ __

4. Cm: __ __ __ __ __ __

5. Bm: __ __ __ __ __ __

Written Assignment (cont.)

D. This assignment is the same as assignment C except that the lowest note may be the root, third, or fifth of the triad.

   1. First, find the root of each triad and blacken the whole note representing it.

   2. Write the analysis of each triad in the blank provided. Remember that the root is the filled-in whole note.

   3. Then, add slurs to connect circle of fifths progressions.

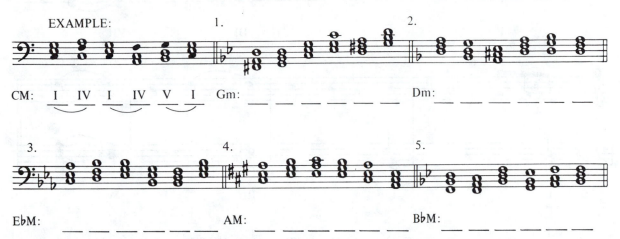

CM: I   IV   I   IV   V   I   Gm: ___ ___ ___ ___ ___ ___   Dm: ___ ___ ___ ___ ___ ___

EbM: ___ ___ ___ ___ ___ ___   AM: ___ ___ ___ ___ ___ ___   BbM: ___ ___ ___ ___ ___ ___

E. In the following exercises, you will identify nonharmonic tones.

   1. Sing each melody and play the triads in simple position (as written).

   2. Repeat the procedure in Step 1, but this time restrike the triad each time you sing a new note.

   3. Circle each melody pitch you think does not agree (is nonharmonic) with the accompaniment triad.

   4. When finished with this procedure, check the answers you determined by sound alone. If the letter name of a melody note is not one of those found in the accompaniment triad, it is nonharmonic.

Franz Schubert (1797–1828), First Movement, *Symphony No. 8* ("Unfinished") (1822)

Patrick Gilmore (1829–1892), "When Johnny Comes Marching Home" (1863)[+]

Gm   i   i   III   VII

i   i   III   V

Traditional Irish Air, "Believe Me, If All Those Endearing Young Charms"

I   IV   I   V   I

Johann Sebastian Bach (1685–1750), Bourrée, *Orchestra Suite No. 1 in C Major* (circa 1720)

C MAJOR: I   I   I   IV   V

F. Each of the following exercises, designed to assist you in identifying cadences, consists of four triads in four-voice harmony. Triads three and four form a cadence.

1. Write each triad in simple position on the blank staff provided.

2. Place the Roman numeral analysis in the blanks provided.

3. In the blank beneath triads three and four write the type of cadence: (1) Perfect Authentic, (2) Imperfect Authentic, (3) Half.

Written Assignment (cont.)

Ear Training Assignment

A. In each exercise the instructor will play seven or eight four-voice triads (a chorale phrase). Each triad may be: I or i (tonic), V (dominant), or some other triad.

    1. Write "I" or "i" in the blanks where you hear a tonic triad.

    2. Write "V" in the blanks where you hear a V (dominant) triad.

    3. Do not write in the other blanks.

1. __ __ __ __ __ __ __   2. __ __ __ __ __ __ __ __

3. __ __ __ __ __ __ __ __   † 4. __ __ __ __ __ __ __ __

† 5. __ __ __ __ __ __ __ __   † 6. __ __ __ __ __ __ __ __

Computer Program Disk: Harmony 3, Lesson B

B. In each exercise your instructor will play a phrase of five triads in four-voice harmony. Identify the I, IV, and V triads by writing their Roman numeral analysis in the appropriate blanks.

1. __ __ __ __ __   2. __ __ __ __ __

3. __ __ __ __ __   † 4. __ __ __ __ __

† 5. __ __ __ __ __   † 6. __ __ __ __ __

Computer Program Disk: Harmony 3, Lesson B

C. The purpose of this assignment is to identify tonic, dominant, and subdominant (i iv V) in seven-chord phrases. Write the appropriate analysis symbols in the blanks provided.

1. __ VI __ __ __ __ __   2. __ __ __ __ __ __ __

3. __ __ __ VI __ __ __   4. __ __ __ __ __ __ __

Computer Program Disk: Harmony 3, Lesson D

D. Each exercise is a short set of chord progressions ending in either an authentic or half cadence. In the blanks provided, write the cadence type (*authentic* or *half*). The example illustrates correct procedure.

You hear:

                        V   I (Authentic)

Answer: 1. Authentic _____   2. _____   3. _____   4. _____

        † 5. _____   † 6. _____   † 7. _____   † 8. _____

Computer Program Disk: Harmony 3, Lesson H

E. In this assignment you are asked to identify *major, minor, diminished,* and *augmented* triads. Each exercise consists of four triads (three-voice, root position). Using the abbreviations (M m d A) label all triads.

1. __ __ __ __   2. __ __ __ __   3. __ __ __ __

4. __ __ __ __   5. __ __ __ __   6. __ __ __ __

7. ___ ___ ___ ___   8. ___ ___ ___ ___   9. ___ ___ ___ ___

†10. ___ ___ ___ ___   †11. ___ ___ ___ ___   †12. ___ ___ ___ ___

†13. ___ ___ ___ ___   †14. ___ ___ ___ ___   †15. ___ ___ ___ ___

Computer Program Disk: Harmony 2, Lessons A and E

F. Each exercise consists of five triads. Only tonic (I), subdominant (IV), and dominant (V) triads are used. Write the Roman numeral analysis in the blanks provided.

Chord
No.   1   2   3   4   5   1   2   3   4   5

   1. ___ ___ ___ ___ ___   2. ___ ___ ___ ___ ___

   3. ___ ___ ___ ___ ___   † 4. ___ ___ ___ ___ ___

† 5. ___ ___ ___ ___ ___   † 6. ___ ___ ___ ___ ___

Computer Program Disk: Harmony 3, Lessons C and D

G. Each exercise consists of five triads played in four-part harmony. Four are correct as played, but one differs from that played. Circle the "wrong" chord and analyze all printed chords (Roman numeral analysis).

1. EXAMPLE (The instructor plays this):   1. EXAMPLE (You see this):

   i   iv   V   i   V   i   V   V   i   V

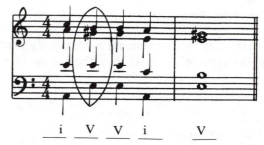

Computer Program Disk: Harmony 3, Lesson D

Chapter 27   Harmonizing a Melody

Accompanying a Melody

Some melodies, like those often found in the tradition of European concert music, are considered to be an integral part of a composition, are interlaced throughout the work, and are seldom regarded out of context. But most folk tunes and popular song melodies represent a vast accumulation of melodic wealth that is often given a personal touch by professional composers, arrangers, and of course musical amateurs. A large majority of these melodies will support different chord progressions and interpretations—to suit individual taste. Whether done by professionals or those who simply enjoy music, the process of providing interesting harmony to accompany a melody is known as **harmonizing.**

Harmonizing "The Yellow Rose of Texas"

You may have heard "The Yellow Rose of Texas" harmonized in several ways, but the way shown here is one of the simplest.

American Folksong, "The Yellow Rose of Texas"+

Triads Reduced:

CM: I   I   I   I   I   V   V   V

Sing the melody in class without accompaniment. Some observations regarding the melody and its harmonization are:

1. While you sing, some possible accompanying triads may come to mind, for often a melody will suggest its own harmony.
2. The notes of the first five measures strongly suggest a tonic (C E G) triad since all, except the nonharmonic tones (circled in the illustration), are notes of that triad.
3. The notes of the last three measures offer a less convincing suggestion of the dominant (G B D) triad. Only the 3rd and 5th (but not the root) of the G B D triad occur in the melody. Furthermore, the increased number of nonharmonic tones weakens the choice.
4. The numbered tones in the example are all nonharmonic tones. These are marked 1, 3, 4, 6, and so on. 1, 3, 4, 6, and 7 are called passing tones because they pass (either up or down) from one triad note to another.
5. Nonharmonic tones 2 and 8 are known as neighboring tones because after departing from the triad note, they return to the same note.
6. Nonharmonic tone No. 5 is called a **suspension** note; it will be discussed later.
7. This short excerpt demonstrates a most important point in harmonizing a folk song: *select triads whose notes are also melody notes.* This may be a slight oversimplification, but remembering it as a rule of thumb is quite important.
8. Also, remember that folk songs require simple accompaniments. The three primary triads, I IV V, can be used to harmonize approximately 50 percent of all folk songs.

Harmonize with Mozart

If you now have the impression that only folk songs contain simple harmony, the next illustration, by Mozart, demonstrates that recognized composers of the past also found primary triads (I, IV, and V) of ample expressive quality.

Wolfgang Amadeus Mozart (1756–1791), *Minuet in F Major for Piano*, K. 2 (1762)

Triads Reduced:

FM: I   IV   I   V   V   I

Sing the melody and play the simplified accompaniment to this excerpt. Perhaps a class member knows this composition and can play it with its more interesting full accompaniment. When you are well acquainted with the example, then observe the following:

1. The first two measures of the melody outline the tonic (I) and subdominant (IV) triads.
2. Measure three beats one and two, clearly outline the tonic triad again.
3. The two melody notes E (fourth bracket) are harmonized by the V triad because the note E is not a part of either I or IV.
4. In measure one the melody calls specifically for tonic harmonization because the entire tonic triad is outlined. However, when melody notes are stepwise, as they are near the end of this phrase, the implied harmony is not as clear.
5. Try playing this excerpt again, substituting other triads for those shown. See if you can find a harmonization that you like better than the chords Mozart selected.

Seventh Chords

While triads consist of two intervals of a third, one stacked above the other, composers often extend triads to include one further interval of a third. When an additional factor above the fifth is added, the new harmonic unit is called a **seventh chord**—so named because the new interval is a seventh above the root. Thus, a seventh chord has four factors: root 3rd 5th 7th.

Seventh chords in the key of C Major

Seventh factor is shown in whole notes

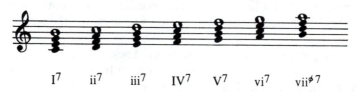

I^7 ii^7 iii^7 IV^7 V^7 vi^7 $vii^{\emptyset 7}$

Like triads, seventh chords exhibit a variety of sound qualities and are named according to the quality of the triad and the seventh. As an example, a seventh chord containing a major triad and a major seventh is termed a major-major seventh chord (MM 7th). While there are theoretically twenty possible seventh chord qualities, only those found within the notes available in the major and minor scales are used often by composers:

Some Diatonic Seventh Chord Qualities

Seventh Chord Qualities in Major Scales

TRIAD QUALITY	+	SEVENTH QUALITY	=	SEVENTH CHORD QUALITY	EXAMPLES	ROMAN NUMERALS
M		M		MM	I^7 and IV^7	Upper case
M		m		Mm	V^7 (only)	Upper case
m		m		mm	ii^7 iii^7 vi^7	Lower case
d		m		dm*	$vii^{ø7}$	Lower case

In this table of seventh chord qualities, the degree sign (°) alone would mean that both the triad and seventh is diminished, but when the slash is added, only the triad is diminished. Here the triad is diminished, but the seventh is minor.

Chord Symbols

Often, especially with popular or folk songs, the melody is printed but the accompanying chords are not. When this is done, you will usually see the *chord symbols* written above the melody. The letters refer to the roots of the chords, and the chord quality follows. Some people place the symbol for the seventh chord on the level with the root name and some use a superscript. The meaning is the same.

Following are some frequently used chord symbols:

CHORD SYMBOL	MEANS	SPELLED
G	Major triad whose root is G	G B D
Gm	Minor triad whose root is G	G B♭ D
G#m	Minor triad whose root is G sharp	G# B D#
G^7	Mm7th chord whose root is G (Triad is major, 7th is Minor)	G B D F
Gm^7	mm7th chord whose root is G (Triad is minor, 7th is minor)	G B♭ D F
$Gmaj^7$	MM7th chord whose root is G (Triad is major, 7th is major)	G B D F#

Observe the use of chord symbols in the following song. In this example the actual chords (in simple position) have been added (bass clef) below the melody, so you can see how the melody would be harmonized. A pianist, familiar with chord symbols, would fashion an interesting accompaniment from these block chords.

First, sing the melody enough times to become familiar with it. Try playing the melody on the piano as well. When you have a good grasp of the melody, accompany it with the printed harmony—there are only three different chords: (1) G major triad, (2) A minor–minor seventh chord, and (3) D major–minor seventh chord.

*The chord with a diminished triad and a minor seventh is known as a *half-diminished seventh chord*.

Illustration of Chord Symbols

American Song, "The Man on the Flying Trapeze"+

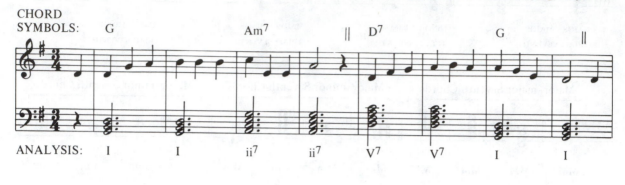

The ‖ indicates the end of a phrase. When a chord symbol is printed it is continued in force until the next symbol appears.

Keyboard and Sight Singing Assignment

A. In the following assignment you will be singing melodies and reading chord symbols.

Suggested procedure for each melody:

1. Play, then sing the melody until you learn it thoroughly.
2. On the piano, play the chord represented by each chord symbol.
3. Option: If you have difficulty playing the chords, write them out (simple position) on the blank staff below the melody.
4. After you have rehearsed the melody and chords separately, sing the melody and accompany it with the block chords played on the piano.
5. If you have had sufficient piano study, play the chords in an accompaniment pattern like one of the following:

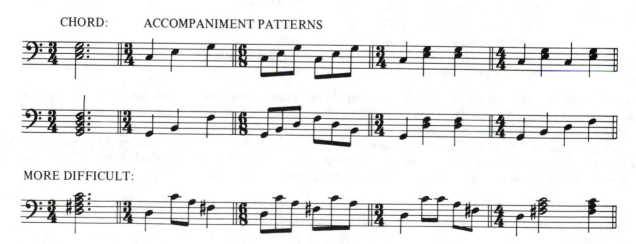

1. Jacques Offenbach (1819–1880), "My Sweetheart," *La Perichole* (1868)

2. American Folksong, "My One Mistake"+

3. American Folksong, "Wabash Cannon Ball"+

4.

American Folksong, "The Land of Arizona"+

5.

American Folksong, "Irene, Goodnight"+

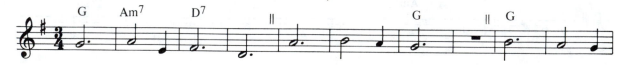

Written Assignment

A. In the following exercises you will be harmonizing melodies.

1. Sing each of the four melodies until they are thoroughly familiar to you.

2. On the staves, write the triad you think best harmonizes the melody.

3. Circle nonharmonic tones—melody notes that do not match triad notes.

4. In the blanks under the score write the triad analysis.

5. Use only the primary triads (I, IV, or V).

Use first the strategy suggested in this chapter for harmonizing each melody. Analyze the melodic segments under each bracket. As an example, in the first piece, "Home on the Range", the first bracket contains seven notes, five of which are also notes of the tonic (I) triad. The logical choice is obviously the I triad. The remaining notes (A and F♯) are passing tones and are thus circled.

When finished with this approach, cover up your answers and go to a piano, guitar, keyboard synthesizer, or some other harmonic instrument. Without any system whatsoever, and remembering that you are restricted to I, IV, and V, pick out the triad harmonization you think *sounds* best. Do the results of both approaches agree? They should! But at least you know what you are doing when you apply the first (strategic) method.

To get the creative urge out of your system, try a third approach. Avoid entirely the I, IV, and V triads, and see if you can come up with another harmonization that you think is exciting—but perhaps unorthodox!

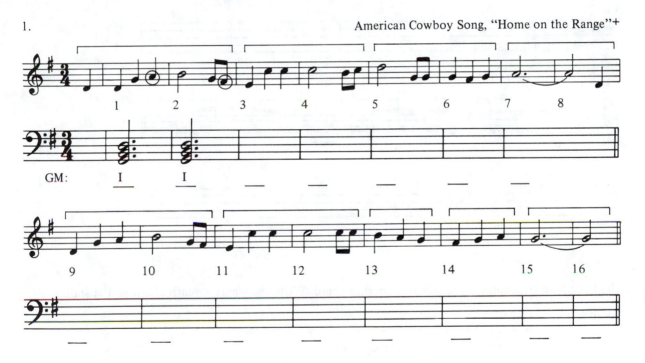

1. American Cowboy Song, "Home on the Range"+

2. Wolfgang Amadeus Mozart (1756–1791), Overture, *Nozze di Figaro (Marriage of Figaro)*, K. 492 (1786)

3. Johann Sebastian Bach (1685–1750). Gigue, *French Suite No. 5 in G Major* (1722)

GM: I

4.   American Popular Tune, "Little Brown Jug"+

CM: I

B. Each of the following notes is the root of a seventh chord. Write the whole seventh chord on the staff.

Remember: 1. Upper case "M" means major
2. Lower case "m" means minor
3. First letter indicates the type of *triad.*
4. Second letter indicates the type of *7th interval.*
5. MM = Major triad and major 7th
6. Mm = Major triad and minor 7th
7. mm = Minor triad and minor 7th

EXAMPLE:

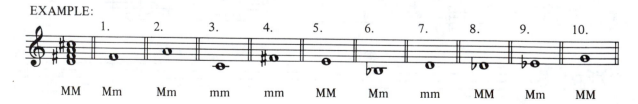

MM   Mm   Mm   mm   mm   MM   Mm   mm   MM   Mm   MM

Written Assignment (cont.)

C. This assignment will assist you in identifying seventh chord types. The possibilities are: MM (Major-Major), Mm (Major-Minor), and mm (Minor-Minor).

1. Rewrite each 7th chord in simple position (root first, then the 3rd above it, then the 5th, and finally the 7th) on the blank staff provided.

2. Write MM, Mm, or mm in the blanks under the staves.

Ear Training Assignment

A. In this assignment you are to identify (Roman numeral analysis) all chords including the V^7. Each exercise consists of five chords (listed below as 1 through 5). Write your analysis in the blanks provided.

Chord
No.   1   2   3   4   5   1   2   3   4   5

1. ___ ___ ___ ___ ___   2. ___ ___ ___ ___ ___

3. ___ ___ ___ ___ ___   † 4. ___ ___ ___ ___ ___

† 5. ___ ___ ___ ___ ___   † 6. ___ ___ ___ ___ ___

Computer Program Disk: Harmony 3, Lesson I

Chapter 28   Further Harmonizations Using I, ii, ii⁷, IV, V, and V⁷

In Chapter 27 you were introduced to the basic steps in harmonizing a melody. Expansion of this process, including some added harmonic possibilities and a few shortcuts, will facilitate and refine the undertaking.

Melody with Chord Symbols

Assuming that only the I, IV, and V^7 chords are available, examine the following short melody and chord symbols:

Friedrich Silcher (1789–1860), "The Lorelei" (Legendary nymphs of the Rhine River)

Regarding "The Lorelei":

Bracket 1   Choices: C or G^7. C was chosen because most conventional melodies such as this often begin on the I (tonic) chord. CEG=I (tonic).

Bracket 2   Choice: F (only). F (FAC) is the only chord both a C and an A.

Bracket 3   Choices: C or G^7. Either could have been used here, but the composer probably chose C (I or tonic) to avoid using the same chord for brackets 3 and 4.

Bracket 4   Choices: F or G^7. Since C is selected for bracket 3, either F or G^7 would be quite musical. Free choice here.

Bracket 5   Choice: C (only). E is the third scale degree, and it can be harmonized only with C (I or tonic). E is not a note of either FAC or GBDF.

Bracket 6   Choice: G^7 (only). The G^7 chord is the only one that contains all three notes, G, F, and D.

Bracket 7   Choices: C or F. Since composers customarily harmonize the final tonic note with a tonic chord, there is little choice here. You will understand this better by playing the melody and harmonizing bracket 7 with an FAC (IV) triad.

Some General Suggestions for Harmonizing Melodies

1. For each melodic segment, choose the chord whose notes match the largest number of melody notes. Example: For a melodic segment, G F E D C, select a C major triad (C E G) in preference to an E minor triad (E G B) because the C major triad contains three melodic notes (G E C) while the E minor triad contains only two (G and E).

2. At the end of each phrase be sure to select chords that form a cadence (authentic, half, or plagal). As an example, don't end a phrase with a ii chord because it does not form an authentic, half, or plagal cadence.

3. Chord tones should match those in the melody that are either preceded or followed by a skip (more than a whole step).

PREFERRED

AVOID

"G" IS FOLLOWED BY SKIP.
"E" IS PRECEDED BY SKIP.
BOTH ARE FOUND IN THE
CHORD.

"E" IS PRECEDED BY SKIP
BUT IS *NOT* A NOTE OF THE
CHORD.

4. Except for Rock style, a V or V⁷ chord followed by a IV triad is seldom found in the harmonization of most melodies. Rock style harmony is an exception.

CHORD	PROCEEDS USUALLY TO	OCCASIONALLY TO
I	to any other chord	
ii	V	I
ii⁷	V	
IV	V	I
V	I	
V⁷	I	

The ii, ii⁷, and IV chords are considered pre-dominant (progressing to the dominant), while the V and V⁷ chords are said to be pre-tonic (most often progress to the I—tonic).

Sight Singing and Keyboard Assignment

A. Harmonize each melody with only the chord symbol choices listed above it. Circled notes are nonharmonic.

1. First, reread the beginning of Chapter 28 and the harmonization of "The Lorelei." Without playing or singing the melody, apply the information gained from the analysis of the seven brackets in "The Lorelei" to each melody in the assignment.

2. Write down your choices in the first (highest) set of blanks provided.

3. Now, play and sing each melody until you can perform it from memory.

4. Also, play the chords to be used for each harmonization until they are also familiar.

5. Play both the melody and chords you selected (from step 1), being critical of any chord progression that sounds unmusical. If you find some you do not like, experiment with other chord combinations.

6. When you are satisfied with any chord changes you have made, write down the new chord symbol choices in the second (lower) set of blanks provided.

7. Bring to class your two sets of harmonizations (1) selected according to calculated choice, and (2) chosen through decisions made after playing and hearing your original preference.

1.

Chord Choices: C   Dm   Dm⁷   G⁷
                (I) (ii) (ii⁷) (V⁷)

2.

Giovanni Paisello (1740–1816), "The Miller"

Chord Choices: C   Dm   Dm⁷   F   G   G⁷
                (I) (ii) (ii⁷) (IV) (V) (V⁷)

3.

German Christmas Carol, "O Tannenbaum," ("Oh Christmas Tree")

Chord Choices: C   Dm   Dm⁷   F   G   G⁷
                (I) (ii) (ii⁷) (IV) (V) (V⁷)

4.   Johannes Brahms (1833–1897), *Hungarian Dance No. 5* (in the 1850's)

Chord Choices: Dm   Gm   A   A⁷
(i)   (iv) (V) (V⁷)

5.   Johannes Brahms (1833–1897), "Weigenlied" ("Lullaby") Op. 49, No. 4 (1868)

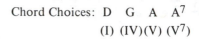

Chord Choices: D   G   A   A⁷
(I) (IV)(V) (V⁷)

B. Select one of your favorite popular or folk songs and sing it while playing the accompanying chord symbols on a piano or guitar. Perform it in class or for your instructor. If there are some chord symbols you do not understand, consult Appendix 1, which provides a list of almost all symbols in present use.

C. Select one of your favorite popular or folk songs and provide a harmonization for it. If chord symbols are already provided, erase them and write your own.

D. Compose a melody of your own in a popular or folk style. Provide a chord symbol harmonization and perform the composition in class.

Ear Training Assignment

A. Each exercise consists of five triads. Harmony in this assignment is limited to the following:

I   ii   IV   V

In the blanks provided, write the Roman numeral analysis of all chords.

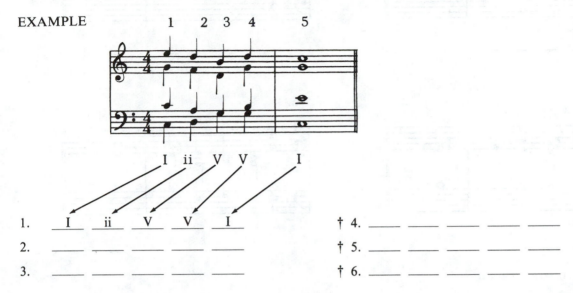

EXAMPLE   1   2   3   4   5

1.   I   ii   V   V   I   † 4. ___ ___ ___ ___ ___

2.   ___ ___ ___ ___ ___   † 5. ___ ___ ___ ___ ___

3.   ___ ___ ___ ___ ___   † 6. ___ ___ ___ ___ ___

Computer Program Disk: Harmony 3, Lesson G; also Lessons E and F

B. Each exercise consists of five triads. The harmony in this assignment is limited to the following:

i   i⁶   ii°⁶   iv   V   vii°⁶

First, write the bass notes on the music staff. Then, in the blanks provided, include a harmonic analysis of all triads. The example illustrates correct procedure.

1. EXAMPLE: 2.

i   i⁶   ii°⁶   V   i

3.

† 4.

† 5.

† 6.

Computer Program Disk: Harmony 3, Lesson G

Appendix 1   Chords in Popular Music

Comprehensive List of Chords Found in Popular Music

Following is a comprehensive list of chords found in popular song accompaniments with the most common symbols used in this style. Note that the symbols are somewhat different from some others you have learned for the same chords. All are based on C but may be transposed to any other tone:

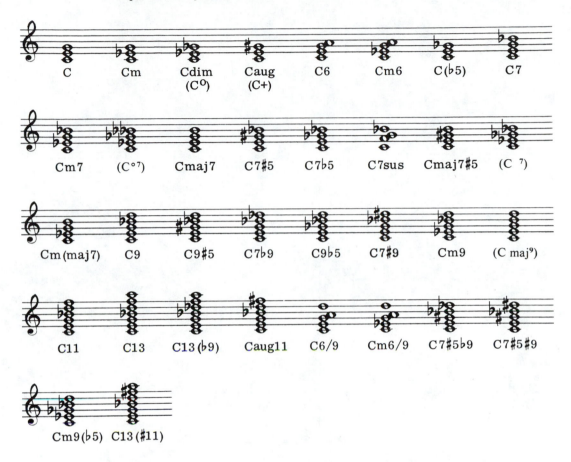

Appendix 2   Nonharmonic Tones

We call the embellishing notes that do not belong to the harmony being sounded *nonharmonic tones*. We have seen such tones in melodies outlining chords in Part V, which covered harmony.

The names we use for nonharmonic tones describe the melodic patterns made by the *note preceding* the nonharmonic tone, the *nonharmonic tone itself*, and the *note to which it moves*. As the nonharmonic tone is normally dissonant with the harmony we can also describe the pattern as:

preparation note————————►nonharmonic tone————————►resolution

Each of the common patterns will be illustrated in the examples that follow. The nonharmonic tones are circled in the examples.

The passing tone is approached and left by step in the same direction. The nonharmonic tone may be accented or unaccented. The pattern may be up or down.

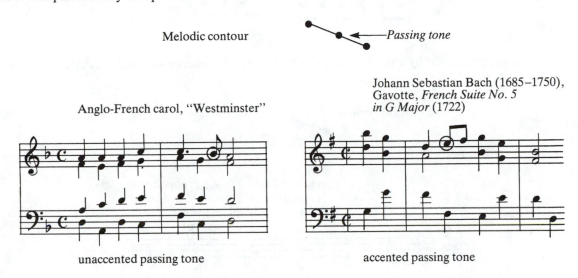

Nonharmonic tones may occur anywhere in the texture—in the top voice, in inner parts, or in the bass. Those in the examples above are both in the top voice, but you will see other examples in which the nonharmonic tones are in some other part of the texture.

The *neighboring tone* is approached and left by step, but it moves back to the original pitch for the resolution note. Neighboring tones may be accented or unaccented, and the pattern may go up or down.

The **appoggiatura** is approached by leap and left by step *downward*.

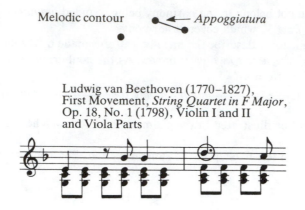

Ludwig van Beethoven (1770–1827),
First Movement, *String Quartet in F Major*,
Op. 18, No. 1 (1798), Violin I and II
and Viola Parts

The **escape tone** is approached by step and left by skip. It is usually unaccented, and it is often approached from below and left by a downward leap.

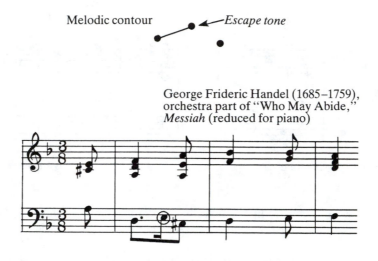

George Frideric Handel (1685–1759),
orchestra part of "Who May Abide,"
Messiah (reduced for piano)

The **suspension** is prepared by a chord tone that is continued into the new chord (either tied or repeated) and which then resolves downward into a chord tone of the new chord. The suspension note itself is on an accented part of the beat.

Giovanni Pierluigi da Palestrina (1525–1594), "Kyrie eleison"
("Lord, Have Mercy"), Mass on *Aeterna Christi Munera* (1590)

The example above also has passing tones in it. Draw a square around each passing tone. The **retardation** is like a suspension except that the resolution is *up* instead of down.

Melodic contour

Chord movement

Retardation
(approached from the same
note and resolves up)

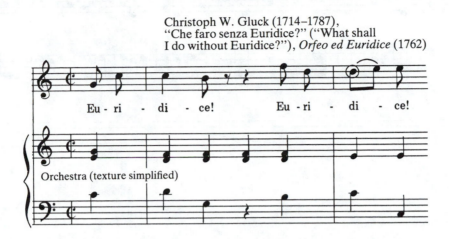

Christoph W. Gluck (1714–1787),
"Che faro senza Euridice?" ("What shall
I do without Euridice?"), *Orfeo ed Euridice* (1762)

Eu - ri - di - ce!   Eu - ri - di - ce!

Orchestra (texture simplified)

This example also has a suspension in it. Draw a square around the suspension note.

The **anticipation** anticipates the chord to come by arriving ahead of the beat on which the chord changes.

Melodic contour

Chord movement

Anticipation
(May be approached
from above or below)

Johann Sebastian Bach (1685–1750),
Gavotte, *French Suite No. 5 in G Major* (1722)

When a long note is held in the bass while harmonic or melodic activity in which it does not participate goes on above it, it is called a **pedal tone,** because in organ music it is very often found in the pedal part, as in the Bach **fugue** below.

Johann Sebastian Bach (1685–1750), *Organ Fugue in G Minor*

Pedal tone

Appendix 3   Introduction to Musical Forms

The materials and patterns studied in the chapters are formed into larger structures that also show coherent patterns. Although the study of these forms in depth is beyond the scope of this book, a brief description of some forms from which examples have been drawn for this book would be handy for you to have. Our description starts with the ways in which phrases are combined to form larger units.

Combination of Phrases: The Period

Phrases can be combined to form a larger structure called the **period.** Most periods contain two phrases which are sometimes called *question* and *answer* phrases. The formal name for the first phrase of a period (the "question") is the **antecedent** (that which goes before); for the second phrase (the "answer"), the **consequent** (that which follows).

Johannes Brahms (1833–1897), Fourth Movement,
Symphony No. 1 in C Minor (1876)

If the two phrases of a period begin alike, the structure is called a *parallel period*.

Wolfgang Amadeus Mozart (1756–1791), First Movement,
Piano Sonata in A Major, K. 330i (1781–83)

Parallel period (first two measures alike)

The two phrases of a period may be related in such a way that melodic motion in one direction is answered by motion in the opposite direction. Sometimes tonic harmonies in the first phrase are answered by dominant harmonies in the second phrase, or vice versa. Either of these types of period construction is called *opposite construction of a period*.

Ludwig van Beethoven (1770–1827), First Movement,
Sonata in D Major for Piano, Op. 28 (1801)

Opposite melodic motion in a period

Ludwig van Beethoven (1770–1827), First Movement,
Sonata in C Minor for Piano, Op. 10, No. 1 (1797)

I   Antecedent phrase   V   V   Consequent phrase   I

Opposite harmonic construction in a period

When the two phrases of a period begin in different ways and use contrasting materials, the period is called a *contrasting period.*

Carl Maria von Weber (1786–1826), Overture,
Der Freischütz (*The Freeshooter*), (1817–1821)

Antecedent phrase   Consequent phrase

Contrasting period (phrases use different materials)

The cadence of the first phrase of a period usually has less feeling of finality than that of the second phrase. Often the cadence of the first phrase uses a note of the dominant triad for the final note of the cadence. This means that the first phrase will be harmonized with a dominant chord on the final note (a *half cadence*). The consequent phrase then answers this with a cadence ending on the tonic chord (*authentic cadence*).

French Folk Song, "On the Bridge at Avignon"

Larger Complete Forms

Since musical forms are intimately connected with the style periods in which they originate, these descriptions will be grouped according to historical periods. Forms first used in one period usually continue to affect music of succeeding eras and often are used in new ways by composers of a later age. It also often happens that a form name will refer to one kind of piece when it is first used and will later come to have a very different meaning.

Form names tell us something about the way a piece of music is organized or structured. They may tell us what to expect as one section follows another, or they may indicate the musical procedures or devices by which it is put together. Some form names also indicate the character or spirit of the piece. Sometimes the name shows the way the music would be used, as in dance music or music for religious services. Another type of form name may tell us that the music is organized as part of a dramatic stage presentation, that it takes its shape from the text, or that some other relationship to another art has helped to shape the musical plan. And, of course, many musical structures are a mixture of several of these aspects.

Medieval Period (ending about 1400 A.D.)

Carol. Although we now use **carol** to mean a Christmas song, in the Middle Ages it was a song with refrains (sections of recurring text and music) that were frequently religious seasonal songs. They were festive in spirit and originally were also *dance songs.*

Mass. The service of the Catholic Church that celebrates the Last Supper is the *mass.* In the Middle Ages the whole service could be sung, and the music for service use, which was sung in unison, was called *Gregorian chant.* The melodies of Gregorian chant have been in use for over a thousand years. A *requiem* is a special mass for the dead.

Round. A composition in which one voice has a melody that is exactly imitated by each succeeding voice which begins the melody at a different time. "Row, Row, Row Your Boat" is a familiar modern example. The oldest round known dates from about 1240 A.D. "Sumer is i-cumin in" (page 163). A *round* can also be called a **canon.**

Renaissance Period (ending about 1600)

Chorale. The hymns sung by the congregation in the Lutheran service from the sixteenth century on (page 53) are called *chorales.* "Sleepers awake" is an example of a *chorale* tune. The first section of the music is usually repeated (with new words) and is followed by a section which is not the same as the first part. These three parts of the tune can be represented by the letters AAB. "A Mighty Fortress is Our God," by Martin Luther, is another well-known example of a chorale.

Madrigal. A term commonly used for sixteenth century polyphonic compositions setting Italian or English poetry. Madrigal does not imply a specific or predictable formal plan; the pieces are often planned to reflect the meaning of the text. Some of you may have sung in a *madrigal group* which sings music like "The Silver Swan," by the English composer Gibbons (see Appendix 4), "Suggested Listening List."

Mass. Fifteenth century composers began to set the portions of the text of the Catholic mass in which the words were always the same as a multisectional musical whole. The practice has continued since that time. Typically five sections of the mass were set with polyphonic music, and in the service, the other portions of the ritual might still be sung with the old melodies of Gregorian chant. On your listening list, masses by Palestrina (a sixteenth century Italian composer of church music) are suggested for you to hear.

Pavan. By the Renaissance many kinds of dance music were being written down. One of the important dances of the time was the *pavan,* a slow stately processional dance in duple time. There is an example for you to sing on page 112.

Baroque Period (ending about 1750)

Dance Forms. New kinds of dances arise with every new style period reflecting changes in taste and fashion. Dance music was used to dance to, but eighteenth century listeners also enjoyed hearing the music by itself. Even when these pieces were not danced, the distinctive rhythms that accompanied the dance remained the basis of the music. Dances of this period usually have a two-part form (also called **binary form**) and each part is repeated. Some of the dances in the musical excerpts in this book include the **sarabande,** **minuet** (*menuet*), and **gavotte.** You may know others from music you have heard or played—**allemande, courante,** and **gigue** are also dances from this period. Listen to J. S. Bach's *French Suite in E Major* for some wonderfully characteristic baroque dances.

Fugue. An imitative contrapuntal piece in which each line enters with a distinctive melodic idea (called a *subject*) that is imitated by each other entering voice, and which appears again and again in the course of the piece. Unlike the round, the strict imitation does not continue throughout. J. S. Bach wrote many fugues. Listen to the first fugue of the *Well-Tempered Clavier* (a collection of preludes and fugues in all keys).

Prelude. **Preludes,** as the name suggests, are intended to precede something. A special type of prelude often preceded the singing of Lutheran chorales; preludes may also be the first movement of a *suite* or other group of movements. The *Well-Tempered Clavier* of Bach precedes each fugue with a prelude; listen to the first prelude. The form name does not indicate a predictable formal pattern, but instead refers to the function as an opening musical event.

Opera and *Oratorio.* These large scale dramatic-musical forms were born in the Baroque era and have been important in all subsequent periods. A **cantata** is a smaller, similar work. **Opera** is performed with stage action and many types of opera are sung throughout. **Oratorio** is usually a dramatic choral work that is performed without stage action. Extended musical pieces for a soloist in opera, oratorio, or cantata are called *arias.* Baroque arias are usually in a **three-part musical form,** with the last part a repeat (*da capo*) of the first part, making a form which can be represented by the letters *ABA*. The best known Baroque oratorio is probably Handel's *Messiah*. The aria "The Trumpet Shall Sound" in *Messiah* is an *ABA form*.

Suite. Dances and other short instrumental pieces were grouped together to form *suites*. Another term which usually means the same thing is **partita**. J. S. Bach's *Orchestra Suite No. 2 in B Minor* is on your listening list.

Concerto. In the early eighteenth century **concerto** meant an orchestral piece in several movements which was sometimes for the orchestra as a whole but usually for one or more soloists and orchestra. Commonly there were three movements of contrasting tempo: fast—slow—fast. You will enjoy hearing a concerto by Vivaldi: "Primavera" (Spring) *Concerto*, which is the first of a group of concertos depicting the four seasons.

Classic Period (ending in the early nineteenth century)

Classic Concerto. Classic concertos are usually for one soloist and orchestra, and frequently the solo instrument is the piano. There are three movements, fast—slow—fast, but the formal patterns found within each movement are new in the late eighteenth century. The first movement is related to the **sonata** and an outline of its formal plan will be found with the discussion of **sonata-form.** Many different patterns might be chosen for the slow movement and the last movement is usually a **rondo** which will also be discussed later. Mozart loved the new woodwind instrument of the period—the clarinet—and wrote a wonderful concerto for it which you should hear.

Rondo. The last movement of many classic sonatas, concertos and symphonies is a rondo, a form in which the opening theme returns again and again after contrasting sections called episodes. A common rondo plan, in which the *rondo theme* is A, would be A B A C A. Its character is usually lively, like the last movement of Haydn's *Trio for Violin, Cello and Piano in C Major,* which is listed in Appendix 4.

Sonata. In the classic era, this is a multimovement instrumental form. It may be for piano or for piano with another instrument. If more than two instruments are involved the name given the piece will indicate how many: thus we speak of *trios, quartets, quintets, octets,* and so on. Such combinations frequently do not use piano. Commonly there are three or four movements using various classic forms. The opening movement (and sometimes other movements as well) uses a form called *sonata-form*, in which the order of events is as shown in the following diagram. The concerto modification of this plan is also shown in the diagram in simplified form. You may listen to the first movement of Beethoven's *Sonata in F Major for Violin and piano, Op. 24* (known as the "Spring" sonata) for an example of sonata-form.

Symphony. A work using classic forms in a multimovement piece for orchestra is called a **symphony.** Commonly symphonies have four movements. The first movement is usually in *sonata-form,* the second movement is usually a slow movement, and the third movement is a dance movement, usually a *minuet*. The minuet in a classic symphony is actually a large *ABA form,* in which each part of the form is a complete *binary form*. This dance is in triple time. The last movement may be a sonata-form, a theme and variations, a rondo, or some other form.

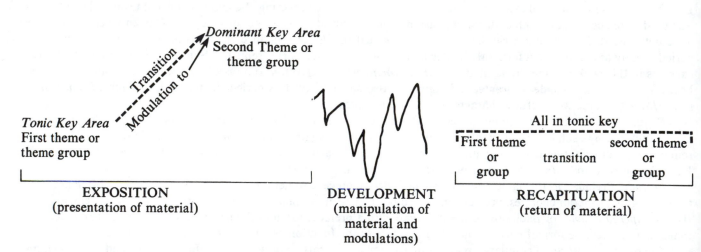

Classical Sonata-form

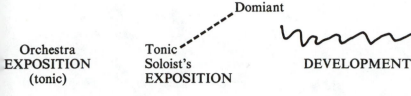

| Orchestra
EXPOSITION
(tonic) | Tonic
Soloist's
EXPOSITION | **DEVELOPMENT** | (tonic)
RECAPITULATION | cadenza | Coda |

Classical Concerto first-movement-form

Romantic Period (nineteenth century)

The romantic period continued to use most of the classic forms. Some new dances appeared, especially the **waltz,** a dizzying dance in triple time which became almost a symbol for Vienna. National dances from other parts of Europe often were used as instrumental pieces, especially for the piano. The Polish composer Chopin uses **mazurkas** and **polonaises** for wonderful piano pieces. Romantic music often stresses representation of extra-musical ideas—something which was *not* new to the 19th century but which acquired the name **program music.**

In the United States, religious songs of black Americans called **spirituals** became widely known, especially after the Civil War.

The Twentieth Century

Musicians of the twentieth century have been free to experiment with all sorts of new designs or to use new materials with any of the formal plans or procedures of the past. Often they will use old terms as in Bartok's *Concerto for Orchestra* which uses the work *concerto* as some Baroque composers did for a piece exploiting the orchestra as a whole rather than to mean a work for soloist and orchestra.

Some important new elements have come from the music of the United States, particularly through Black influences. *Ragtime* was a syncopated style of the early twentieth century employed especially in piano *rags* with very regular formal plans based on the 16-bar period (or **strain**) similar to marches and dances of the end of the 19th century. Scott Joplin's "Maple Leaf Rag" is in the form AABBACCDD. **Blues** is a term that describes the spirit and expressive devices used to perform music as well as the blues form harmonic progression and scale.

Appendix 4   Suggested Listening List

This list includes many of the works from which examples in the text have been drawn.

Medieval
Gregorian chant

Renaissance
Palestrina, Pierluigi da. *Missa Aeterna Christi Munera* or *Pope Marcellus Mass*
Gibbons, Orlando. "The Silver Swan"

Baroque
Bach, Johann Sebastian. *French Suite VI in E Major* (harpsichord or piano recording)
　　Prelude and Fugue in C Major, No. 1, Well-Tempered Clavier, Book I
　　Orchestra Suite No. 2 in B Minor for Flute and Strings
Handel, George Frideric. *Messiah*
Vivaldi, Antonio, "Primavera" (Spring), from *The Seasons* concertos

Classic
Mozart, Wolfgang Amadeus. *Symphony No. 41 in C Major*
　　Piano Sonata No. 11 in A Major, K. 331
　　Concerto for Clarinet and Orchestra
　　Music from the soundtrack of the movie *Amadeus*
Haydn, Joseph. Trio in C Major, H. XV:25
　　The Creation

Romantic
Beethoven, Ludwig van. *Sonata in F Major for Violin and Piano* ("Spring"), Op. 24
　　Symphony No. 5 in C Minor
　　Leonore Overture No. 3
Chopin, Fryderik. "Minute" Waltz
　　Mazurkas
Brahms, Johannes. *Liebeslieder Waltzer* (Lovesong Waltzes)
Mendelssohn, Felix. *Symphony No. 4 in A Major* ("Italian")
Mussorgsky, Modest. *Pictures at an Exhibition* (either the original piano version or Ravel's orchestration)
Strauss, Johann (Jr.). "Blue Danube Waltz"
Schumann, Clara. *Trio in G Minor for Violin, Cello, and Piano*
Dvořák, Antonin, *Symphony No. 9 in E Minor*, "New World"
Tchaikovsky, Pyotr Il'yich, *Symphony No. 4*
Sor, Fernando. *Variations on a theme of Mozart* for guitar
Verdi, Giuseppe. *La Traviata* (excerpts)

American (pre-World War I)
Billings, William. "Chester" and "When Jesus Wept"
Foster, Stephen. Selected songs
Sousa, John Philip. Selected marches
Joplin, Scott. Piano rags

Impressionism
Debussy, Claude. *Prélude à l'apres-midi d'un faune (Prelude to The Afternoon of a Faun)*
　　Selected piano preludes
Ravel, Maurice. *String Quartet*

Twentieth Century
Bartók, Béla, *Concerto for Orchestra*
Stravinsky, Igor. *Petrouchka Suite* or *Rite of Spring*

Copland, Aaron. *Appalachian Spring* or *Billy the Kid*
Schoenberg, Arnold. String Quartet No. 4 or *6 Little Piano Pieces*
Schuman, William. *Chester Overture*
Ives, Charles. *The Unanswered Question* or Variations on *America*
Ligeti, György. *Atmospheres*
Varèse, Edgar. *Deserts*
Smithsonian Classic Jazz Collection

Appendix 5 Chronology

The Old World (musical events in bold)

800 B.C.	Rise of Greek city-states
753 B.C.	Founding of Rome
c. 4 A.D.	Birth of Jesus
70	Destruction of the Temple of Jerusalem
112	**Pliny reports hymn-singing among Christians**
313	Emperor Constantine issues edict of toleration for Christianity
	Gradual development of Catholic liturgy and Church Chant
476	Fall of Rome
590	*Gregory the Great* becomes Pope (Gregorian Chant subsequently named for him)
1025	**Musical staff developed by Guido of Arezzo**
1163	Building of Notre Dame Cathedral begins in Paris
	Troubadours, Trouvères, and Minnesingers produce love songs
1260	**Sumer Is Icumen In—the earliest music round**
1307	Dante's *Divine Comedy*
c.1400	**Triads become the basis of harmony**
1431	Joan of Arc burned at the stake during Hundred Years War
1456	Gutenberg prints Bible with moveable type
1492	Queen Isabella finances Columbus's first voyage to New World
1501	**First music printed with moveable type**
1517	Martin Luther posts his 95 theses; **subsequently he composed hymns for Lutheran worship services**
1530	Copernicus's study of the solar system
1558	Elizabeth I becomes Queen of England
1588	Defeat of the Spanish Armada. **First English madrigals.**
	Palestrina and Gabrieli flourish in Italy Byrd and Morley flourish in England
1594	Shakespeare's *Romeo & Juliet*
1600s	**Beginning of opera in Italy. Composers include Giulio Caccini, Francesca Caccini, and Claudio Monteverdi**
1602	Galileo Galilei discovers law of falling bodies
1618	30 Years' War begins in Germany
1643	Louis XIV King of France (until 1715)
1667	Milton's *Paradise Lost*
1680s	**Corelli composing in Rome, François Couperin and Elizabeth Jacquet De La Guerre active in France**
1685	**Johann Sebastian Bach, George Friderick Handel, and Domenico Scarlatti born**
1690	**Antonio Stradiarius's career as a violin maker at its height**
1714	George I King of England **Handel composing opera in London**
1720s	Voltaire flourishing in France
1729	Birth of Moses Mendelssohn, philosopher and grandfather of **Felix and Fanny Mendelssohn. First performance of Bach's *St. Matthew Passion* in Leipzig**
1737	**First sonatas of Domenico Scarlatti published**
1742	**Handel, *Messiah***
1750	**J. S. Bach dies**
1757	**Joseph Haydn begins writing string quartets**
1776	American War of Independence begins
1780s	**Wolfgang Mozart in Vienna**
1789	Fall of the Bastille begins French Revolution
1790	**Haydn visits London**
1793	Reign of Terror in France
1798	**Haydn, *The Creation***
1800	Napoleon crowned Emperor
1807	**Beethoven, *Fifth Symphony***
1808	Goethe, *Faust, Part I*

1815	Battle of Waterloo. **Metronome invented**
1827	**Death of Beethoven**
1839	**Chopin, *Preludes* for Piano, written while on Majorca with novelist George Sand**
1840	**Marriage of Clara Wieck and Robert Schumann. Invention of the saxophone in France**
1848	Revolutions in Europe. Karl Marx and Friedrich Engels, *Communist Manifesto*
1853	Crimean War, nursing work of Florence Nightingale. **Verdi's opera *La Traviata* written.**
1864	Tolstoy, *War and Peace*. **Brahms active in. Vienna Waltzes of Johann Strauss, Jr. popular**
1870	Franco-Prussian War
1876	**First Wagner Festival at Bayreuth**
1888	Pasteur Institute in Paris opens, continuing the work of Louis Pasteur. **Tchaikovsky, *Fifth Symphony***
1894	**Antonin Dvořák, *New World Symphony*. Claude Debussy, *Afternoon of a Faun***
1900	Sigmund Freud, *The Interpretation of Dreams*
1902	Discovery of radium by Marie and Pierre Curie
1905	Albert Einstein, special relativity theory
1910	**Composers active include: Debussy, Ravel, Bartók, Mahler, Schoenberg, Stravinsky, Vaughan Williams, Richard Strauss, Sibelius**
1914–18	World War I
1920s	**Schoenberg discusses method of composing with 12 tone row, Nadia Boulanger teaches at Fountainbleau. Composers active include Hindemith, Berg, Webern, Shostakovich, Prokofiev, Milhaud, Honegger, Poulenc**
1929	Beginning of Great Depression
1930s	Beginnings of World War II, rise of Hitler to power
1941	**Young composers active include Benjamin Britten (England) and Oliver Messiaen (France)**
1945	End of World War II
1960	**Composers Active: Stravinsky, Poulenc, Hindemith, Orff, Messiaen, Britten, Stockhausen, Penderecki, Ligeti, Nono, Boulez. The Beatles rock group formed in Liverpool**
1971	**Stravinsky dies in New York and is buried in Venice**
1985	Mikhail Gorbachov takes power in the USSR

The New World

1492	Columbus lands in New World
1518	Cortes conquers Mexico
1565	St. Augustine, Florida settled by Spain
1607	English settlement at Jamestown
1619	Blacks first brought to Jamestown as indentured servants
1620	Plymouth colony founded. Colonists bring **Psalm books for congregational singing**
1630	**First polyphonic music published in the New World in Lima, Peru by Bocanegra (Catholic music in the Inca language)**
1640	*Bay Psalm Book* **first book printed in English colonies**
1692	Salem Witchcraft trials
1756	French and Indian Wars
1761	**Benjamin Franklin invents musical instrument (Glass Armonica). His musical friends include Francis Hopkinson and Thomas Jefferson**
1770	**William Billings publishes** *The New England Psalm Singer*
1776	Declaration of Independence
1780s	**Musical activities flourish in Moravian settlements at Bethlehem, Pennsylvania and Winston-Salem, North Carolina. Composers include John Frederick Peter and John Antes**
1789	George Washington becomes president
1803	Louisiana Purchase
1827	Mormon Church founded
1836	Independence of Texas
1839	**New York Philharmonic founded**
1845	**Louis Gottschalk writing music in Louisiana**
1846	Smithsonian Institution founded

1850	Hawthorne writes *Scarlet Letter;* Longfellow writes *Evangeline*
1851	**Stephen Foster writing songs**
1854	Thoreau writes *Walden*
1861	Beginning of Civil War. **Great outpouring of popular songs in both North and South**
1863	Emancipation Proclamation
1865	Assassination of Lincoln
1875	Mary Baker Eddy writes *Science and Health*
1877	**Thomas Edison invents the phonograph**
1892–95	**Antonin Dvořák teaches in United States, hears black American music sung by his American student Henry T. Burleigh, writes *New World Symphony***
1894	**Charles Ives enrolls at Yale**
1891	**John Philip Sousa, "The Stars and Stripes Forever"**
1899	**Scott Joplin, "Maple Leaf Rag"**
1903	Wright brothers' first air flight
1908	First Model T Ford
1909	Frank Lloyd Wright active as architect. **Gustav Mahler comes to U.S. to conduct New York Philharmonic**
1914	**W. C. Handy, "St. Louis Blues".** World War I begins
1917	U.S. enters World War I
1924	**George Gershwin's "Rhapsody in Blue"**
1920s	**Tin Pan Alley composers active: Jerome Kern, George M. Cohan, George Gershwin, Irving Berlin: Jelly Roll Morton's *Red Hot Peppers* Great Jazz Group. Many young Americans study with Nadia Boulanger in Paris—Aaron Copland, Walter Piston, Roy Harris**
1930	**Edward Kennedy (Duke) Ellington, "Mood Indigo"**
1930s	**Long careers of Louis Armstrong, Ella Fitzgerald, Billie Holliday, Benny Goodman, Duke Ellington underway**
1940s	**Many European composers in United States as refugees: Bartók, Hindemith, Stravinsky, Milhaud, Kurt Weill, Schoenberg. Young Americans active: Samuel Barber, William Schuman, John Cage**
1941	Pearl Harbor bombed; U.S. enters World War II
1940s	**Latin American composers include Heitor Villa-Lobos (Brazil), Carlos Chávez (Mexico), and Alberto Ginastera (Argentina)**
1944	**Aaron Copland, *Appalachian Spring* written for Martha Graham (American modern dancer)**
1945	First atomic bomb dropped. End of World War II
1945	**Charlie Parker joins forces with Dizzy Gillespie—Rise of Be-Bop style and small combos**
1950	Korean War. **Gian-Carlo Menotti, *The Consul***
1958	**Varèse, *Poeme Electronique* (composition with electronic music)**
1960	First working laser beam
1963	Assassination of President J. F. Kennedy
1965	**First performance of Ives' *Fourth Symphony***
1960s	Civil Rights issues. Involvement in Vietnam War
1968	Assassination of Robert Kennedy and Martin Luther King. **Woodstock Festival**
1969	Americans land on the moon
1970s	**Younger composers active in U.S. include: George Crumb, David Del Tredici, Thea Musgrave, Paul Chiharra**
1977	**Zubin Mehta conducts *Star Wars Suite* in Los Angeles Hollywood Bowl using laser beams for a mixed media event**
1986	Seven astronauts die in space shuttle

Appendix 6　Keyboard Harmony Supplement

In both Part IV and Part V of this text, suggestions have been made for playing common progressions on the keyboard, and for using model progressions to transpose to all keys. A group of common progressions is given here in one place for convenience. Each progression is given in both C major and C minor, and can be played in all major and minor keys.

It is quite helpful to practice keyboard harmony progressions as rhythmically as possible, so these examples are metrically notated. You may practice them with other rhythmic patterns of your own invention once you have learned the progression. They can be practiced all in one mode or as given here, with the minor immediately following the form of the progression in the same meter and tempo.

Play the following progressions as notated and then play them substituting the V⁷ for the V chord in each progression.

Notice that this progression is like no. 2, with ii^6 (ii_o^6) substituted for IV (iv).

Appendix 7 Fingerboard Harmony for Guitar

The guitar is tuned as follows:

When guitar music is written on a staff, it is notated an octave higher and is read in treble clef.

When guitar music is notated to show fingering and finger patterns instead of pitches, the notation is called *tablature.* Each vertical line corresponds to a string with the lowest string at the left. Each horizontal line represents a *fret,* with the top line representing the end of the string.

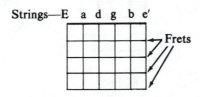

An "X" above a string means that the string is not to be sounded; the black dots show the placement of each finger (just behind the fret). Arabic numbers show a common way of fingering each chord (index finger "1," middle finger "2," ring finger "3," and little finger "4") and "o" means an *open string* (with no fingers stopping the string).

Actual notes played

X 3 2 0 1 0

Simple position of the triad

Thus, a C major chord could be notated in these three ways shown.

When chords are strummed on the guitar they do not necessarily follow the same principles of doubling or voice-leading as in keyboard harmony. Strummed guitar chords are so arranged that a note of the chord will be on every string from the bottom string played up. One may begin a chord above the lowest string, but from the lowest note played no higher strings are skipped. The chords given in this supplement are so arranged that they sound good strummed on the guitar and are easy to reach with the hand. The chords in these progressions make very limited use of the bar fingering (in which the first finger is laid flat across more than one string, stopping two or more strings at once), and keys using this fingering can easily be omitted if desired.

When letter notation is used, a capital letter stands for a major triad; a capital letter followed by "m" stands for a minor triad, and a capital letter with "7" stands for a major-minor (dominant type) seventh chord. The easiest and most frequently used major keys on the guitar are F, C, G, D, A, and E. The easiest and most often used minor keys are d, a, and e, but c, g, and f minor are also given here.

The Commonly Used Triads

First, learn to strum these common triads, starting with the bottom string to be played and brushing across the strings with the right thumb. For some chords alternate fingerings are given. Use the one you find easiest and most comfortable.

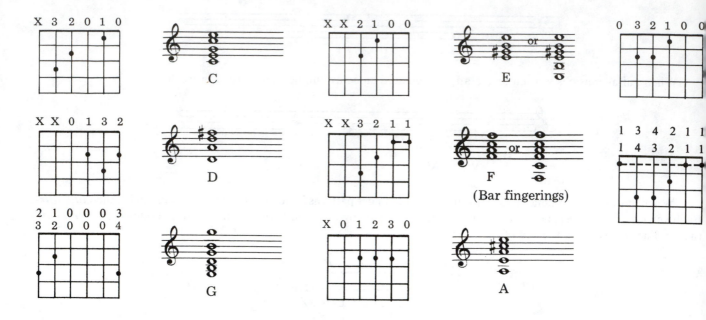

Here are the most commonly used triads.

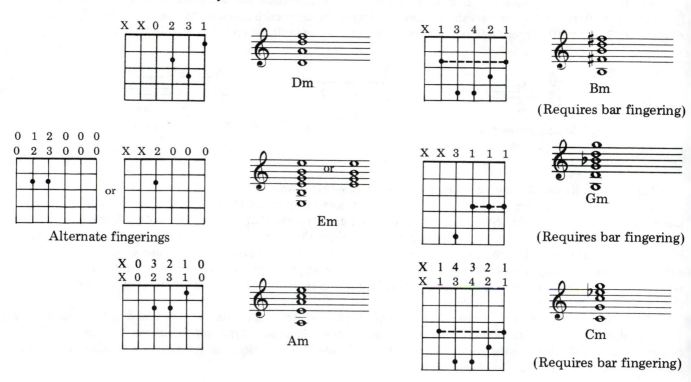

The Dominant Seventh Chord

The V^7 in the commonly used keys for the guitar is notated as follows:

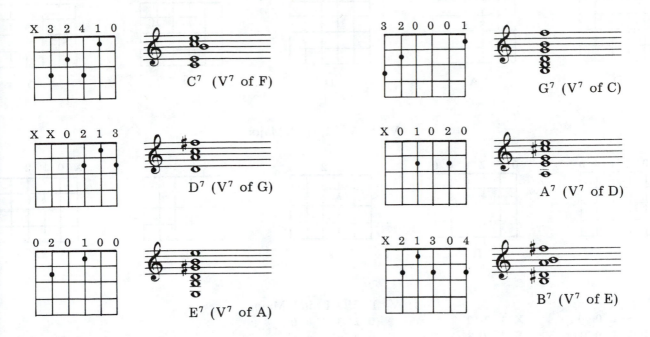

The I V I and I V^7 I Progressions

By playing the progression I V I V^7 I in all keys used, you can become familiar with the use of both the dominant chord and the dominant seventh chord. (In guitar chords the V^7 is used very frequently and is usually used instead of the vii° so no progressions for the use of the diminished triad are found in this book. For fingerings for diminished and augmented triads consult more advanced books on guitar playing.)

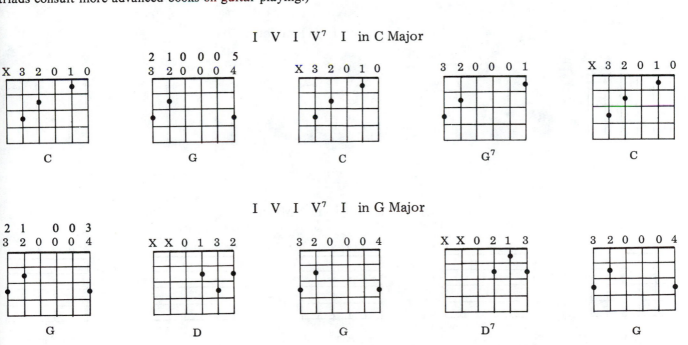

Remember that fingerings can be chosen or altered to fit your own hand. These fingerings are *suggestions*.

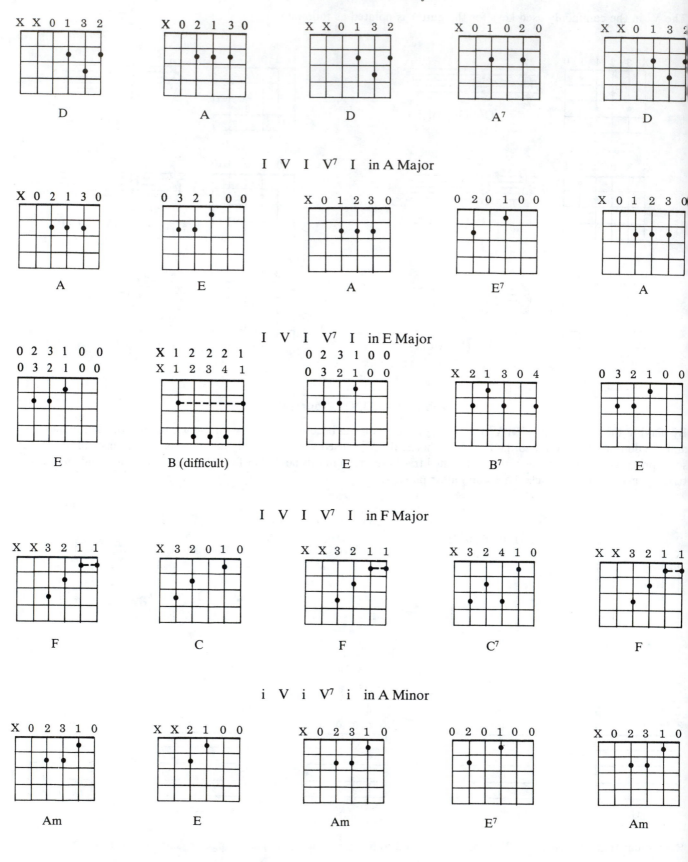

I V I V⁷ I   in D Major

X X 0 1 3 2   X 0 2 1 3 0   X X 0 1 3 2   X 0 1 0 2 0   X X 0 1 3 2

D   A   D   A⁷   D

I V I V⁷ I   in A Major

X 0 2 1 3 0   0 3 2 1 0 0   X 0 1 2 3 0   0 2 0 1 0 0   X 0 1 2 3 0

A   E   A   E⁷   A

I V I V⁷ I   in E Major

0 2 3 1 0 0   X 1 2 2 2 1   0 2 3 1 0 0   X 2 1 3 0 4   0 3 2 1 0 0
0 3 2 1 0 0   X 1 2 3 4 1   0 3 2 1 0 0

E   B (difficult)   E   B⁷   E

I V I V⁷ I   in F Major

X X 3 2 1 1   X 3 2 0 1 0   X X 3 2 1 1   X 3 2 4 1 0   X X 3 2 1 1

F   C   F   C⁷   F

i V i V⁷ i   in A Minor

X 0 2 3 1 0   X X 2 1 0 0   X 0 2 3 1 0   0 2 0 1 0 0   X 0 2 3 1 0

Am   E   Am   E⁷   Am

308   APPENDIX 7 FINGERBOARD HARMONY FOR GUITAR

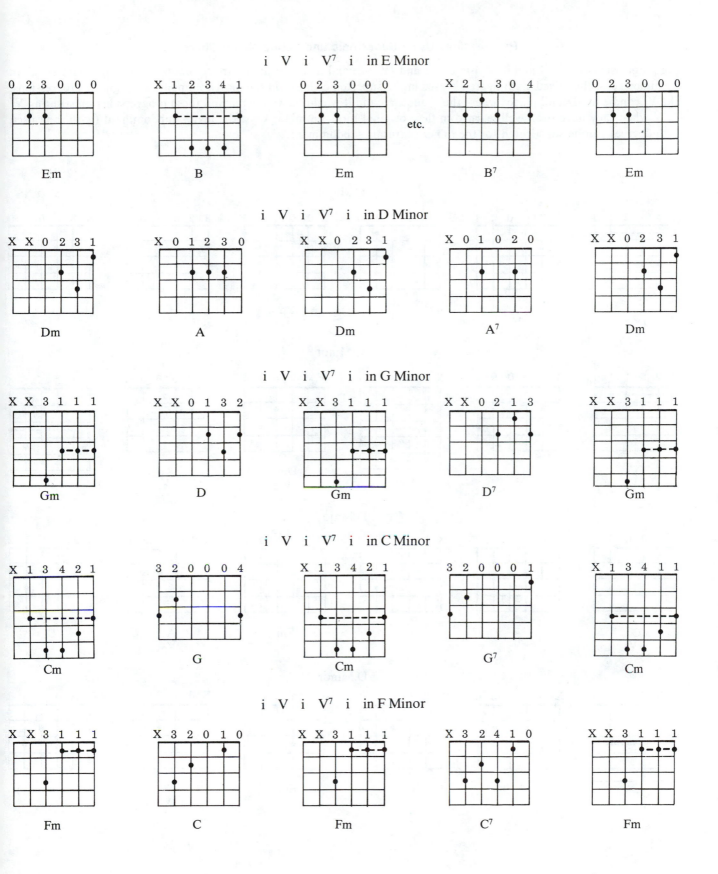

Progressions Using Supertonic and Subdominant Chords

The progressions IV V I and ii V I in major and IV V i and ii V i in minor are common and useful progressions. In the minor keys, the raised sixth degree is used in the supertonic chords in the most commonly used guitar progressions. The V^7 can be used in all places where the V appears, and it would be well to play all these progressions substituting V^7 for V when they have been well learned in their original form. In minor keys, the major subdominant (with the raised sixth degree) can be substituted for the minor (natural) subdominant.

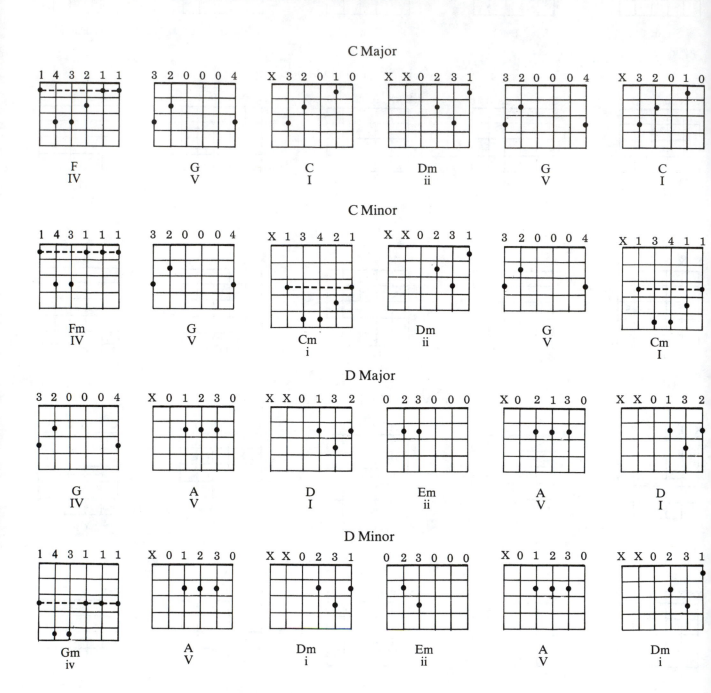

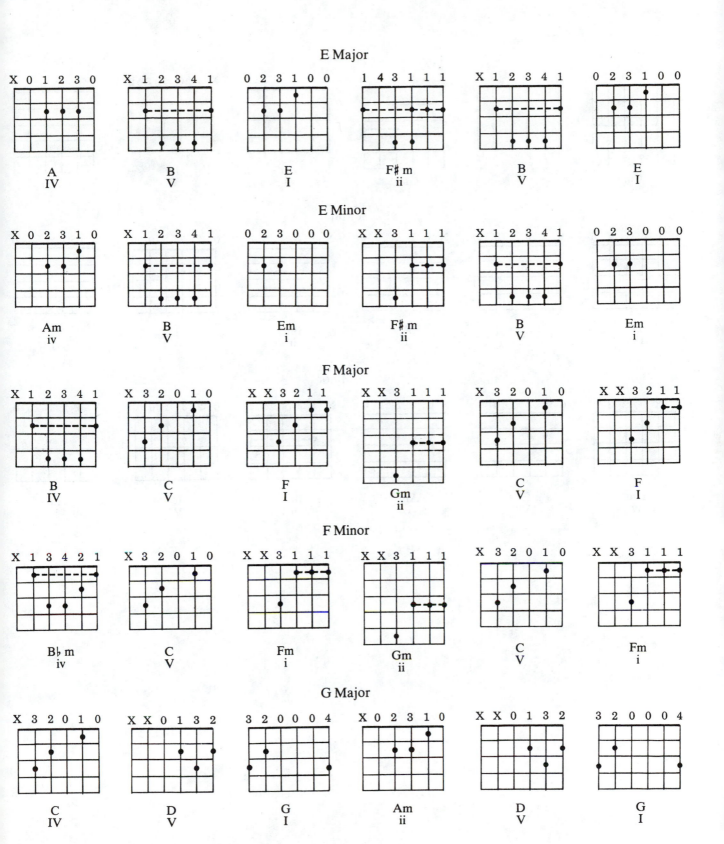

E Major

X 0 1 2 3 0	X 1 2 3 4 1	0 2 3 1 0 0	1 4 3 1 1 1	X 1 2 3 4 1	0 2 3 1 0 0
A IV	B V	E I	F♯m ii	B V	E I

E Minor

X 0 2 3 1 0	X 1 2 3 4 1	0 2 3 0 0 0	X X 3 1 1 1	X 1 2 3 4 1	0 2 3 0 0 0
Am iv	B V	Em i	F♯m ii	B V	Em i

F Major

X 1 2 3 4 1	X 3 2 0 1 0	X X 3 2 1 1	X X 3 1 1 1	X 3 2 0 1 0	X X 3 2 1 1
B IV	C V	F I	Gm ii	C V	F I

F Minor

X 1 3 4 2 1	X 3 2 0 1 0	X X 3 1 1 1	X X 3 1 1 1	X 3 2 0 1 0	X X 3 1 1 1
B♭m iv	C V	Fm i	Gm ii	C V	Fm i

G Major

X 3 2 0 1 0	X X 0 1 3 2	3 2 0 0 0 4	X 0 2 3 1 0	X X 0 1 3 2	3 2 0 0 0 4
C IV	D V	G I	Am ii	D V	G I

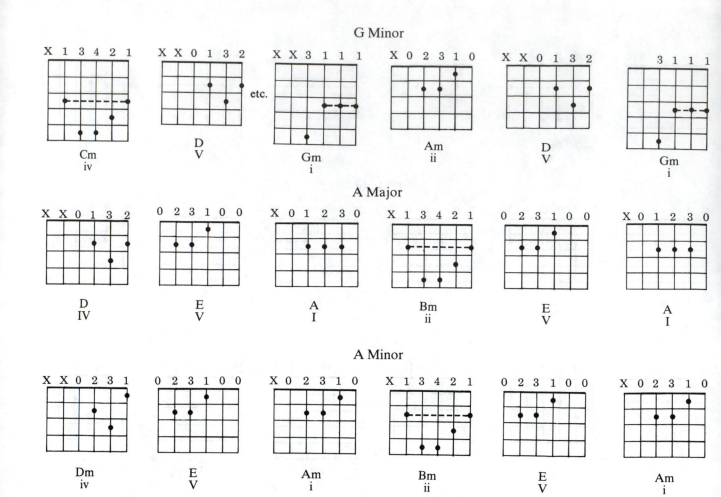

Glossary

Accent—Usually, to make a tone or tones sound louder.

Accelerando—To accelerate or increase the tempo (usually it is gradual).

Accidentals—Flat, sharp, or natural signs.

Acoustics—The branch of physics that deals with sound and sound waves.

Alla Breve—$\frac{2}{2}$ or ¢ meter. Also referred to as "cut time." The beat is in half-note values.

Allegro—Quick tempo.

Allemande—A sixteenth- through eighteenth-century dance in moderate duple time.

Alto—The voice range below the highest range. Usually the lower range of female or children's voices. In four part music, the second part is the alto part.

Anacrusis—Upbeat. The third beat of $\frac{3}{4}$ or fourth beat of $\frac{4}{4}$ meter.

Andante—A slow, walking tempo.

Antecedent—The first of two phrases in an antecedent–consequent (question–answer) relationship.

Anticipation—A nonharmonic tone that anticipates a note of the chord to follow.

Appoggiatura—A nonharmonic tone that features a leap to the dissonant note.

Asymmetric meters—Meters (or meter signatures) whose beats cannot be divided into two, three, or four equal parts.

Atonal—Without a tonal center. Used in some twentieth century music.

Augmented interval—Equal to a perfect or major interval plus one-half step. Example: P4th=C to F. Augmented 4th=C to F♯.

Authentic cadence—Cadence consisting of V to I, occasionally, vii°⁶ to I.

Bar—Same as measure.

Bar line—A vertical line drawn through a staff (or staves) to indicate the end of one measure and the beginning of the next.

Bass—The lowest voice range. The lowest range of men's voices. In four-part music, the bottom part is the bass part.

Bass clef—Also known as the "F clef," this indicates that the second line (down) of the staff is the F below middle C.

Beam—A thick straight line that connects two notes at the end of the stems. Notation: ♫ Beam.

Beat—A unit of metric (rhythmic) meter.

Beat unit—The note value that receives a single beat in a measure.

Binary form—Two-part form.

Breve—A note found in music before the end of the seventeenth century and equal to two whole notes in value.

Blues—A stylistic song developed by black Americans that often features a major scale with flatted third and seventh (and sometimes others).

Cadence—A melodic–harmonic formula that occurs at the end of a composition, section, or phrase indicating a pause—a momentary or permanent conclusion of the musical content.

Canon—A device (sometimes a complete composition) that features strict melodic imitation.

Cantata—A vocal form since the seventeenth century that is based on a continuous but sectional text of a sacred or secular nature. Frequently contains arias, recitatives, duets, choruses, and sometimes organ or orchestral accompaniment.

Carol—Most often, a traditional song celebrating Christmas. Less often a piece that celebrates Easter or other sacred or secular holidays or events.

C clef—Also known as the "movable clef," this indicates that middle C is located wherever the clef is placed. The C clef may be placed on any line or space of the staff. Notation: ⸿K

Changing meters—Meter signatures change during the course of a composition. Example: begins with $\frac{4}{4}$ meter, changing to $\frac{3}{4}$, and eventually to $\frac{5}{4}$, and so on.

Chorale—A hymn tune, from which a *setting* (harmonization or arrangement) is made by an individual composer. Bach harmonized a number of chorale melodies and used them often in cantatas and other sacred works.

Chord—Technically, the simultaneous sounding of any three or more pitches. For this text, intervals of a third are stacked one on top of the other to produce triads and seventh chords.

Chord symbols—Symbols, usually placed above the staves to indicate the use of particular chords. Example: A7 D bm em A D G. Not to be confused with Roman numeral analysis symbols (usually placed below the staves): I IV V, and so on.

Chord tones—Notes or pitches that are part of the harmony. Nonharmonic tones are notes that are *not* a part of the harmony.

Chromatic—Sometimes refers to half-step melodic movement in which the letter name does not change but the pitch does: C C♯ or D♭ to D. Occasionally designates pitches that are not part of a diatonic scale: F♯ is a chromatic in the key of C major.

Chromatic scale—The scale made up of all the half-steps within an octave.

Circle of fifths—Pitches (often tonic) in a pattern of descending perfect fifths (B E A D G C F, and so on). Displayed often to help in memorizing key signatures.

Circle progressions—A harmonic progression or progressions whose roots proceed by descending perfect fifths: A D G C are all circle of fifth progressions.

Clef—A symbol placed upon a staff to indicate the name and pitch of the notes corresponding to its lines and spaces. Most common clefs are the treble and bass. Notation: Treble 𝄞 Bass 𝄢 .

Common time—$\frac{4}{4}$ meter.

Compound intervals—Intervals larger than a single octave. Example: Major tenth is the equivalent of a major third and a perfect octave.

Compound meter—Meters containing a background of three subbeats instead of two. Example: $\frac{6}{8}$ meter, with two main beats (1 and 4) but three subeats: 1 2 3 and 4 5 6. In contrast, $\frac{2}{4}$ also with two main beats (1 and 2) by subbeats in groups of 2: 1 and 2 and. Some other compound meters are: $\frac{9}{8}$, $\frac{12}{8}$, $\frac{6}{4}$, and $\frac{9}{4}$.

Concerto—A composition featuring a solo instrument such as piano, violin, trumpet, or clarinet and an orchestra. The orchestra is on an equal basis with the solo instrument—*not* an accompaniment.

Conjunct motion—Notes in succession in which adjacent notes are no further apart than a major second.

Consequent (phrase)—The second phrase of a period in antecedent–consequent (question–answer) relationship.

Consonance—A smooth or agreeable sounding interval. The consonances are unisons, thirds, fourths, fifths, sixths, and octaves, in contrast to the dissonant intervals (see **dissonance**).

Courante—An early (seventeenth and eighteenth century) type of dance $\frac{3}{4}$, $\frac{3}{8}$, or $\frac{3}{2}$ meter.

Crescendo—Becoming gradually louder.

Decrescendo—Becoming gradually softer.

Diminished interval—An interval created by reducing a perfect or minor interval by one-half step while maintaining the same letter names.

Diminuendo—Becoming gradually softer.

Disjunct motion—Melodic movement where the interval between adjacent pitches is greater than a major second. The opposite of disjunct is conjunct.

Dissonance—A harsh or restless sounding interval. The dissonances are seconds, sevenths, and the tritone (augmented fourth, diminished fifth).

Dominant—The fifth scale degree. In the key of C major, G is the dominant.

Dot—Adds half again the durational value to the note immediately before it.

Double bar—Two vertical lines drawn through a staff or staves. Most often it designates the end of a composition or section thereof.

Double flat—Two flat signs before a note that lower the pitch two half-steps below its original. Example: B♭♭ is the same pitch as A.

Double sharp—A decorated "X" before a note. Raises the pitch two half-steps above its original. Example: C✖ is the same pitch as D.

Downbeat—The first beat of a measure—an accented beat.

Duple meter—$\frac{2}{2}$, $\frac{2}{4}$, $\frac{2}{8}$, and so on. A measure contains two beats.

Duration—The length of time a musical sound continues or exists.

Dynamic—Intensity of loudness or softness.

Eighth note—A note with half the value of a quarter note. To notate, add a flag to a quarter note. It also is notated through the use of a single beam (which connects the eighth note to another note).

Embellishments—Ornamental notes (most often in small notation) such as trills or turns.

Enharmonic—Pitches that sound the same but that are spelled differently. Example: The note B is enharmonic with C flat.

Escape tone—A nonharmonic tone approached by step and left by skip.

Fermata—The sign: ⌢. Placed above or below the note, the performer plays the pitch with about twice its designated length.

Fifth—Interval of a fifth. C up to G is a fifth.

Fifth of the triad—The fifth factor of a triad or a fifth above the root of a triad.

First inversion—The position of a triad when the third factor is the lowest sounding pitch. Example: E G C is the first inversion of the C major triad.

Flag—A rhythmic notational sign. Note without flag: ♩ . Note with flag: ♪ . One flag designates an 8th note; two flags, a 16th note; three flags, a 32nd note; and so on.

Flat—Flat sign: ♭. Placed before a note on the staff, it directs the player to play the pitch one half step lower.

Forte—Designated by the sign: *f*. Means loud.

Forte piano—Loud, then suddenly soft, notated *fp*.

Fortissimo—Designated by the sign: *ff*. Means very loud.

Fourth—Interval of a fourth. C up to F is a fourth.

Fret—The small metal strips or gut placed across on the fingerboard of stringed instruments like the mandolin and guitar. Frets guide the player in placing fingers on the fingerboard. The violin, viola, cello, and string bass are nonfretted instruments.

Fugue—An instrumental composition (often for keyboard instruments) of contrapuntal design, featuring considerable imitation, and popular in the eighteenth century.

Gavotte—An old French dance in $\frac{4}{4}$ meter and strongly accented.

Gigue—A jig. A very fast dance, usually in $\frac{6}{8}$ meter, of English origin.

Glissando—The playing of rapid scales (as on the piano using the thumb), or continuous ascending or descending sounds (possible on the violin or trombone).

Grace notes—A type of ornament in vocal and instrumental music. In modern notation, grace notes are written as very small notes with a slash through the stem.

Grand staff—The two staves combining the treble and bass clefs.

Half cadence—A cadence that ends with a dominant chord. The most common progressions are I to V or IV to V.

Half note— ♩ is the symbol for a half note. It has half the value of a whole note, twice the value of a quarter note.

Half step—The smallest interval on the piano keyboard, or the interval between two adjacent frets on the guitar. C to C♯ is a half step. The only half steps between adjacent white keys on the piano are E to F and B to C.

Harmonic—Relating to harmony; simultaneous sounds. Sometimes used as a synonym for upper partials or overtones.

Harmonic interval—The interval between two pitches that sound at the same time (simultaneously).

Harmonic minor (Scale)—A minor scale that uses an accidental to raise the seventh degree of the scale by one half step. This produces a leading tone (half step tending to move upwards) between the seventh and eighth notes of the scale.

Harmonizing—The process of selecting chords to accompany and support a melody.

Harmony—In general, any combination of simultaneous sounding tones. The vertical aspect of music—chords.

Hemiola—In $\frac{6}{8}$ meter rhythmic accents sometimes shift from the first and fourth beats to the first, third, and fifth (giving the effect of $\frac{3}{4}$ meter). Frequently found in the compositions of Brahms.

Imperfect cadence—An authentic cadence, but one that differs from the perfect authentic only in that the final chord (tonic) does not contain the tonic in its highest sounding voice.

Intensity—The loudness or softness of a musical sound.

Interval—The difference in pitch between two tones. The interval between C and D is two half steps (one whole step) and is called a *major second*.

Inversion of an interval—An interval can be inverted by placing the lowest of the two pitches above the upper pitch or placing the upper of the two pitches below the lower one.

Inversion of a triad—A triad placed in any arrangement where the root is not the lowest-sounding pitch.

Key signature—Flats or sharps that are arranged in a particular order at the beginning of each staff to indicate the key of a composition.

Leading tone—Seventh scale degree (pitch) in major, harmonic minor, and ascending melodic minor scales. In the natural minor the seventh scale step is called the subtonic because it is a whole step from the adjacent tonic.

Leger lines—Short horizontal lines above or below a clef upon which to write notes not within the normal range of the clef.

Legato—A term indicating phrasing. Perform legato passages as if each note were slurred to the next. No interruption (silence) between notes.

Major scale—A seven-note scale with half step intervals between scale degrees 3–4 and 7–8. (Other intervals are whole steps.)

Mass—The highest ceremony of the Catholic Church—may be spoken or set to music. The Ordinary (always a part of the Mass) consists of the Kyrie, Gloria, Credo, Sanctus, and Agnus Dei. The texts of other parts of the mass (known as the Proper) vary.

Mazurka—A dance originating in Poland, usually in $\frac{3}{4}$ meter with a characteristic accent on the third beat.

Measure—A group of meter beats separated by bar lines (vertical lines, known as *measure bars,* drawn through the staff or staves). Example: In $\frac{3}{4}$ meter a measure consists of three beats.

Mediant—The third scale degree. Example: In C major "E" is the mediant scale degree.

Melodic contour—The general contour (ascending or descending) of a melody.

Melodic interval—The difference in pitch between two tones that are sounded one after the other (melodically).

Melodic minor (Scale)—Ascending form contains half-step intervals between the second and third, and seventh and eighth scale degrees. The descending form consists of half-step intervals from the sixth to fifth, and the third to second scale degrees. The descending form is the same as the natural minor scale.

Melodic motive—A very short but identifiable fragment of melody that is often repeated exactly or in a modified state throughout a composition or shorter section thereof. A motive (also motif) consists of as few as two notes and generally does not exceed eight or ten.

Melody—A succession (horizontally) of musical tones that possess shape or pattern.

Meter—The basic system of regularly recurring pulses. Example: Each unit of $\frac{3}{4}$ meter contains three steady pulses with a steady accent on the first pulse of each group. The 3 means three beats per group (measure), and the 4 indicates that the quarter note value is the basic pulse.

Metric—Refers to meter.

Metronome—A mechanical device with a pendulum that "clicks" the basic pulse (meter). A weight on the pendulum permits different tempi to be selected.

Mezzo forte—Literally medium loud. Notated: *mf* .

Mezzo piano—Literally medium soft. Notated: *mp* .

Middle C—The note C nearest the middle of the keyboard. As written, it is the C written on the leger line between the bass and treble clef. Indicated as c′.

Minor key—A key based on any of three scales: natural minor, harmonic minor, melodic minor. *Key* indicates the beginning note of the scale. Example: "F minor" means a minor key using the scales beginning on the pitch F.

Minor scale—Generic term that may refer to any of three scales: natural minor, harmonic minor, or melodic minor.

Minor triad—Triad made up of a minor third from root to third and a perfect fifth from root to fifth.

Minuet—A French court dance of moderate tempo and $\frac{3}{4}$ meter. So named because of the small steps involved.

Mixed meters—Occasionally two (or more) meters are indicated in a meter signature signifying some kind of alternation of the two in the composition to follow. This condition is called *mixed meters*.

Moderato—Moderate (usually tempo).

Modified repetition—Applied to two related phrases in which the second is basically the same as the first but contains some nonessential melodic decorations or slight harmonic changes.

Modified sequence—A sequence in which subsequent segments are altered slightly so as to provide additional interest without destroying the basic sequential nature of the passage.

Motive—A distinctive melodic or rhythmic figure. See also Melodic Motive and Rhythmic motive.

Music—The art of sound in time which expresses ideas and emotions in significant forms through the elements of harmony, melody, rhythm, and tonal color.

Music appreciation—In this text the term means to increase the taste and love for music through study.

Music history—In this text, includes the general history of music, musical styles, musicians, notation, musical instruments, performance practices, etc.

Music literature—In this text, refers to the vast literature of music scores and compositions written or printed in musical notation.

Music theory—The study of patterns (melodic, harmonic, rhythmic, and formal) in music.

Natural—A symbol used to cancel a sharp or flat. Notated: ♮ .

Natural (pure) minor—A scale made up of a mixture of whole and half steps with the half steps occurring from scale degrees 2 to 3 and 5 to 6.

Neighboring tone—One of the nonharmonic devices that is found between two tones of the same pitch. Under proper circumstances in the pattern "D to C to D" the middle note "C" is a neighboring tone.

Nonharmonic tone—A general category signifying a tone (or tones) that is not a factor of the accompanying or prevailing triad or chord. Passing tones, neighboring tones, suspensions, anticipations, and so on are all nonharmonic tones.

Nonmetric—Compositions or passages therein that have no defined steady meter or metric pulse.

Note(s)— Written symbols indicating the pitch and duration of a musical sound or sounds such as ♩ , ♪, and so on.

Note head—The oblong portion of a note. Note head: ● . Lacks a stem (line drawn up or down from the note head). One note that is made up entirely of a note head is the whole note.

Octave—The interval of eight notes. From C to the next C is an octave.

Opera—A staged musical drama which is usually sung throughout.

Opus—Literally, a work or composition. One of the compositions by a composer, usually numbered according to the order of publication. Example: Opus 23 precedes Opus 25. Abbreviated Op. in this text.

Oratorio—A dramatic literary work, often of sacred or heroic content, set musically for choruses, soloists, and an orchestra.

Organum—A very early (as early as 900 A.D.) type of melodic accompaniment consisting often simply of parallel perfect fourths or perfect fifths. Later organum took on the barest hint of independence of voice leading.

Parallel intervals—Two pitches, each moving melodically and maintaining the exact same intervallic distance.

Example: D E F♯ G. Parallel perfect fifths.

              G A B C.

Parallel major—A major scale beginning on the same pitch (tonic) as a minor scale. Example: C major is parallel to C minor.

Parallel minor—A minor scale beginning on the same pitch (tonic) as a major scale. Example: C minor is parallel to C major.

Partita—A seventeenth-century term applied to a collection of dance tunes or other movements.

Passing tone—A nonharmonic tone that "passes" from one chord tone to another. Example: C D E. Under proper harmonic circumstances the D is a passing tone.

Pavan—A word derived from ancient Spain, a pavan is a stately processional dance in moderate to slow duple meter.

Pedal tone—A note of extended length, usually in the bass voice, over which various harmonic progressions (both dissonant and consonant) are sounded.

Perfect cadence—Perfect authentic (V to I) cadence, where, in the final chord (I), the tonic note is both the highest and lowest sounding tone.

Perfect consonance—The name given to perfect intervals (P8, P5, P4, and P Unison). The perfect 4th, although considered a consonance in abstraction, is actually treated as a dissonance in harmonic practice.

Perfect intervals—P octave, P5, P4, and P unison.

Period—A combination of two or more related phrases culminating in closure (usually a perfect authentic cadence).

Phrase—The "sentence" of musical speech. Phrases tend to be about four measures long; they end with some kind of cadence.

Piano—Soft. Notation: $\boldsymbol{p}$.

Pianissimo—Very soft. Notation: $\boldsymbol{pp}$.

Pitch—A sound made up of steady vibrations. The note a′ (middle "A" on the piano) has a rate of 440 vibrations per second.

Polonaise—A processional dance in $\frac{3}{4}$ meter of Polish origin.

Position—The arrangement of a triad—root position, first inversion, or second inversion.

Prelude—An introductory section of music preceding the main portion of the composition. Also, a separate short composition.

Preparation note—A consonant pitch that prepares a suspension (nonharmonic) figure.

Primary triads—The I, IV, and V triads.

Program music—Music written to conform to or express an extramusical idea, program, poetic idea, or imaginative scheme.

Progression—The succession of one chord to the next. Sometimes refers to an entire series of chord movements.

Quadruple meter—Indicates meters containing four beats: $\frac{4}{2}, \frac{4}{4}, \frac{4}{8}$. May sometimes be extended to include compound meters such as $\frac{12}{8}, \frac{12}{16}$, and so on.

Quarter note—The notation ♩ means a note that is the equivalent of one pulse in $\frac{4}{4}$ meter.

Quality—A general term that usually applies to harmony, but that may on occasion also include intervals. Examples: "The chord quality is major.", "The interval qualities were consistently dissonant."

Rags—Ragtime compositions.

Ragtime—Originally a type of highly syncopated piano music later to become jazz.

Relative major—A major key that shares the same key signature with a minor key. The tonic of the relative major is the third degree of the relative minor scale.

Relative minor—A minor key that shares the same key signature with a major key. The tonic of the relative minor is the sixth degree of the relative major scale.

Repeat sign—A double bar with two dots beside it; the symbol means that a section should be repeated. Notated: :||

Resolution—To relieve dissonance by following it with an appropriate consonance.

Rest—A rest is a silence indicated by a musical symbol. The sign for this measured silence is also called a rest.

Retardation—Similar to a suspension except that the retardation resolves upward by step. Suspensions resolve downward by step.

Rhythm—The time relationships in music.

Rhythmic motive—A motive whose distinguishing features are provided primarily by rhythm rather than conspicuous pitch relationships.

Ritardando—Gradual reduction of tempo. Same as rallentando.

Rondo—A larger musical form featuring a recurring main theme interspersed with one or more contrasting elements. Example of form: A B A C A B A. A is the main theme, while B and C are the contrasting elements.

Root—The generating pitch upon which a triad is based. Example: In the triad C E G, C is the root.

Root position—A triad or chord position in which the root is the lowest sounding pitch.

Round—A composition consisting of imitating voices whose entrances are spaced at regular intervals. A particular type of canon at the unison.

Sarabande—A dance of Spanish origin, usually with a slow tempo, in triple meter.

Scales—The various notes of a particular tonality arranged stepwise.

Scale degree—Particular note of a scale. Example: In C major the third scale degree is E.

Second—The interval formed by adjacent notes of a major or minor scale. Seconds may be major (two half steps), minor (one half step), diminished (no half steps), or augmented (three half steps).

Seventh chord—A chord formed by a triad to which an additional third (above the fifth) is added. Example: G B D is a triad. G B D F is a seventh chord.

Second inversion—The position of a triad in which the lowest sounding tone is the fifth factor. Example: G C E is the second inversion of the C E G triad.

Sequence—A musical device in which a short section of music is repeated on different scale degrees. Example: C D E D E F E F G. D E F is a sequence of C D E as is E F G.

Sevenths—The interval formed by a note seven letter names above or below a given pitch. Example: C up to B and B down to C are both intervals of a seventh.

Sforzando—Sudden accent. (Also sforzato). Notation: *sf* (or) *sfz* .

Sharp—(1) The symbol (♯) meaning to raise the pitch of a note by one half step. (2) Sometimes employed in regard to tuning. Example: "The C you are playing is too sharp."

Simple intervals—Intervals no greater than an octave.

Simple meter—Meter in which there are two subdivisions of the beat.

Simple position—Closest possible arrangement of a triad or chord in root position. Example: C E G is the simple position of the C major triad.

Sixteenth note—The notation ♪ means half the rhythmic value of an eighth note. Four sixteenth notes equal one quarter note.

Sixths—The interval formed by a note six letter names above or below a given pitch. Example: C up to A or A down to C is a sixth.

Sixty-fourth note—The notation ♬ means half the rhythmic value of a 32nd note. Sixteen notes equal a quarter note value.

Slur— A curved line above or below a series of notes indicating that the notes should be played legato (closely connected with no time lapse between notes). Notation: ♩♩♩♩♩ .

Sonata—An instrumental composition (often solo piano or piano and violin) usually consisting of three or four individual pieces (movements).

Sonata form—The form of a particular movement of a sonata, symphony, string quartet, or of a variety of individual compositions. Sonata form consists of three main sections, exposition, development, and recapitulation.

Soprano—The highest voice range. Usually the higher range for voices of women and children. The top part of four-part music.

Spirituals—Religious folk or composed songs. Spirituals in general are the cultural heritage of black Americans. More recent spirituals are often called gospel songs.

Staccato—Notation consists of a dot directly above or below a note. A staccato note is to be played with much less than its notated value. Thus, a staccato quarter note might be played as an eighth note value with silence consuming the remainder of the quarter note value.

Staff—The five parallel lines across a page of music permitting the placement of notes. The plural is staves.

Staves—Plural of staff.

Stem—The part of a note (except the whole note) that consists of a straight line that connects to the note head.

Step—Adjacent letter name. A step up from C is D. A step down from C is B. Step usually connotes no more than two half steps.

Strain—A small portion of music, possibly a phrase or period. Also, a verse or chorus of a song.

Submediant—The sixth scale step of major and minor scales. Example: A is the submediant step of the C major scale.

Subdominant—The fourth scale step of major and minor scales. Example: F is the subdominant step of the C major scale.

Subtonic—The note a whole tone below the tonic. The seventh note of the natural minor scale is a subtonic.

Suite—From the seventeenth through the nineteenth century a suite was a collection of dances. During the twentieth century the term has been broadened to include a collection of shorter compositions of any type.

Supertonic—Second scale step of major or minor scales. Example: D is the supertonic step of the C major scale.

Suspension—An accented nonharmonic tone preceded by repetition and followed by a tone one step lower. Example: C C B. Assuming the second C to be dissonant, it is a suspension note.

Symphony—A composition played by a symphony orchestra usually with several movements. Also, a full orchestra consisting usually of string, woodwind, brass, and percussion sections.

Syncopation—A shift from the normal metric accent to one not usually accented. Example: In $\frac{4}{4}$ meter, an accent on the fourth beat is considered a syncopation.

Tablature—A system of notation where notes are not placed on a staff but are indicated by letters, figures (like drawings of a fingerboard), or other symbols. Example: Guitar tablature shows the fingerboard of the guitar and places dots where fingers are to be placed.

Tempo—The speed at which the beat moves. Allegro is a fast tempo; adagio is a slow tempo.

Tenor—The upper voice range of male voices. In four-part writing, the third voice down is the tenor voice.

Third of the triad—The note a major or minor 3rd above the root of the triad.

Thirds—Intervals of a third (major, minor, diminished, or augmented).

Thirty-second note—Half the value of a 16th note. Eight 32nd notes equal a quarter note value. Notation: ♬ .

Three-part musical form—Made up of three sections each a complete (comes to closure) composition in itself. The third section is a repeat (or modified repeat) of the first section. Thus, the form: A B A. Found often as the Minuet–Trio–Minuet movement of classical symphonies.

Tie—A curved line extending between two adjacent notes of the same pitch signifying that the second of the two notes is held rather than sounded again. Notation: ♩♩ .

Timbre—The tone color or quality of a sound. The difference between the sound of a violin and the sound of a clarinet is a difference in timbre.

Time signature—Also known as meter signature. Two numbers one above the other, placed on the staff at the beginning of a composition (and elsewhere when needed) indicates the meter. The upper number displays the number of beats per measure, and the lower number shows the note value that gets one beat. Example: $\frac{3}{4}$. 3 means three beats per measure, and the 4 means that a quarter note gets one beat.

Tonal center—For music referred to in this text the tonal center and the tonic note are the same.

Tonality—For music referred to in this text the tonality of a composition is the same as the tonic note. Example: In the key of C major the tonality is C and the tonic is C. The term tonality describes a hierarchical music system where one note is the center (point of maximum repose) of the system and all other notes gravitate around it (and eventually lead toward it).

Tonic—The first step of a major or minor scale.

Transpose—To move to another pitch; in practicality, *transposition* refers to the process of rewriting a composition or parts thereof a specified interval above or below the original. Example: A composition in the key of C major may be transposed to the key of G major by copying all notes a perfect fifth above their original pitch in C major.

Treble clef—Also known as the G clef. Indicates that the second line (up) of the staff is G above middle C. Notation: 𝄞 .

Triad—Three pitches harmonically arranged (one above the other) in thirds. Three common types: Major (M3rd and P5th), minor (m3rd and P5th), diminished (minor 3rd and diminished 5th), augmented (M3rd and augmented 5th).

Triple meter—$\frac{3}{2}$, $\frac{3}{4}$, $\frac{3}{8}$, and so on. Any meter with three beats per measure. Compound meters may also be included: $\frac{9}{16}$, $\frac{9}{8}$, $\frac{9}{4}$.

Triplet— Three notes in the rhythmic space regularly provided for only two notes—thus the 3 above or below the notes. The complete triplet must take up only the time allotted to two pitches. Typical notation: ♪♪♪ .

Tritone—An interval of three whole steps. Both the diminished 5th (like B up to F) and the augmented fourth (like D up to G♯) are tritones.

Twelve tone row—All twelve notes of the octave, arranged melodically in such a way that no pitch is duplicated until all have been sounded. Found in atonal (lacking tonality) compositions.

Unison—The interval formed by two or more notes with the same pitch. In some ways a unison is not an interval at all, but for convenience in musical calculation it is listed as such.

Upbeat—Immediately precedes an accented beat. So called because a conductor's baton is raised on an upbeat in preparation for the downbeat (accented) to follow.

Waltz—A dance in moderate triple meter (usually $\frac{3}{4}$).

Whole note—The notation o means the note has the value of a full measure of $\frac{4}{4}$ meter or twice the value of a half-note.

Whole step—The interval equal to two half steps. On the piano keyboard there is a whole step between each pair of adjacent white keys except for E to F and B to C. Thus, whole steps may be found between C and D, D and E, F and G, G and A, and A and B.

Whole tone scale—A scale made up entirely of whole steps. This scale has one less note (6) than the major and minor scales (7). Example of a whole tone scale: C D E F♯ G♯ A♯ C.

Index

values for duration of note, 28–30
whole rest, 38
Note(s)
dot or a tie to add length to, 29–30
grace, 45
names of, 6
parts of, 28–29
values for duration of, 28–30
Note head, 28

O

Octave(s)
abbreviation of an, 8
interval of the, 67
middle, 17
piano, 17
Opera, in historical context, 293–94
Opus number(s)
abbreviation for, 31
and other ordering, 124
Oratorio, in historical context, 293–94
Organum sound, 83

P

Passing tone, 287. *See also* Tone
Pavan in historical context, 293
Pedal tone, 290
Percussion instruments, types of, 2
Perfect fourth, definition of, 119
Perfect interval(s)
arranged in order, 117
definition of, 67
Period, 291–92
Phrase(s)
beginning the, 216–17
cadence, as beginning of the, 216
contrasting, 292
examples of, 215–17
question and answer, 291
Piano, pitch and the keyboard of the, 17–25
Prelude, in historical context, 293
Preparation note, 287
Progressions of chords, fifths, and triads, 255

R

Repeat sign, 44
Resolution, 287
Rest, 29–30, 38, 39, 40, 43, 175
Rest tones, 219
Retardation, 289
Rhythm, 27–47. *See also* Accent; Beat; *and* Tempo
definition of, 27

hemiola, 207–208
modified repetition of melodic, 238
Rhythmic syllables, 173
Rock style harmony, 280
Rondo in historical context, 294
Root position, 246
Round in historical context, 293

S

Scale(s)
chromatic, 19
degree, definition of, 54
dominant, 218
major, definition of, 53
major and minor, table of, 108
minor, definition of, 53
mode type, 50
names of the notes in a, 217–18
notes, table of, 218
parallel, definition of, 108
relative, definition of, 108
sequence within an octave, 19
and the tonal center, 48, 217–18
tonal production of, 49
Scotch Snap, 176
Semitone. *See* Half steps
Sequence, definition of, 238. *See also* Melody
Sevenths
creating, 268
diatonic, qualities of, 269
half-diminished, 269
major and minor, keyboard fingerings for, 133
melodies set with, 134
qualities of, in major scales, 269
types of, 134
Sfortzando (sfp), 188
Sharp notation on piano keyboard, 18, 21–22
Sixths, 133–34 *See also* Consonances *and* Intervals
Slur sign, 197
Sonata in historical context, 294
Soprano voice as part of four-voice arrangement, 245
Staff notation, 5. *See also* Notation of musical sounds
Staccato, 45, 47, 175
Stem, 28
Stress, 27
String instruments
timbres produced by, 1
types of, 2
Subdominant, 218
Submediant, 218
Suggested listening list, 297–98
Suite in historical context, 294
Supertonic, 218
Suspension, 288
Syllable system, 57

Symphony, in historical context, 294
Syncopation, 187–96

T

Tempo. *See also* Beat
accelerando, 44
allegro, 33
andante, 33
definition of, 33
moderato, 33
recognition of, 41
ritardando (rit.), 44
ritenuto, 44
Tenor voice as part of four-voice arrangement, 245
Thirds
identifying major and minor, 73
locating major and minor on the guitar, 75
major and minor, definition of, 68. *See also* Intervals
melodies set with, 68
placing major and minor on the keyboard, 74
writing major and minor, 73
Tie, 29–30
Time. *See also* Meter *and* Beat
and beat units, 30–32
nonmetric organization of 28
signature, 30
Tonal center
definition of, 49
introduction to the, 48–51
major and minor scales to create the, 53
in relation to other names in a scale, 48, 217–18
symbol for, 269
Tonality. *See* Tonal center
Tones
active and rest, in a key, 219
arrangement of, to produce scale, 49
half step and minor second, 56
names of triad, 82
neighboring, 287
nonharmonic, 246, 255, 287–90
passing, 246, 287
Tonic. *See* Tonal center
Treble clef
notations, definition of, 5
on the piano keyboard, 15–16
Triad(s). *See also* Chord(s)
augmented and diminished, 151–60
augmented, in minor scales, 153
commonly used for the guitar, 306